THEN. NOW. FOREVER.

VOLUME TWO

BOOM!
STUDIOS

**ROSS RICHIE** CEO & Founder
**MATT GAGNON** Editor-in-Chief
**FILIP SABLIK** President, Publishing & Marketing
**STEPHEN CHRISTY** President, Development
**LANCE KREITER** Vice President, Licensing & Merchandising
**PHIL BARBARO** Vice President, Finance & Human Resources
**ARUNE SINGH** Vice President, Marketing
**BRYCE CARLSON** Vice President, Editorial & Creative Strategy
**SCOTT NEWMAN** Manager, Production Design
**KATE HENNING** Manager, Operations
**SPENCER SIMPSON** Manager, Sales
**SIERRA HAHN** Executive Editor
**JEANINE SCHAEFER** Executive Editor
**DAFNA PLEBAN** Senior Editor
**SHANNON WATTERS** Senior Editor
**ERIC HARBURN** Senior Editor
**WHITNEY LEOPARD** Editor
**CAMERON CHITTOCK** Editor
**CHRIS ROSA** Editor
**MATTHEW LEVINE** Editor
**SOPHIE PHILIPS-ROBERTS** Assistant Editor
**GAVIN GRONENTHAL** Assistant Editor
**MICHAEL MOCCIO** Assistant Editor
**AMANDA LaFRANCO** Executive Assistant
**KATALINA HOLLAND** Editorial Administrative Assistant
**JILLIAN CRAB** Design Coordinator
**MICHELLE ANKLEY** Design Coordinator
**KARA LEOPARD** Production Designer
**MARIE KRUPINA** Production Designer
**GRACE PARK** Production Design Assistant
**CHELSEA ROBERTS** Production Design Assistant
**ELIZABETH LOUGHRIDGE** Accounting Coordinator
**STEPHANIE HOCUTT** Social Media Coordinator
**JOSÉ MEZA** Event Coordinator
**HOLLY AITCHISON** Operations Coordinator
**MEGAN CHRISTOPHER** Operations Assistant
**RODRIGO HERNANDEZ** Mailroom Assistant
**MORGAN PERRY** Direct Market Representative
**CAT O'GRADY** Marketing Assistant
**CORNELIA TZANA** Publicity Assistant
**LIZ ALMENDAREZ** Accounting Administrative Assistant

**R**elive **E**xplore **A**dventure **D**iscover

**WWE: THEN. NOW. FOREVER. Volume Two, October 2018.**
Published by BOOM! Studios, a division of Boom Entertainment,
Inc. WWE is ™ & © 2017, 2018 WWE. All WWE programming,
talent names, images, likenesses, slogans, wrestling moves,
trademarks, logos and copyrights are the exclusive property
of WWE and its subsidiaries. All other trademarks, logos and
copyrights are the property of their respective owners. ©
2018 WWE. All Rights Reserved. Originally published in single
magazine form as WWE: Survivor Series 2017 Special and
WWE: Royal Rumble 2018 Special. © 2018 WWE. All Rights
Reserved. BOOM! Studios™ and the BOOM! Studios logo are
trademarks of Boom Entertainment, Inc., registered in various
countries and categories. All characters, events, and institutions
depicted herein are fictional. Any similarity between any of the
names, characters, persons, events, and/or institutions in this
publication to actual names, characters, and persons, whether
living or dead, events, and/or institutions is unintended and
purely coincidental. BOOM! Studios does not read or accept
unsolicited submissions of ideas, stories, or artwork.

BOOM! Studios, 5670 Wilshire Boulevard, Suite 400, Los
Angeles, CA 90036-5679. Printed in China. First Printing.

ISBN: 978-1-68415-257-5, eISBN: 978-1-64144-119-3

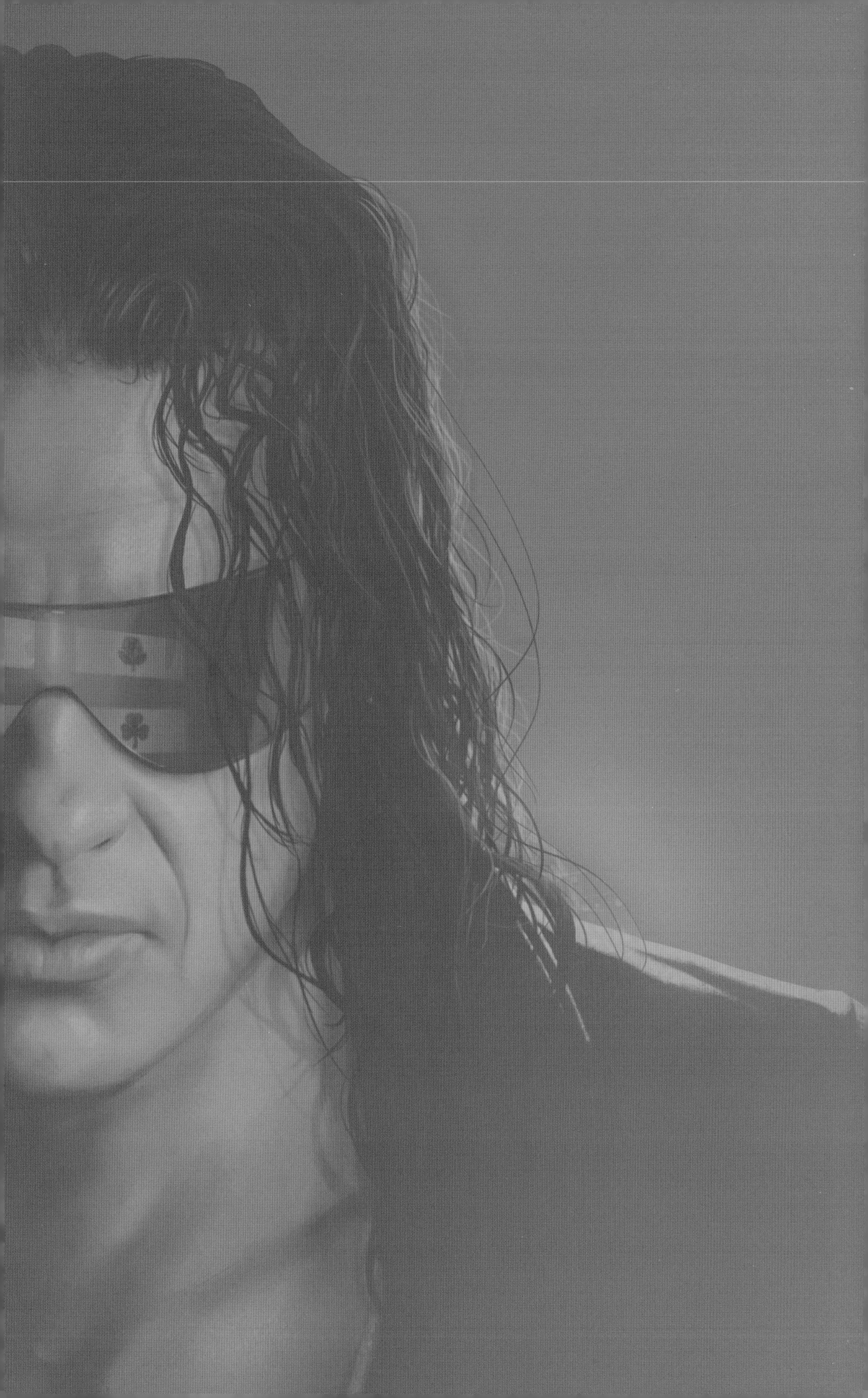

## THE MONTREAL SCREWJOB
WRITTEN BY
**DENNIS HOPELESS**
ILLUSTRATED BY
**LUCAS WERNECK**
COLORED BY
**JEREMY LAWSON**

## DEBUT
WRITTEN BY
**BOX BROWN**
ILLUSTRATED BY
**RODRIGO LORENZO**
COLORED BY
**DOUG GARBARK**

## DOWN THE HATCH
WRITTEN & ILLUSTRATED BY
**DEREK FRIDOLFS**
COLORED BY
**FRED C. STRESING**

## 1 MINUTE, 26 SECONDS
WRITTEN BY
**KEVIN PANETTA**
ILLUSTRATED BY
**KENDALL GOODE**

## THE ROOT OF ALL EVIL
WRITTEN BY
**LAN PITTS**
ILLUSTRATED BY
**KELLY WILLIAMS**
COLORED BY
**DEE CUNNIFFE**

## THE SHIELD: CALLED UP
WRITTEN BY
**AARON GILLESPIE**
ILLUSTRATED BY
**TIM LATTIE**
COLORED BY
**DOUG GARBARK**

## TO BE NUMBER ONE
WRITTEN BY
**LAN PITTS**
ILLUSTRATED BY
**RODRIGO LORENZO**
COLORED BY
**DOUG GARBARK**

## MR. ROYAL RUMBLE
WRITTEN BY
**KEVIN PANETTA**
ILLUSTRATED BY
**DOMINIKE "DOMO" STANTON**
COLORED BY
**JEREMY LAWSON**

## I AM PHENOMENAL
WRITTEN BY
**AJ STYLES & MICHAEL KINGSTON**
ILLUSTRATED BY
**DANIEL BAYLISS**

## YOU CAN HATE ME NOW
WRITTEN BY
**JULIAN MAY**
ILLUSTRATED BY
**MICHEL MULIPOLA**
COLORED BY
**DOUG GARBARK**

## OUT OF THE SHADOW
WRITTEN BY
**G. BRETT WILLIAMS**
ILLUSTRATED BY
**KELLY WILLIAMS**

## BECKY LYNCH: PUN-ISHER
WRITTEN BY
**ANTHONY BURCH**
ILLUSTRATED BY
**BECCA FARROW**
COLORED BY
**REBECCA NALTY**

## VIPER

WRITTEN BY
**MAIRGHREAD SCOTT**
ILLUSTRATED BY
**RODRIGO LORENZO**
COLORED BY
**DOUG GARBARK**

## BIG RED MONSTER

WRITTEN BY
**JULIAN MAY**
ILLUSTRATED BY
**RODRIGO LORENZO**
COLORED BY
**DOUG GARBARK**

## RANDY SAVAGE: NOT SHOW KING

WRITTEN BY
**RYAN FERRIER**
ILLUSTRATED BY
**KENDALL GOODE**

## WHEN A MACHO MAN LOVES A WOMAN

WRITTEN BY
**RYAN FERRIER**
ILLUSTRATED BY
**KENDALL GOODE**

## SECOND NATURE

WRITTEN BY
**JULIAN MAY**
ILLUSTRATED BY
**RODRIGO LORENZO**
COLORED BY
**DOUG GARBARK**

## 'TWAS THE NIGHT BEFORE RUSEV DAY

WRITTEN BY
**KEVIN PANETTA**
ILLUSTRATED BY
**DOMINIKE "DOMO" STANTON**
COLORED BY
**DOUG GARBARK**

LETTERED BY
**JIM CAMPBELL**

COVER BY
**XERMÁNICO**

SERIES DESIGNER
**GRACE PARK**

COLLECTION DESIGNER
**JILLIAN CRAB**

ASSISTANT EDITOR
**GAVIN GRONENTHAL**

EDITORS
**ERIC HARBURN**
**CHRIS ROSA**

SPECIAL THANKS TO
**STEVE PANTALEO**
**CHAD BARBASH**
**BEN MAYER**
**JOHN JONES**
**STAN STANSKI**
**LAUREN DIENES-MIDDLEN**
AND EVERYONE AT **WWE**

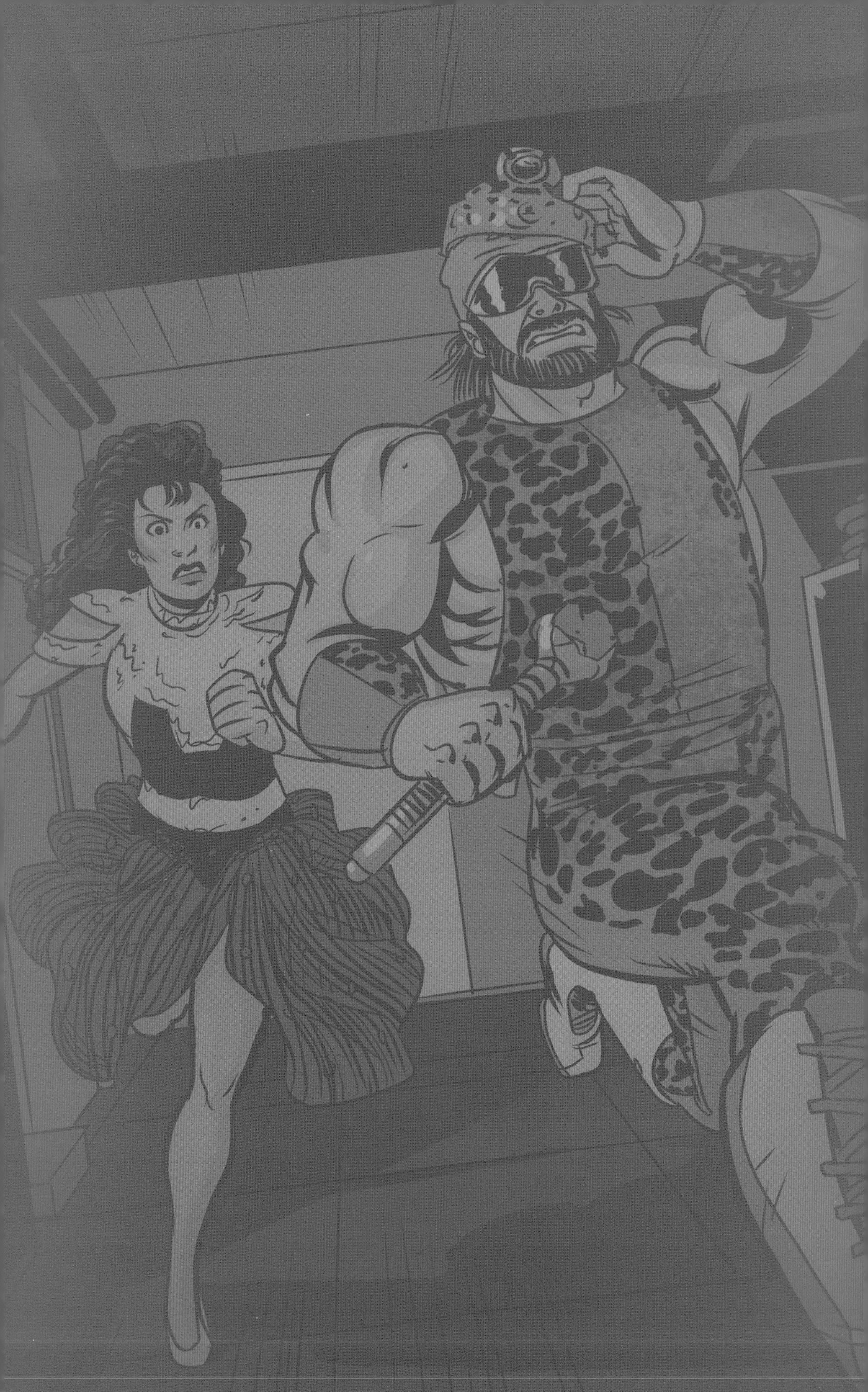

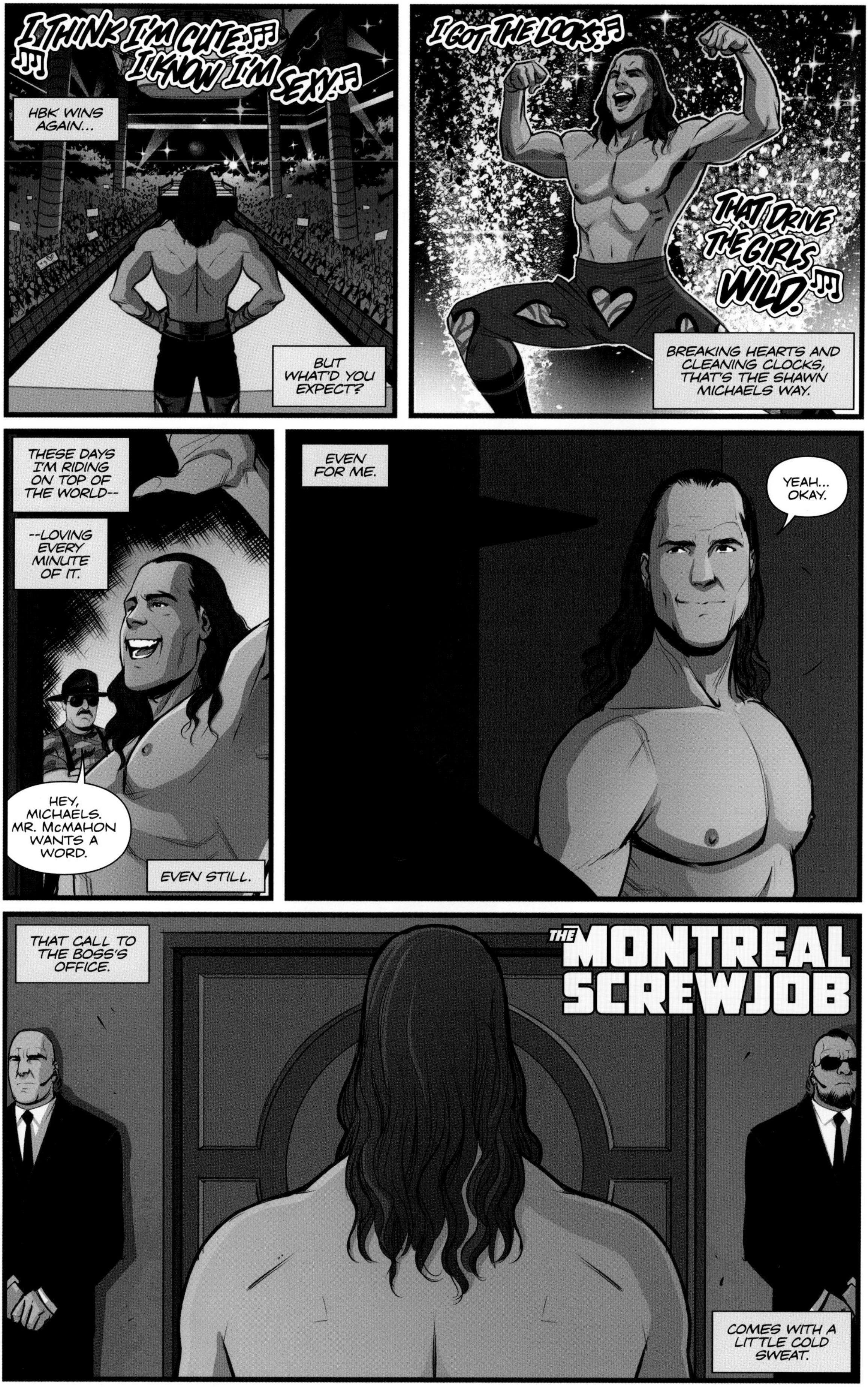
I THINK I'M CUTE.
I KNOW I'M SEXY.
HBK WINS AGAIN...
BUT WHAT'D YOU EXPECT?
I GOT THE LOOKS.
THAT DRIVE THE GIRLS WILD.
BREAKING HEARTS AND CLEANING CLOCKS, THAT'S THE SHAWN MICHAELS WAY.
THESE DAYS I'M RIDING ON TOP OF THE WORLD--
--LOVING EVERY MINUTE OF IT.
HEY, MICHAELS. MR. McMAHON WANTS A WORD.
EVEN STILL.
EVEN FOR ME.
YEAH... OKAY.
THAT CALL TO THE BOSS'S OFFICE.
THE MONTREAL SCREWJOB
COMES WITH A LITTLE COLD SWEAT.

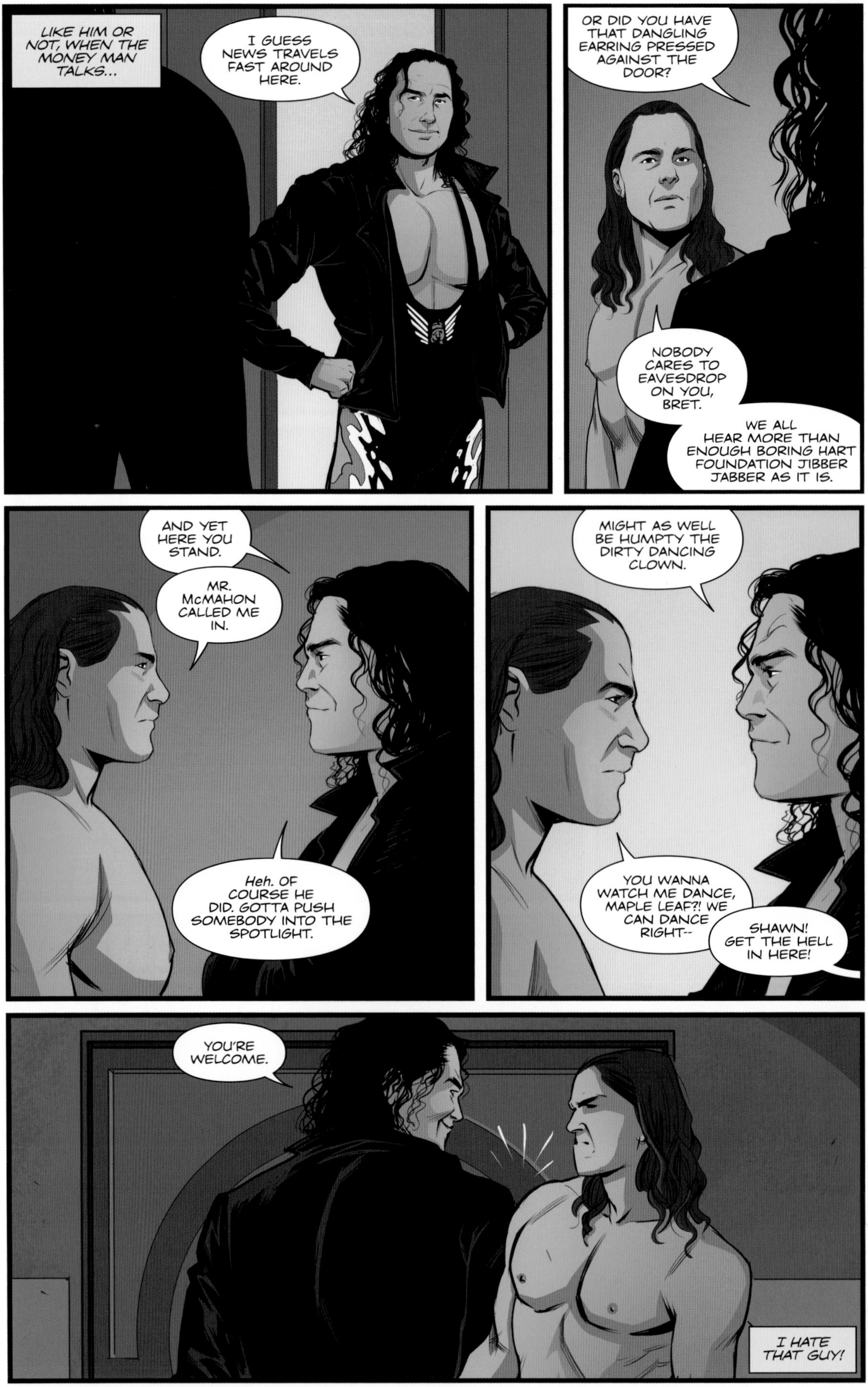
LIKE HIM OR NOT, WHEN THE MONEY MAN TALKS...
I GUESS NEWS TRAVELS FAST AROUND HERE.
OR DID YOU HAVE THAT DANGLING EARRING PRESSED AGAINST THE DOOR?
NOBODY CARES TO EAVESDROP ON YOU, BRET.
WE ALL HEAR MORE THAN ENOUGH BORING HART FOUNDATION JIBBER JABBER AS IT IS.
AND YET HERE YOU STAND.
MR. McMAHON CALLED ME IN.
Heh. OF COURSE HE DID. GOTTA PUSH SOMEBODY INTO THE SPOTLIGHT.
MIGHT AS WELL BE HUMPTY THE DIRTY DANCING CLOWN.
YOU WANNA WATCH ME DANCE, MAPLE LEAF?! WE CAN DANCE RIGHT--
SHAWN! GET THE HELL IN HERE!
YOU'RE WELCOME.
I HATE THAT GUY!

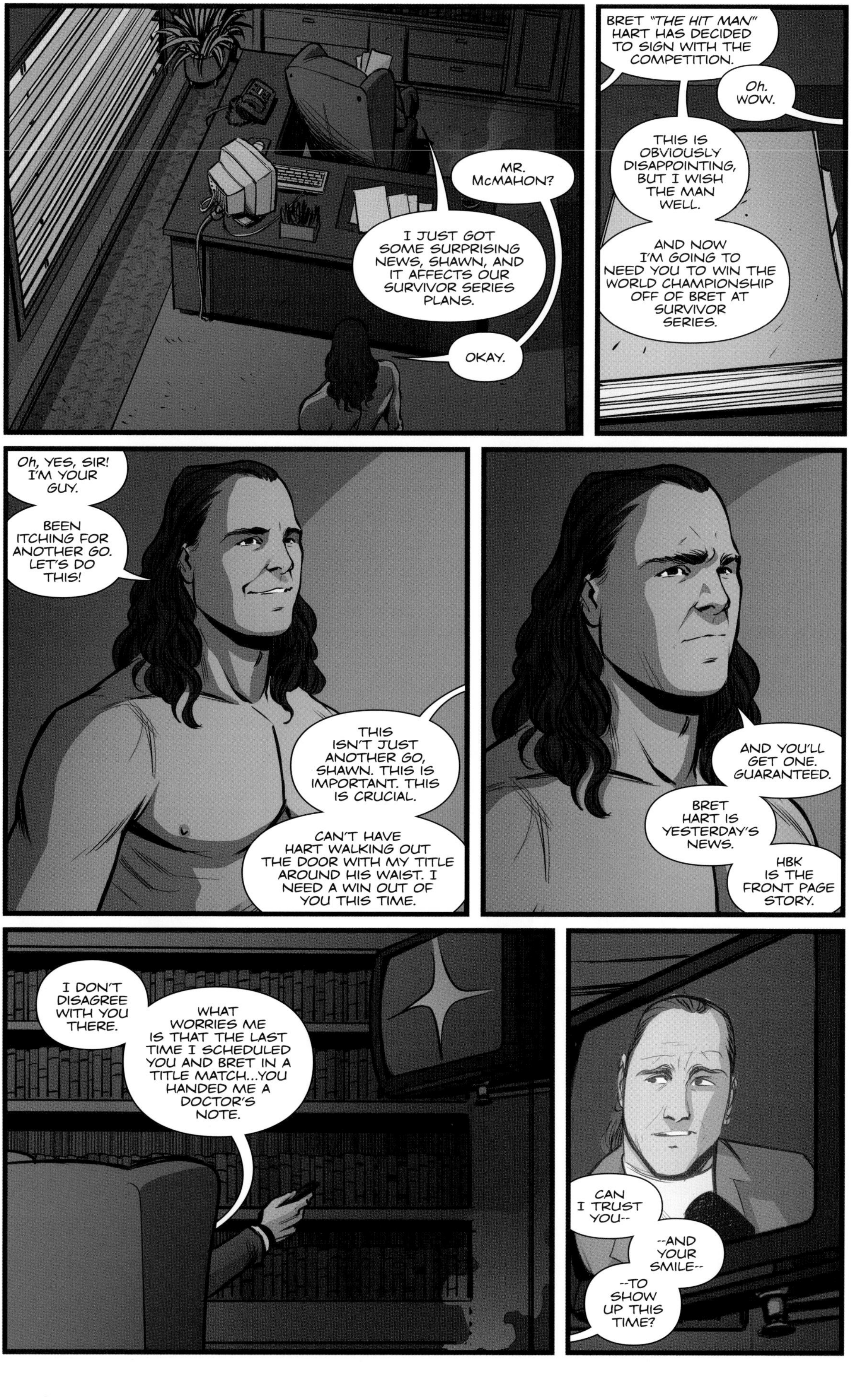
MR. McMAHON?
I JUST GOT SOME SURPRISING NEWS, SHAWN, AND IT AFFECTS OUR SURVIVOR SERIES PLANS.
OKAY.
BRET "THE HIT MAN" HART HAS DECIDED TO SIGN WITH THE COMPETITION.
Oh. WOW.
THIS IS OBVIOUSLY DISAPPOINTING, BUT I WISH THE MAN WELL.
AND NOW I'M GOING TO NEED YOU TO WIN THE WORLD CHAMPIONSHIP OFF OF BRET AT SURVIVOR SERIES.
Oh, YES, SIR! I'M YOUR GUY.
BEEN ITCHING FOR ANOTHER GO. LET'S DO THIS!
THIS ISN'T JUST ANOTHER GO, SHAWN. THIS IS IMPORTANT. THIS IS CRUCIAL.
CAN'T HAVE HART WALKING OUT THE DOOR WITH MY TITLE AROUND HIS WAIST. I NEED A WIN OUT OF YOU THIS TIME.
AND YOU'LL GET ONE. GUARANTEED.
BRET HART IS YESTERDAY'S NEWS.
HBK IS THE FRONT PAGE STORY.
I DON'T DISAGREE WITH YOU THERE.
WHAT WORRIES ME IS THAT THE LAST TIME I SCHEDULED YOU AND BRET IN A TITLE MATCH...YOU HANDED ME A DOCTOR'S NOTE.
CAN I TRUST YOU--
--AND YOUR SMILE--
--TO SHOW UP THIS TIME?

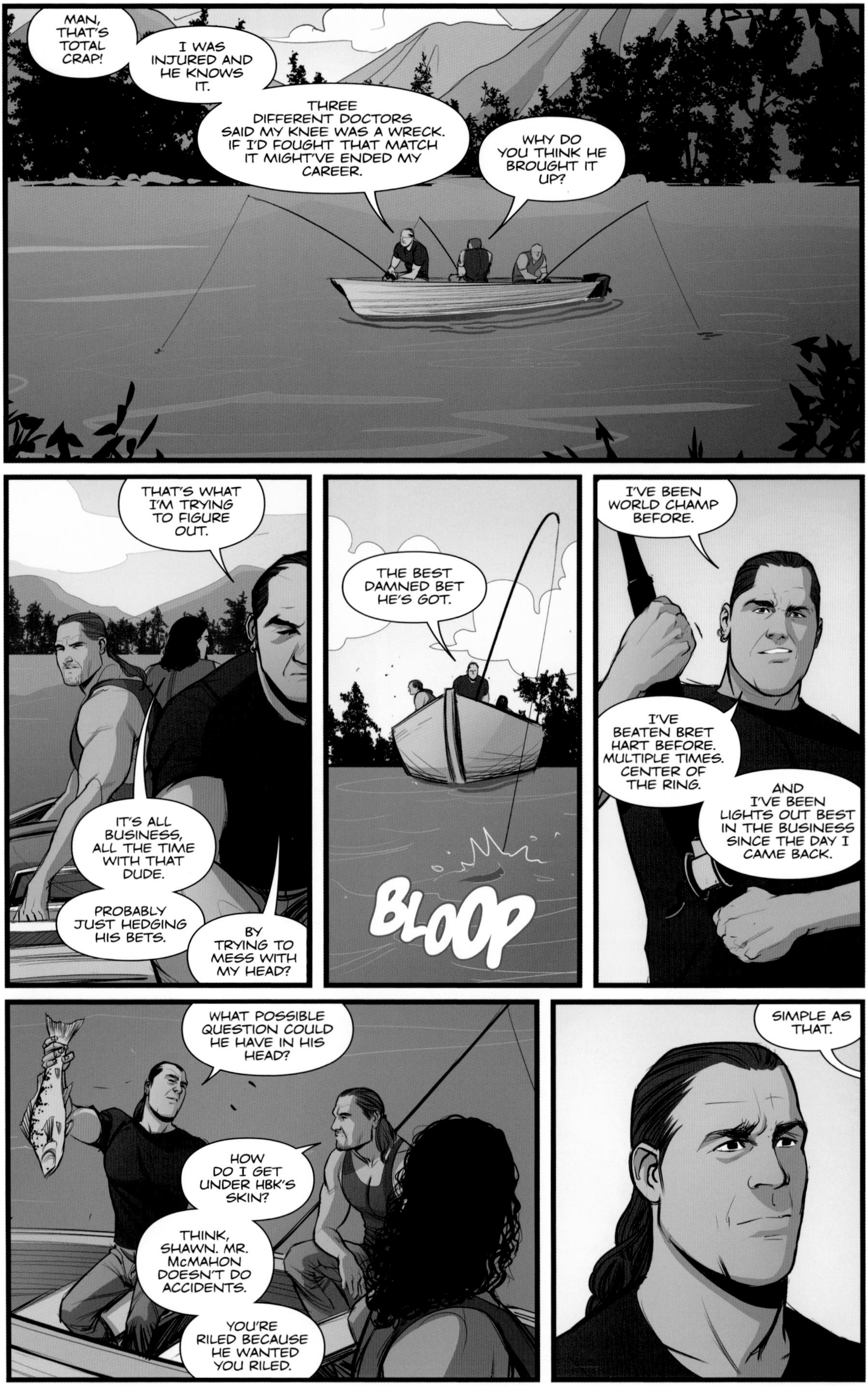
MAN, THAT'S TOTAL CRAP!
I WAS INJURED AND HE KNOWS IT.
THREE DIFFERENT DOCTORS SAID MY KNEE WAS A WRECK. IF I'D FOUGHT THAT MATCH IT MIGHT'VE ENDED MY CAREER.
WHY DO YOU THINK HE BROUGHT IT UP?
THAT'S WHAT I'M TRYING TO FIGURE OUT.
IT'S ALL BUSINESS, ALL THE TIME WITH THAT DUDE.
PROBABLY JUST HEDGING HIS BETS.
BY TRYING TO MESS WITH MY HEAD?
THE BEST DAMNED BET HE'S GOT.
BLOOP
I'VE BEEN WORLD CHAMP BEFORE.
I'VE BEATEN BRET HART BEFORE. MULTIPLE TIMES. CENTER OF THE RING.
AND I'VE BEEN LIGHTS OUT BEST IN THE BUSINESS SINCE THE DAY I CAME BACK.
WHAT POSSIBLE QUESTION COULD HE HAVE IN HIS HEAD?
HOW DO I GET UNDER HBK'S SKIN?
THINK, SHAWN. MR. McMAHON DOESN'T DO ACCIDENTS.
YOU'RE RILED BECAUSE HE WANTED YOU RILED.
SIMPLE AS THAT.

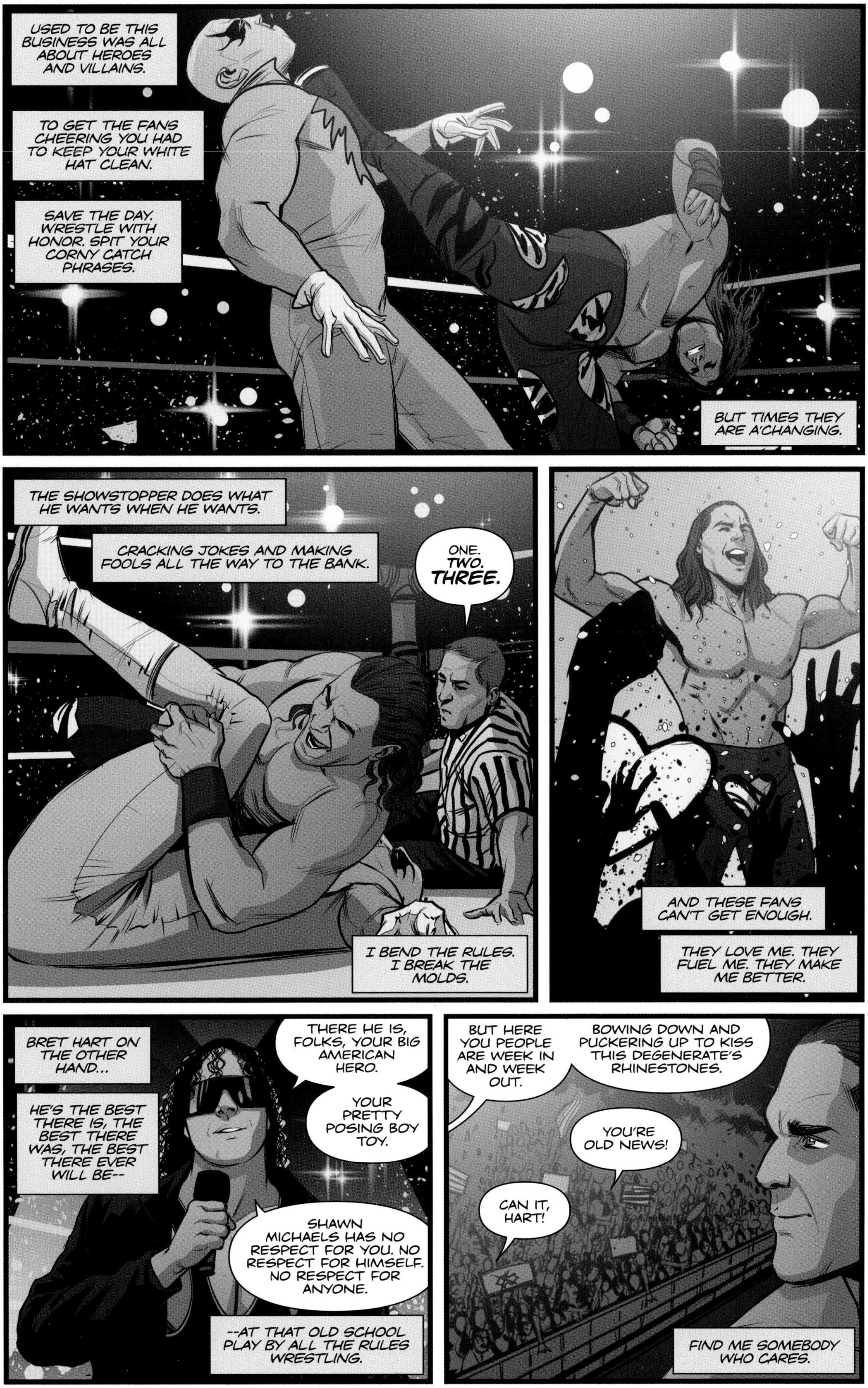
USED TO BE THIS BUSINESS WAS ALL ABOUT HEROES AND VILLAINS.
TO GET THE FANS CHEERING YOU HAD TO KEEP YOUR WHITE HAT CLEAN.
SAVE THE DAY. WRESTLE WITH HONOR. SPIT YOUR CORNY CATCH PHRASES.
BUT TIMES THEY ARE A'CHANGING.
THE SHOWSTOPPER DOES WHAT HE WANTS WHEN HE WANTS.
CRACKING JOKES AND MAKING FOOLS ALL THE WAY TO THE BANK.
ONE. TWO. THREE.
I BEND THE RULES. I BREAK THE MOLDS.
AND THESE FANS CAN'T GET ENOUGH.
THEY LOVE ME. THEY FUEL ME. THEY MAKE ME BETTER.
BRET HART ON THE OTHER HAND...
HE'S THE BEST THERE IS, THE BEST THERE WAS, THE BEST THERE EVER WILL BE--
THERE HE IS, FOLKS, YOUR BIG AMERICAN HERO.
YOUR PRETTY POSING BOY TOY.
SHAWN MICHAELS HAS NO RESPECT FOR YOU. NO RESPECT FOR HIMSELF. NO RESPECT FOR ANYONE.
--AT THAT OLD SCHOOL PLAY BY ALL THE RULES WRESTLING.
BUT HERE YOU PEOPLE ARE WEEK IN AND WEEK OUT.
BOWING DOWN AND PUCKERING UP TO KISS THIS DEGENERATE'S RHINESTONES.
YOU'RE OLD NEWS!
CAN IT, HART!
FIND ME SOMEBODY WHO CARES.

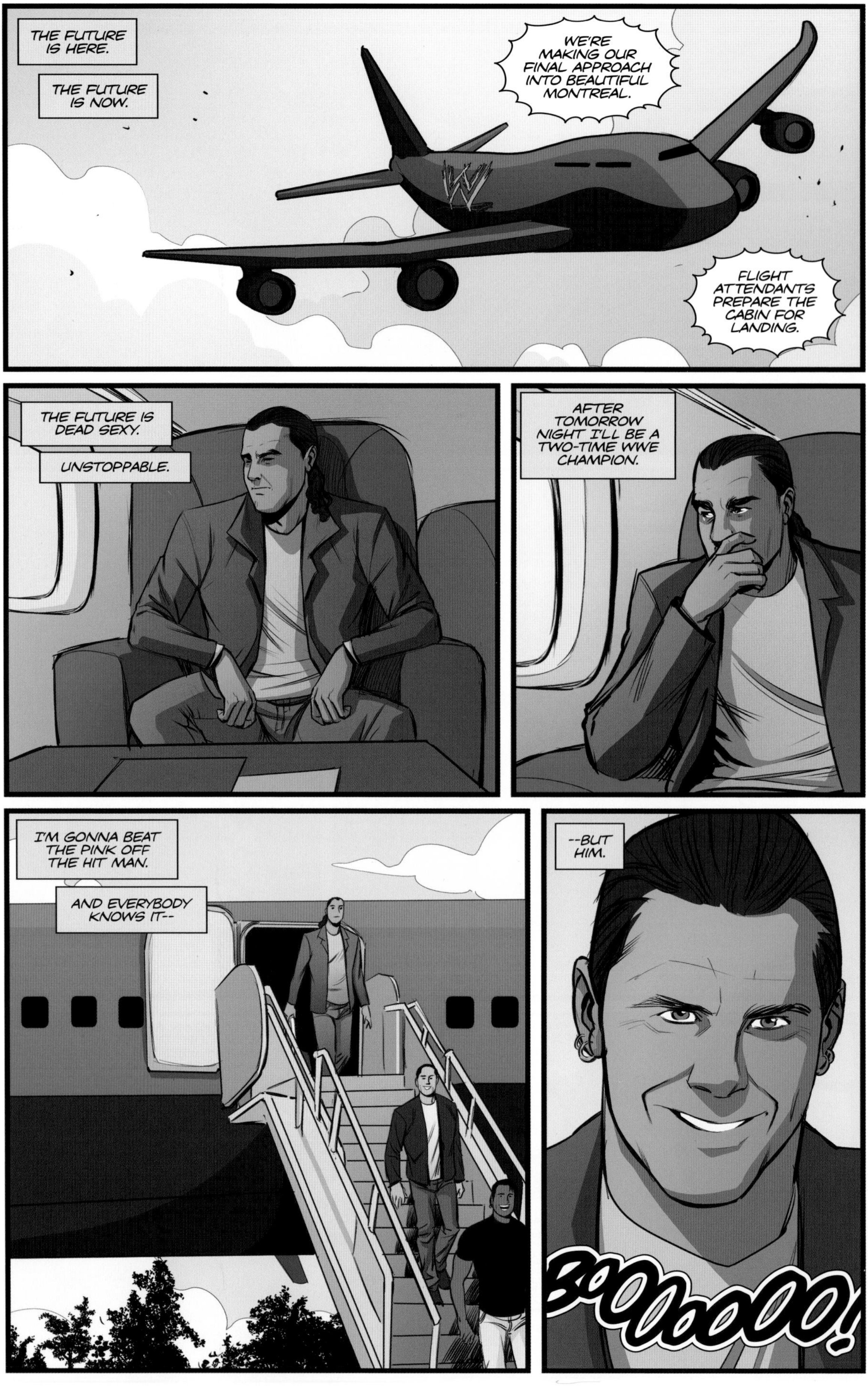
THE FUTURE IS HERE.
THE FUTURE IS NOW.
WE'RE MAKING OUR FINAL APPROACH INTO BEAUTIFUL MONTREAL.
FLIGHT ATTENDANTS PREPARE THE CABIN FOR LANDING.
THE FUTURE IS DEAD SEXY.
UNSTOPPABLE.
AFTER TOMORROW NIGHT I'LL BE A TWO-TIME WWE CHAMPION.
I'M GONNA BEAT THE PINK OFF THE HIT MAN.
AND EVERYBODY KNOWS IT--
--BUT HIM.
BOOOOOOO!

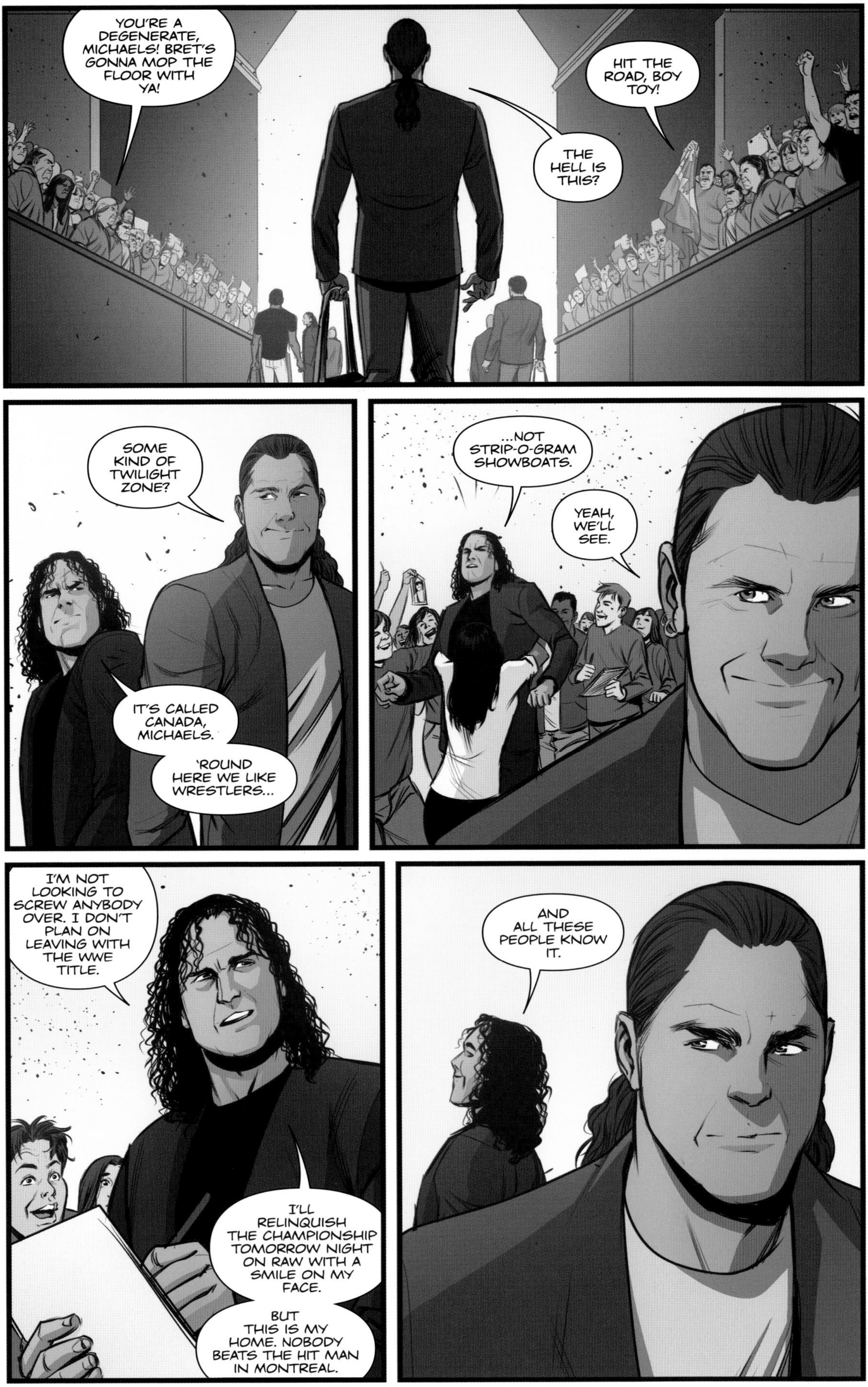
YOU'RE A DEGENERATE, MICHAELS! BRET'S GONNA MOP THE FLOOR WITH YA!
HIT THE ROAD, BOY TOY!
THE HELL IS THIS?
SOME KIND OF TWILIGHT ZONE?
IT'S CALLED CANADA, MICHAELS.
'ROUND HERE WE LIKE WRESTLERS...
...NOT STRIP-O-GRAM SHOWBOATS.
YEAH, WE'LL SEE.
I'M NOT LOOKING TO SCREW ANYBODY OVER. I DON'T PLAN ON LEAVING WITH THE WWE TITLE.
I'LL RELINQUISH THE CHAMPIONSHIP TOMORROW NIGHT ON RAW WITH A SMILE ON MY FACE.
BUT THIS IS MY HOME. NOBODY BEATS THE HIT MAN IN MONTREAL.
AND ALL THESE PEOPLE KNOW IT.

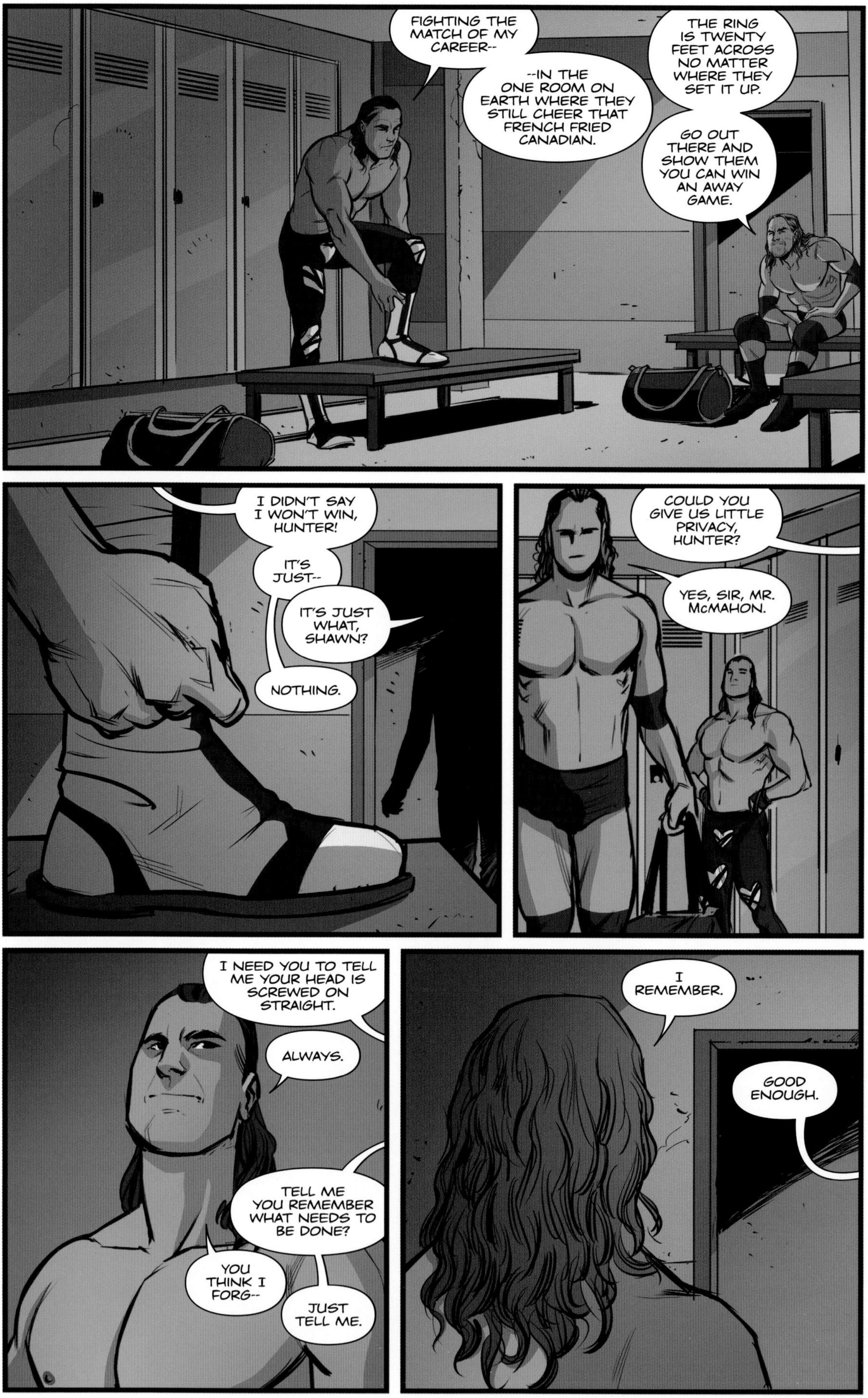
FIGHTING THE MATCH OF MY CAREER--
--IN THE ONE ROOM ON EARTH WHERE THEY STILL CHEER THAT FRENCH FRIED CANADIAN.
THE RING IS TWENTY FEET ACROSS NO MATTER WHERE THEY SET IT UP.
GO OUT THERE AND SHOW THEM YOU CAN WIN AN AWAY GAME.
I DIDN'T SAY I WON'T WIN, HUNTER!
IT'S JUST--
IT'S JUST WHAT, SHAWN?
NOTHING.
COULD YOU GIVE US LITTLE PRIVACY, HUNTER?
YES, SIR, MR. McMAHON.
I NEED YOU TO TELL ME YOUR HEAD IS SCREWED ON STRAIGHT.
ALWAYS.
TELL ME YOU REMEMBER WHAT NEEDS TO BE DONE?
YOU THINK I FORG--
JUST TELL ME.
I REMEMBER.
GOOD ENOUGH.

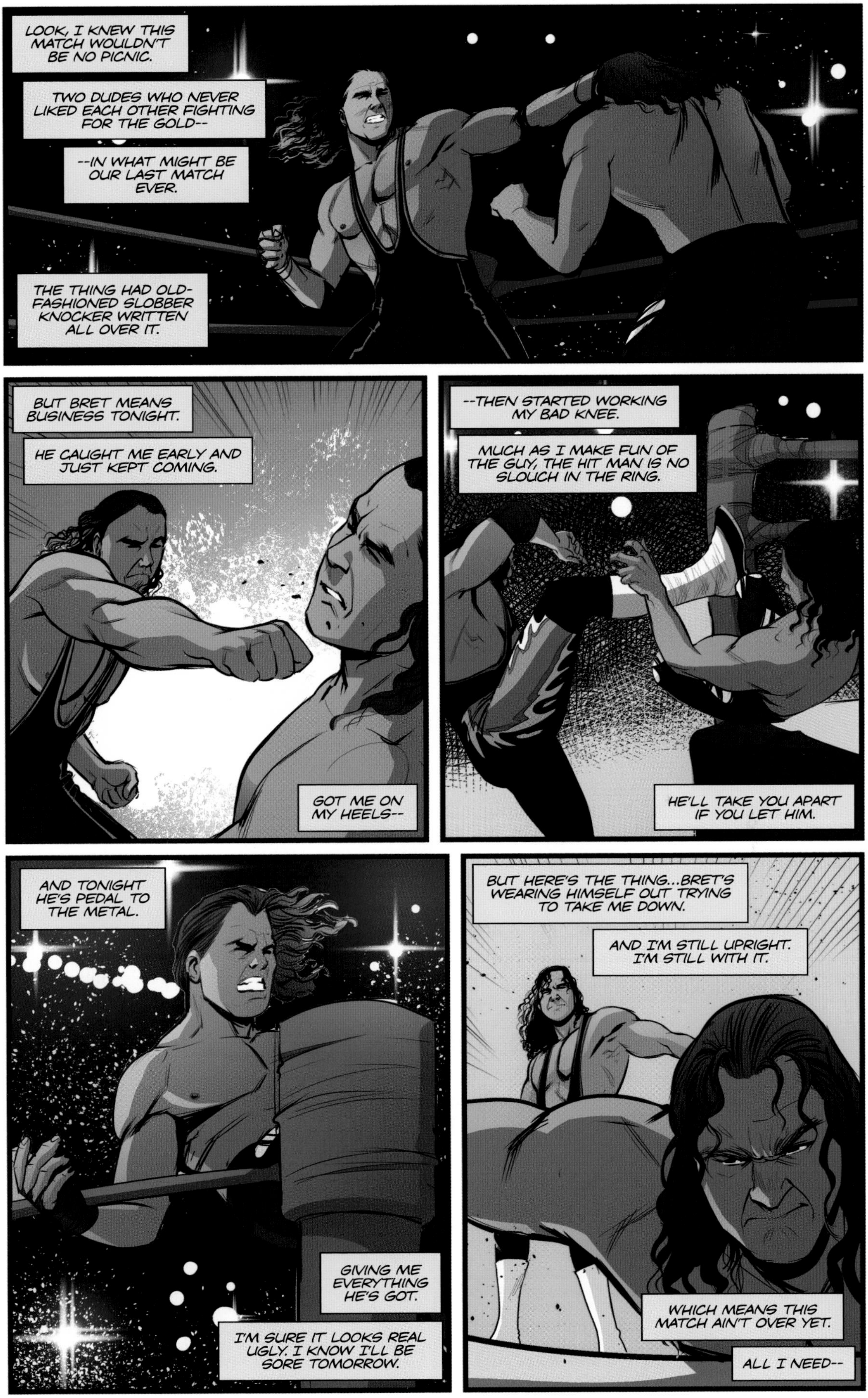
LOOK, I KNEW THIS MATCH WOULDN'T BE NO PICNIC.
TWO DUDES WHO NEVER LIKED EACH OTHER FIGHTING FOR THE GOLD--
--IN WHAT MIGHT BE OUR LAST MATCH EVER.
THE THING HAD OLD-FASHIONED SLOBBER KNOCKER WRITTEN ALL OVER IT.
BUT BRET MEANS BUSINESS TONIGHT.
HE CAUGHT ME EARLY AND JUST KEPT COMING.
GOT ME ON MY HEELS--
--THEN STARTED WORKING MY BAD KNEE.
MUCH AS I MAKE FUN OF THE GUY, THE HIT MAN IS NO SLOUCH IN THE RING.
HE'LL TAKE YOU APART IF YOU LET HIM.
AND TONIGHT HE'S PEDAL TO THE METAL.
GIVING ME EVERYTHING HE'S GOT.
I'M SURE IT LOOKS REAL UGLY. I KNOW I'LL BE SORE TOMORROW.
BUT HERE'S THE THING...BRET'S WEARING HIMSELF OUT TRYING TO TAKE ME DOWN.
AND I'M STILL UPRIGHT. I'M STILL WITH IT.
WHICH MEANS THIS MATCH AIN'T OVER YET.
ALL I NEED--

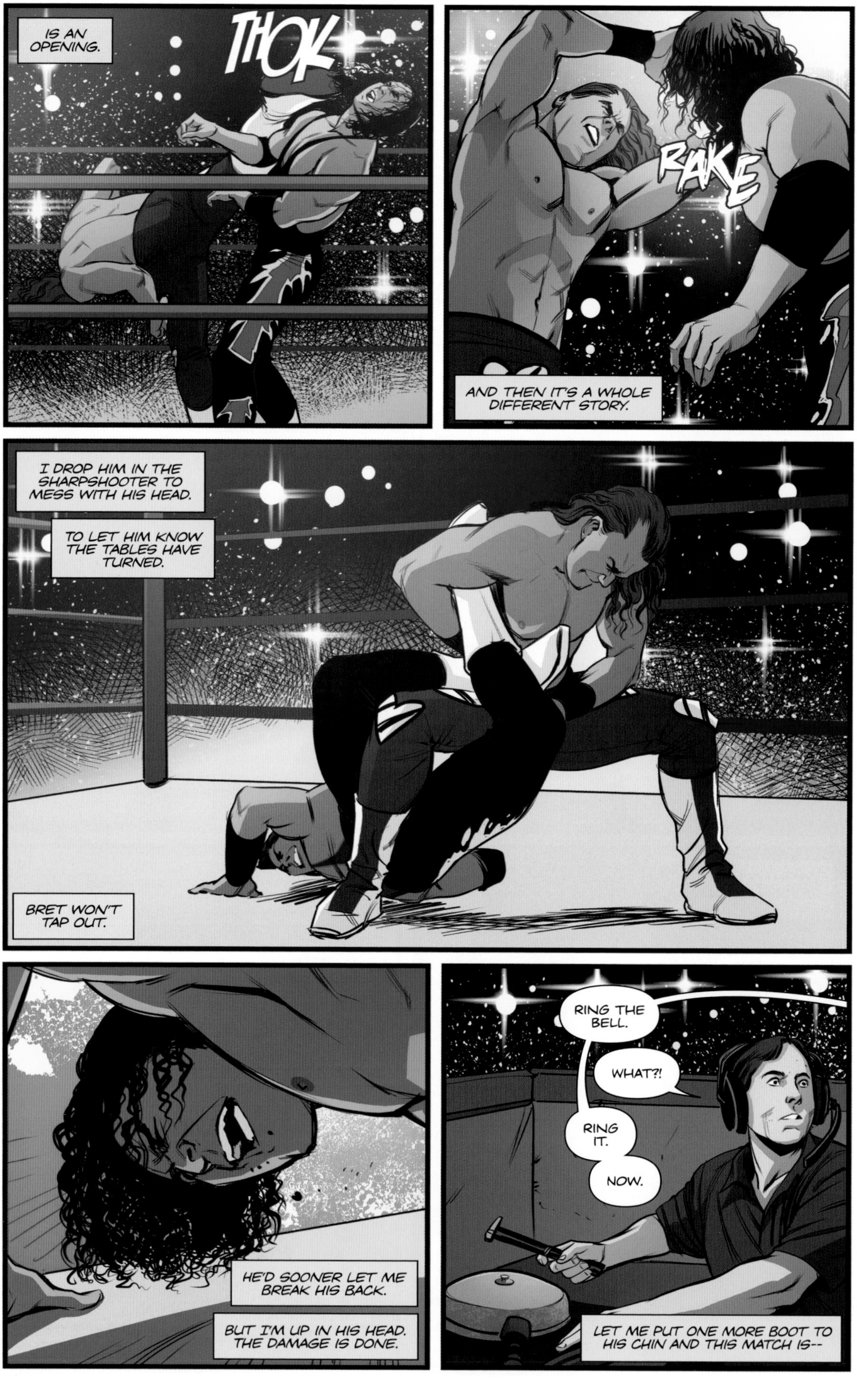
IS AN OPENING.
THOK
RAKE
AND THEN IT'S A WHOLE DIFFERENT STORY.
I DROP HIM IN THE SHARPSHOOTER TO MESS WITH HIS HEAD.
TO LET HIM KNOW THE TABLES HAVE TURNED.
BRET WON'T TAP OUT.
HE'D SOONER LET ME BREAK HIS BACK.
BUT I'M UP IN HIS HEAD. THE DAMAGE IS DONE.
RING THE BELL.
WHAT?!
RING IT.
NOW.
LET ME PUT ONE MORE BOOT TO HIS CHIN AND THIS MATCH IS--

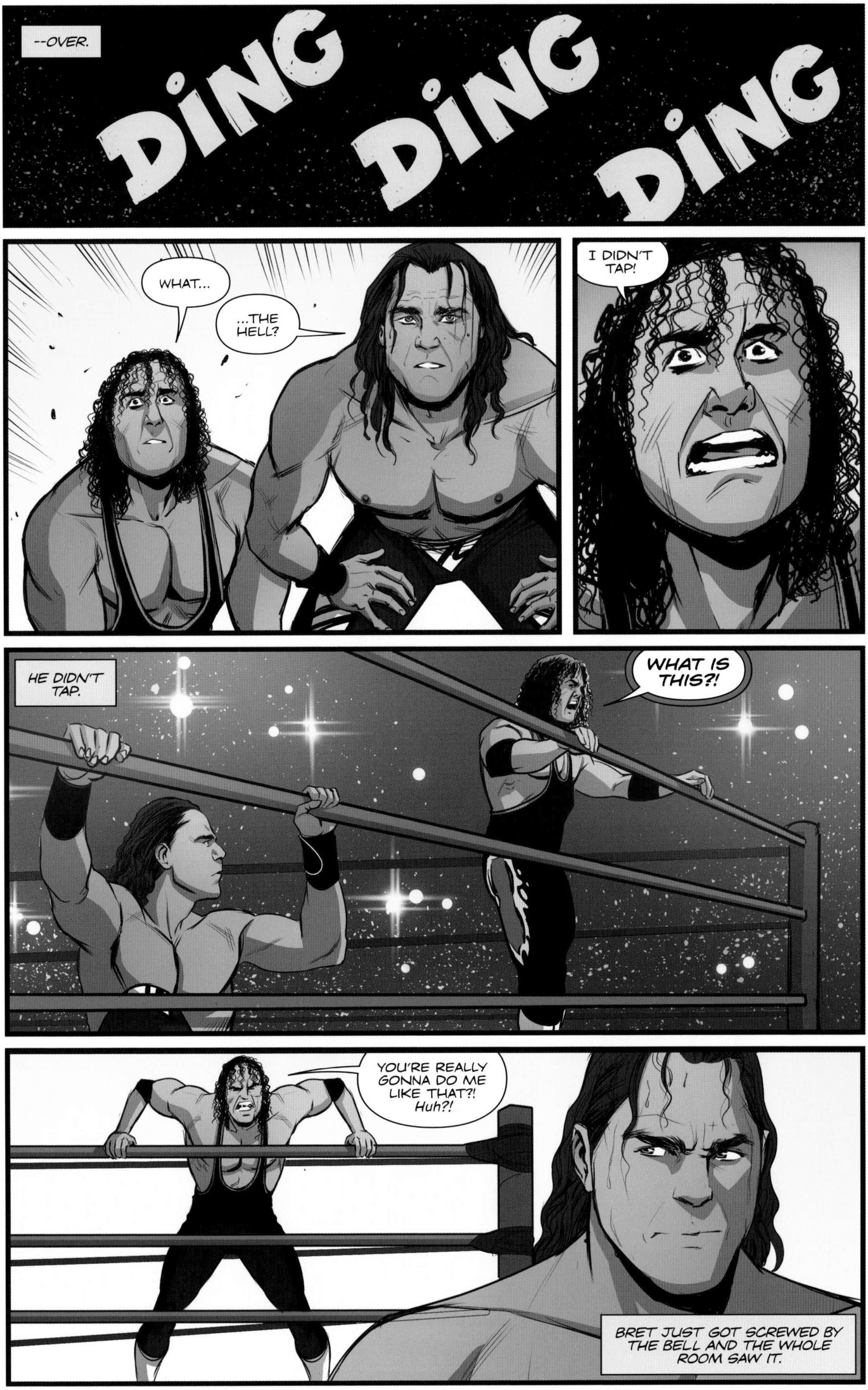
--OVER.
DING DING DING
WHAT...
...THE HELL?
I DIDN'T TAP!
HE DIDN'T TAP.
WHAT IS THIS?!
YOU'RE REALLY GONNA DO ME LIKE THAT?! Huh?!
BRET JUST GOT SCREWED BY THE BELL AND THE WHOLE ROOM SAW IT.

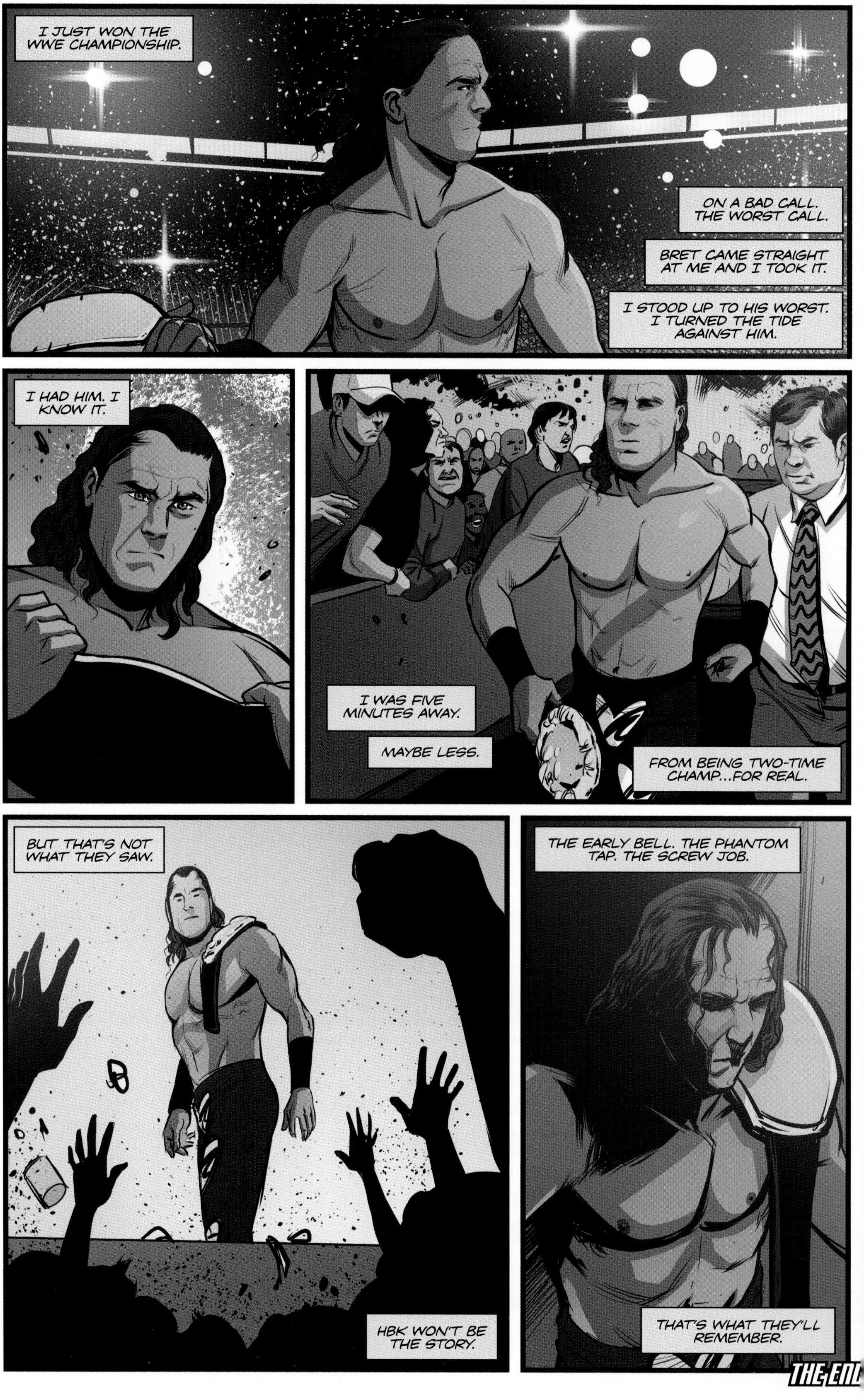
I JUST WON THE WWE CHAMPIONSHIP.
ON A BAD CALL. THE WORST CALL.
BRET CAME STRAIGHT AT ME AND I TOOK IT.
I STOOD UP TO HIS WORST. I TURNED THE TIDE AGAINST HIM.
I HAD HIM. I KNOW IT.
I WAS FIVE MINUTES AWAY.
MAYBE LESS.
FROM BEING TWO-TIME CHAMP...FOR REAL.
BUT THAT'S NOT WHAT THEY SAW.
HBK WON'T BE THE STORY.
THE EARLY BELL. THE PHANTOM TAP. THE SCREW JOB.
THAT'S WHAT THEY'LL REMEMBER.
THE END

ONLY OLYMPIC GOLD MEDALIST TO COMPETE IN WWE.

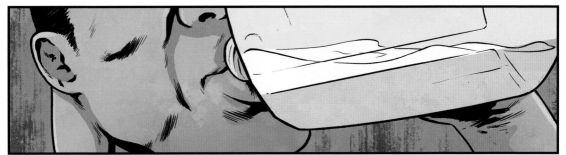

THESE PEOPLE ARE GONNA GO NUTS FOR ME TONIGHT.

DEBUT

I BET THE ROOF POPS OFF THE PLACE.

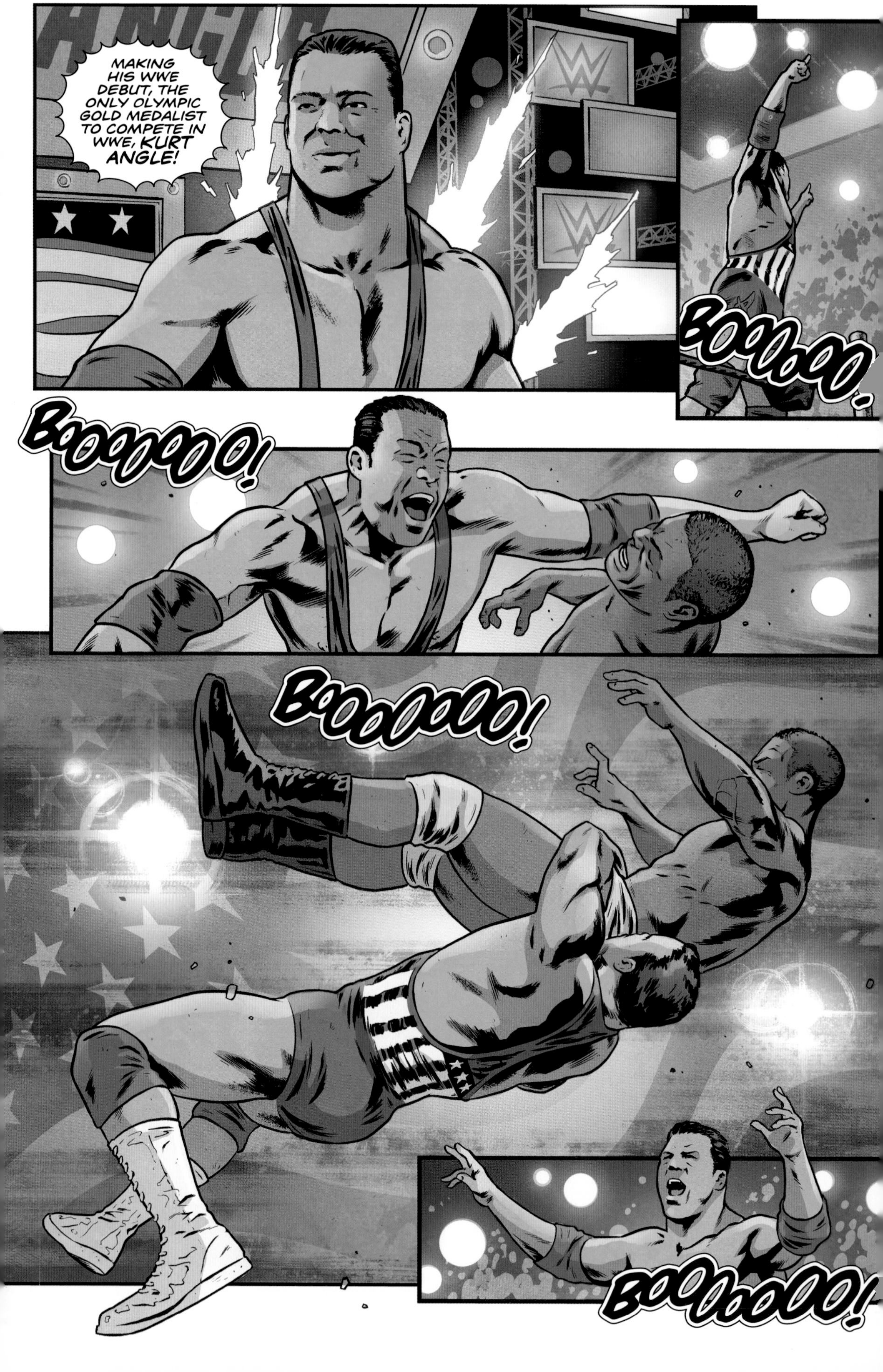
MAKING HIS WWE DEBUT, THE ONLY OLYMPIC GOLD MEDALIST TO COMPETE IN WWE, KURT ANGLE!
BOOOOOO.
BOOOOOOO!
BOOOOOOO!
BOOOOOOO!

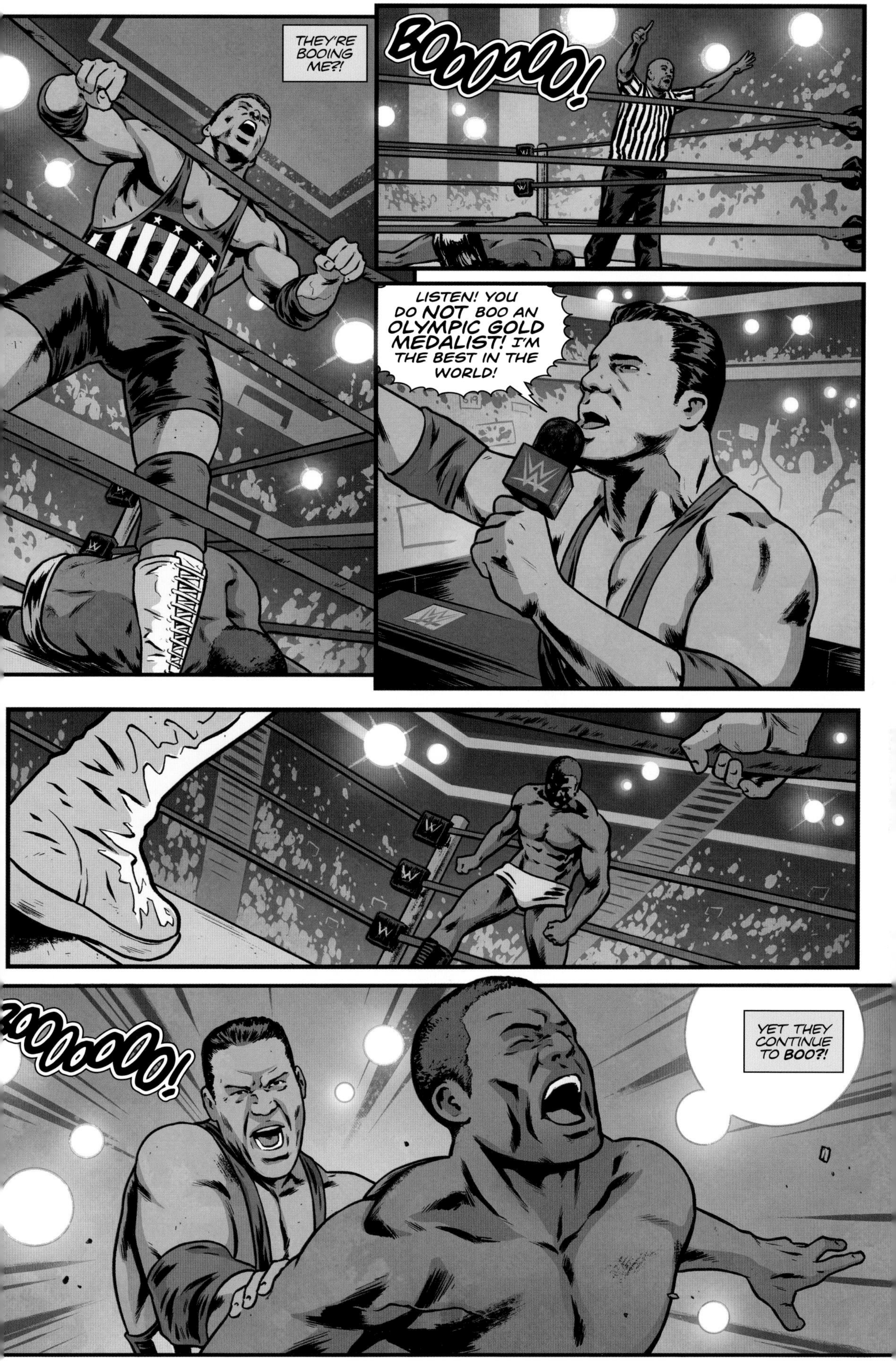
THEY'RE BOOING ME?!
BOOOOOOO!
LISTEN! YOU DO NOT BOO AN OLYMPIC GOLD MEDALIST! I'M THE BEST IN THE WORLD!
OOOOOOO!
YET THEY CONTINUE TO BOO?!

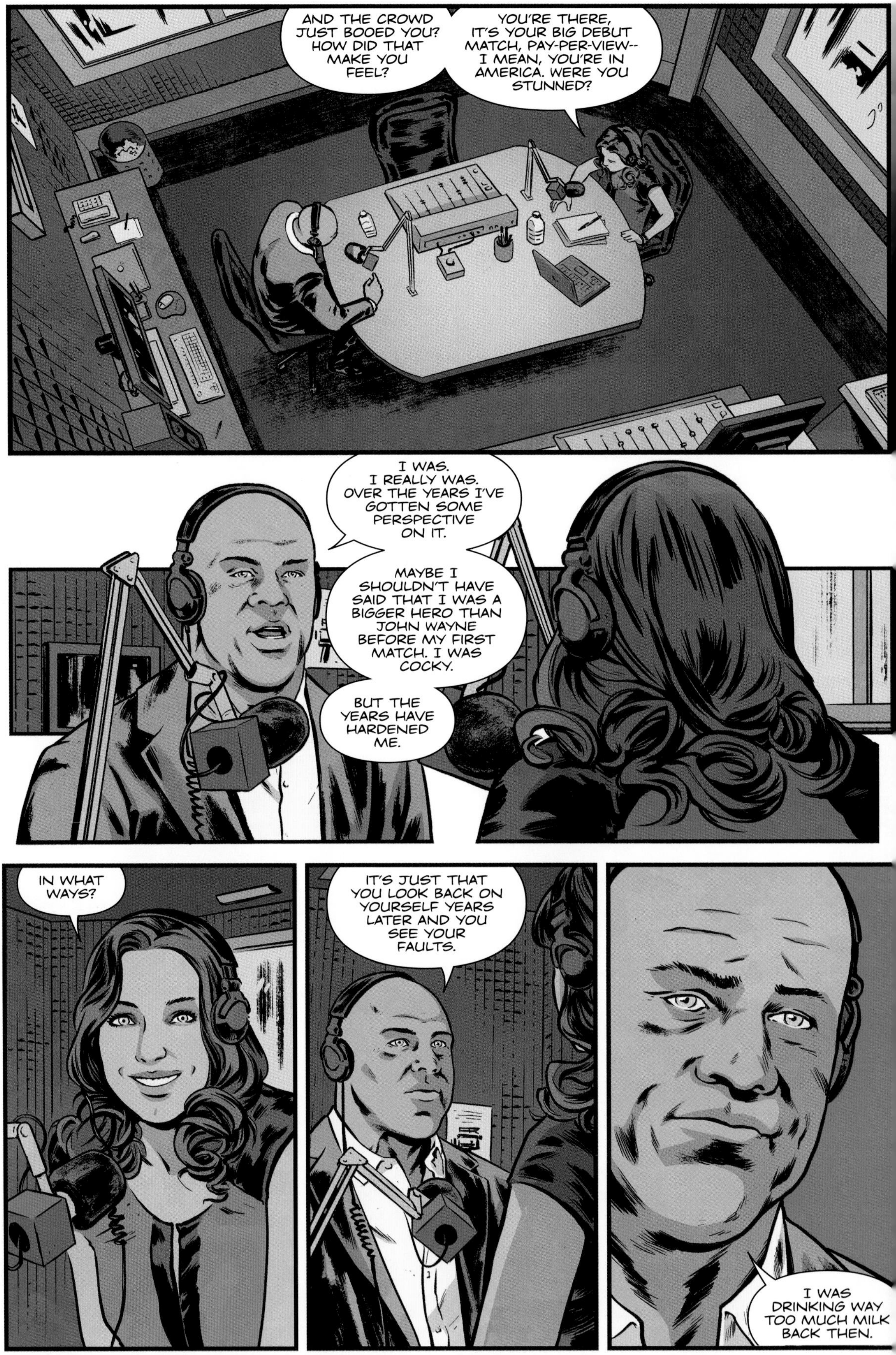
AND THE CROWD JUST BOOED YOU? HOW DID THAT MAKE YOU FEEL?
YOU'RE THERE, IT'S YOUR BIG DEBUT MATCH, PAY-PER-VIEW-- I MEAN, YOU'RE IN AMERICA. WERE YOU STUNNED?
I WAS. I REALLY WAS. OVER THE YEARS I'VE GOTTEN SOME PERSPECTIVE ON IT.
MAYBE I SHOULDN'T HAVE SAID THAT I WAS A BIGGER HERO THAN JOHN WAYNE BEFORE MY FIRST MATCH. I WAS COCKY.
BUT THE YEARS HAVE HARDENED ME.
IN WHAT WAYS?
IT'S JUST THAT YOU LOOK BACK ON YOURSELF YEARS LATER AND YOU SEE YOUR FAULTS.
I WAS DRINKING WAY TOO MUCH MILK BACK THEN.

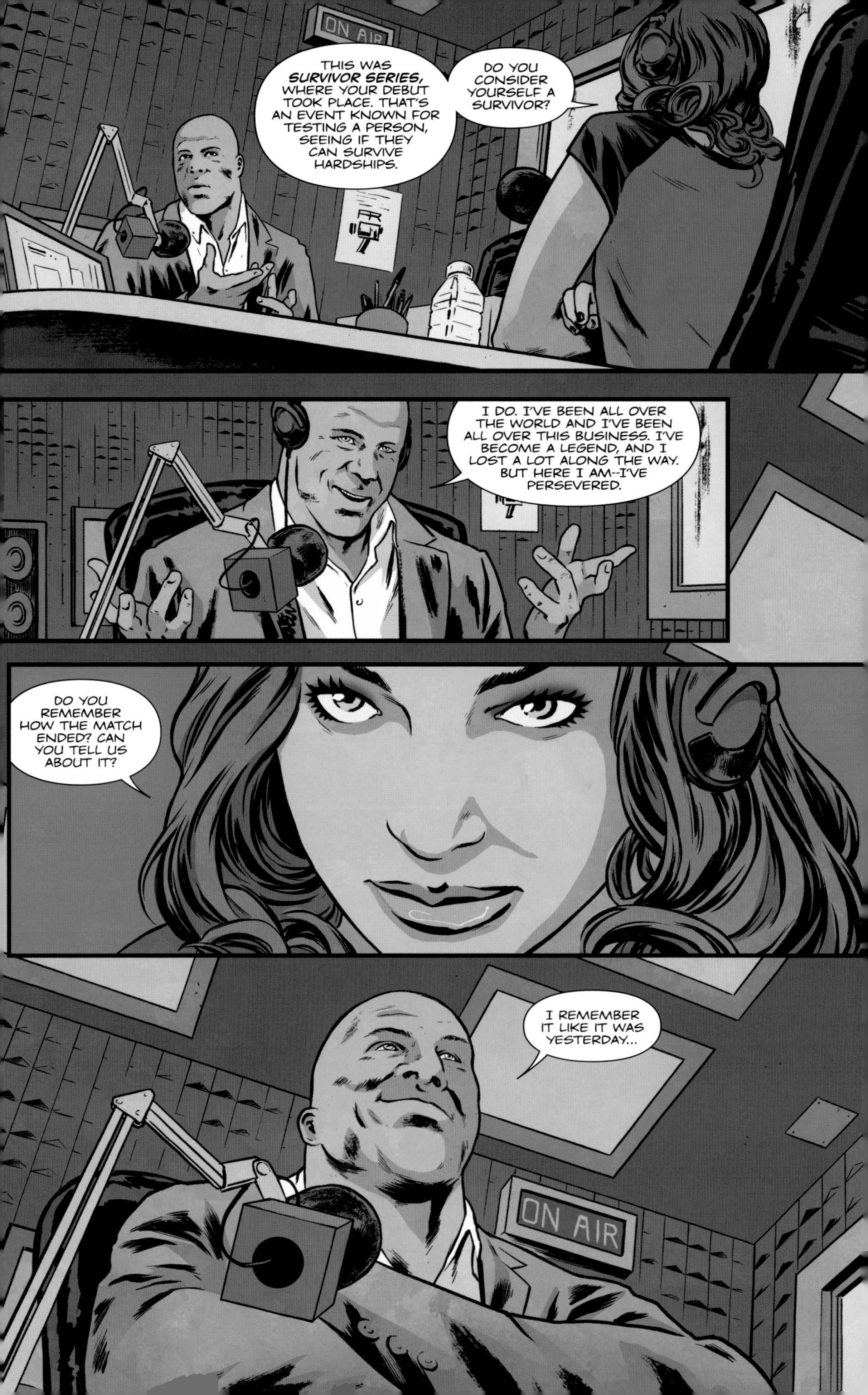
ON AIR
THIS WAS **SURVIVOR SERIES,** WHERE YOUR DEBUT TOOK PLACE. THAT'S AN EVENT KNOWN FOR TESTING A PERSON, SEEING IF THEY CAN SURVIVE HARDSHIPS.
DO YOU CONSIDER YOURSELF A SURVIVOR?
I DO. I'VE BEEN ALL OVER THE WORLD AND I'VE BEEN ALL OVER THIS BUSINESS. I'VE BECOME A LEGEND, AND I LOST A LOT ALONG THE WAY. BUT HERE I AM--I'VE PERSEVERED.
DO YOU REMEMBER HOW THE MATCH ENDED? CAN YOU TELL US ABOUT IT?
I REMEMBER IT LIKE IT WAS YESTERDAY...
ON AIR

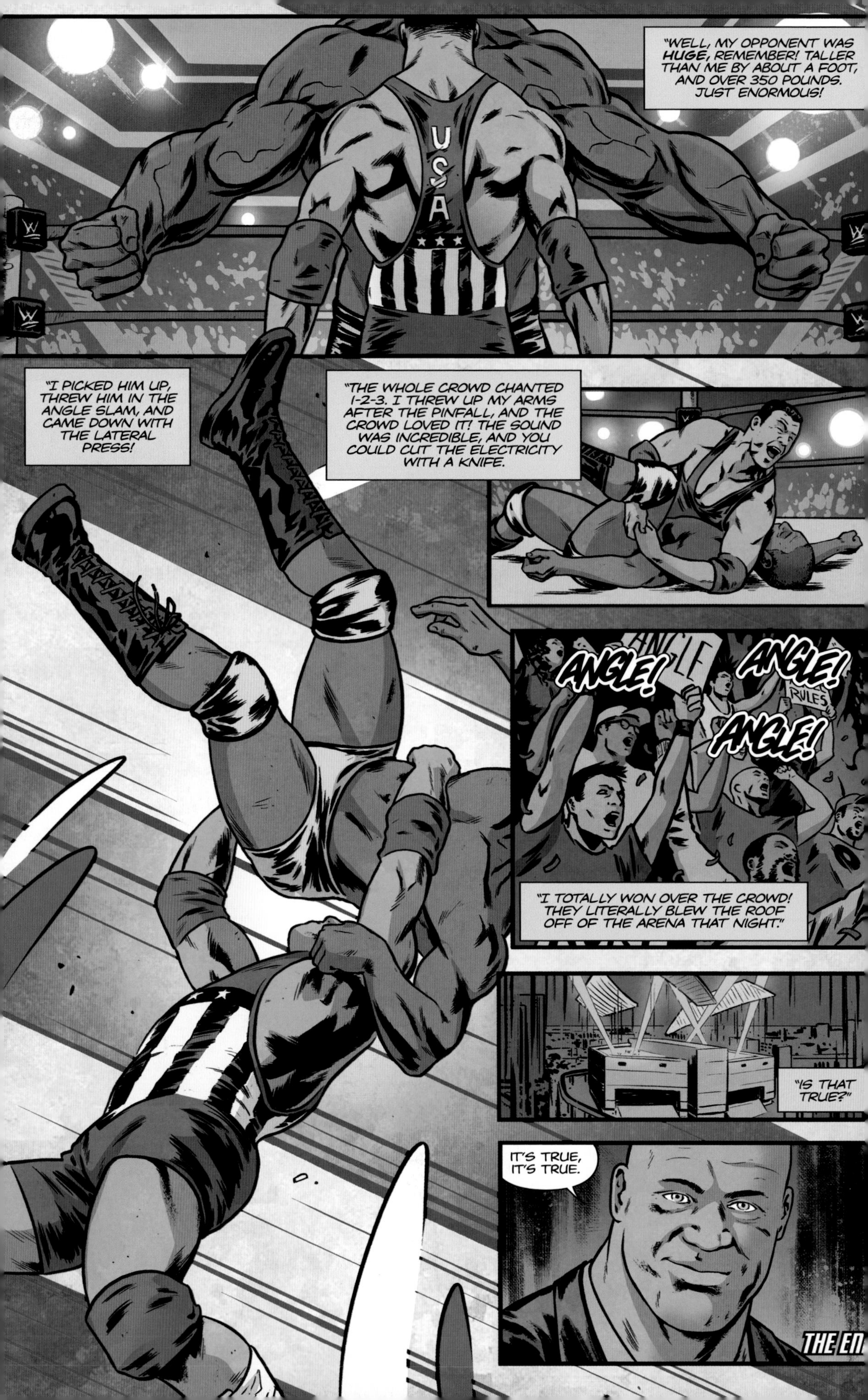
"WELL, MY OPPONENT WAS HUGE, REMEMBER! TALLER THAN ME BY ABOUT A FOOT, AND OVER 350 POUNDS. JUST ENORMOUS!
USA
"I PICKED HIM UP, THREW HIM IN THE ANGLE SLAM, AND CAME DOWN WITH THE LATERAL PRESS!
"THE WHOLE CROWD CHANTED 1-2-3. I THREW UP MY ARMS AFTER THE PINFALL, AND THE CROWD LOVED IT! THE SOUND WAS INCREDIBLE, AND YOU COULD CUT THE ELECTRICITY WITH A KNIFE.
ANGLE!
ANGLE!
ANGLE!
RULES
"I TOTALLY WON OVER THE CROWD! THEY LITERALLY BLEW THE ROOF OFF OF THE ARENA THAT NIGHT."
"IS THAT TRUE?"
IT'S TRUE, IT'S TRUE.
THE EN

# DOWN THE HATCH

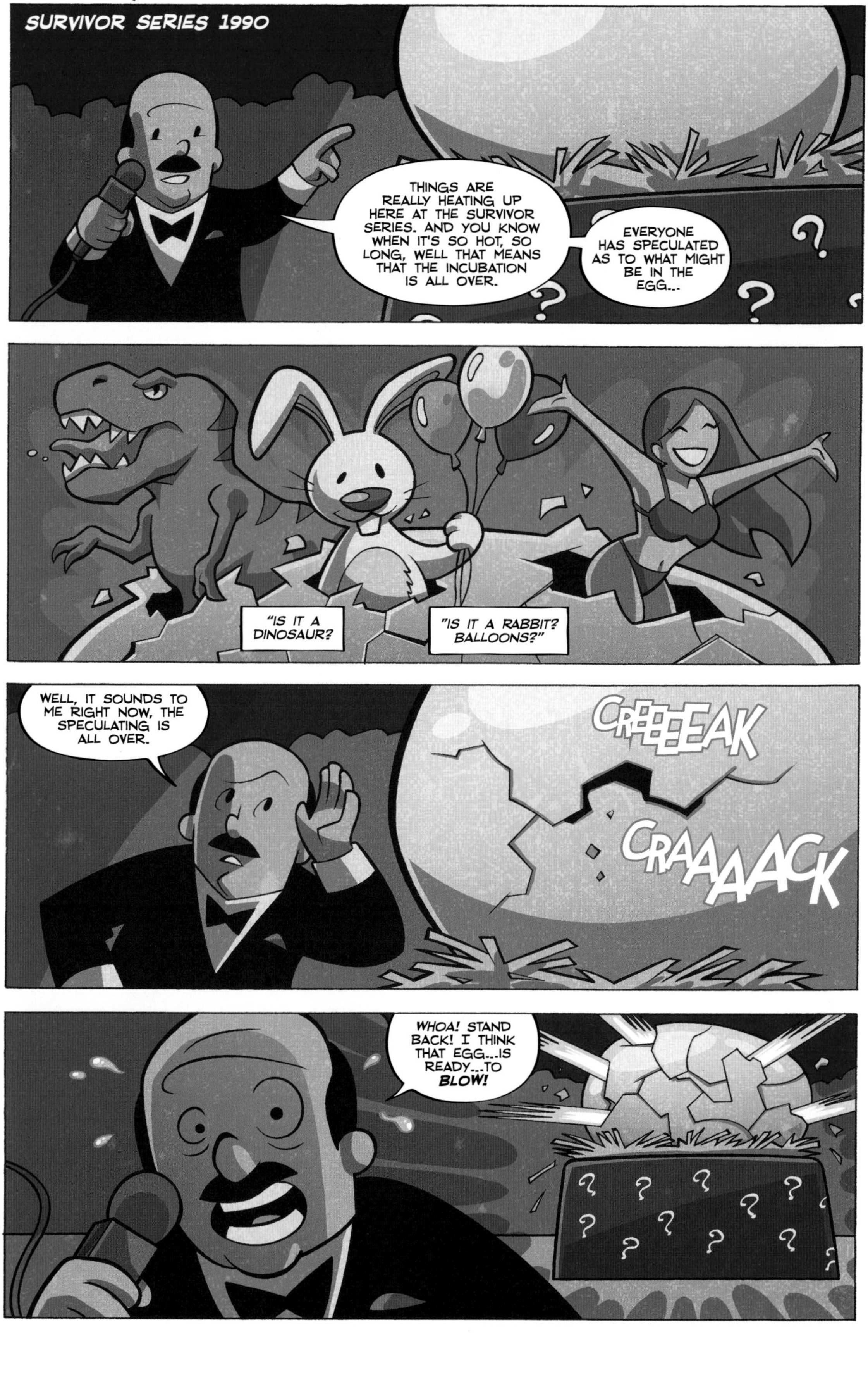
SURVIVOR SERIES 1990
THINGS ARE REALLY HEATING UP HERE AT THE SURVIVOR SERIES. AND YOU KNOW WHEN IT'S SO HOT, SO LONG, WELL THAT MEANS THAT THE INCUBATION IS ALL OVER.
EVERYONE HAS SPECULATED AS TO WHAT MIGHT BE IN THE EGG...
"IS IT A DINOSAUR?
"IS IT A RABBIT? BALLOONS?"
WELL, IT SOUNDS TO ME RIGHT NOW, THE SPECULATING IS ALL OVER.
CREEEEAK
CRAAAACK
WHOA! STAND BACK! I THINK THAT EGG...IS READY...TO BLOW!

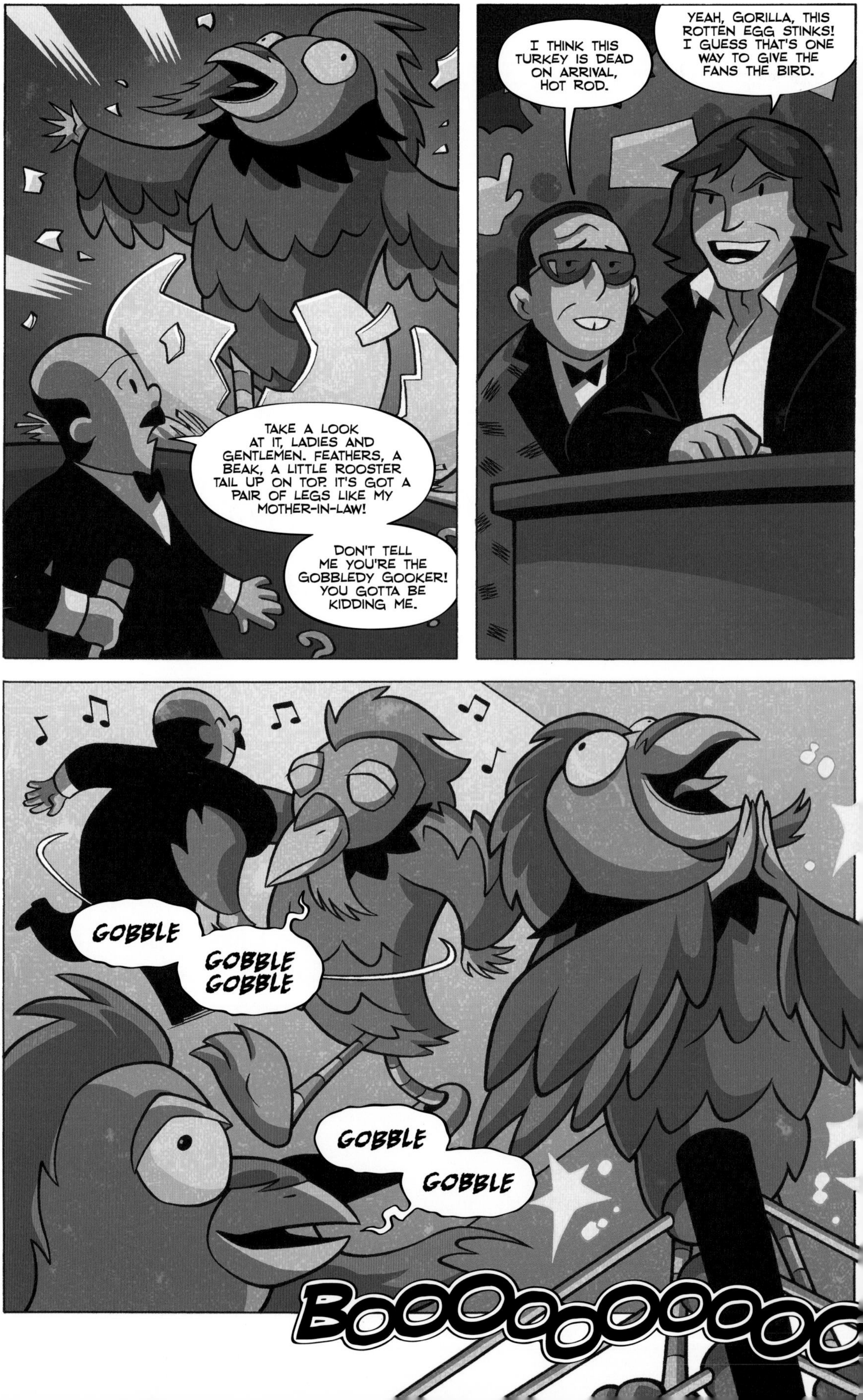
TAKE A LOOK AT IT, LADIES AND GENTLEMEN. FEATHERS, A BEAK, A LITTLE ROOSTER TAIL UP ON TOP. IT'S GOT A PAIR OF LEGS LIKE MY MOTHER-IN-LAW!
DON'T TELL ME YOU'RE THE GOBBLEDY GOOKER! YOU GOTTA BE KIDDING ME.
I THINK THIS TURKEY IS DEAD ON ARRIVAL, HOT ROD.
YEAH, GORILLA, THIS ROTTEN EGG STINKS! I GUESS THAT'S ONE WAY TO GIVE THE FANS THE BIRD.
GOBBLE
GOBBLE GOBBLE
GOBBLE
GOBBLE
BOOOOOOOOOOOO

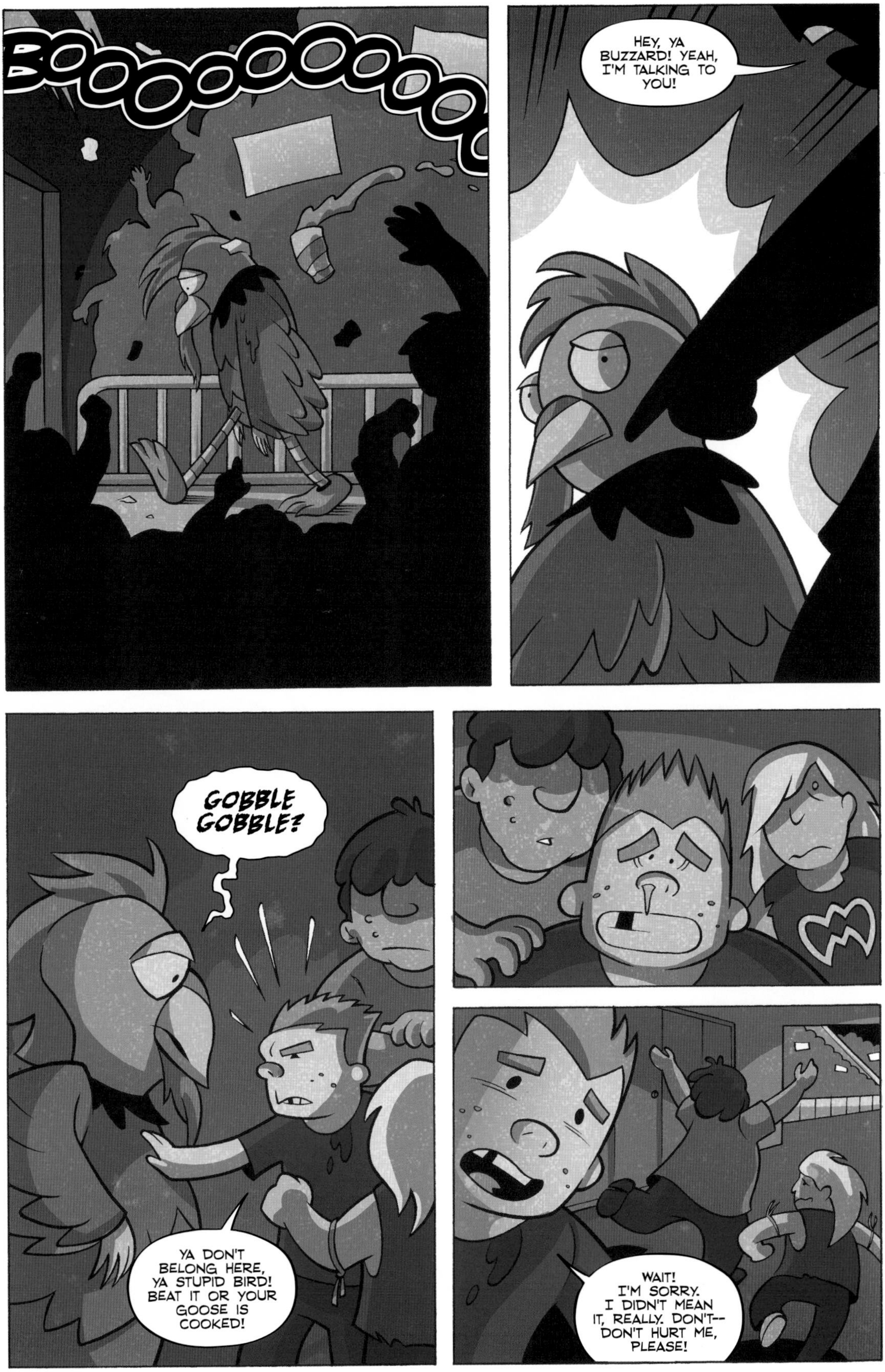
BOOOOOOOOOOO
HEY, YA BUZZARD! YEAH, I'M TALKING TO YOU!
GOBBLE GOBBLE?
YA DON'T BELONG HERE, YA STUPID BIRD! BEAT IT OR YOUR GOOSE IS COOKED!
WAIT! I'M SORRY. I DIDN'T MEAN IT, REALLY. DON'T-- DON'T HURT ME, PLEASE!

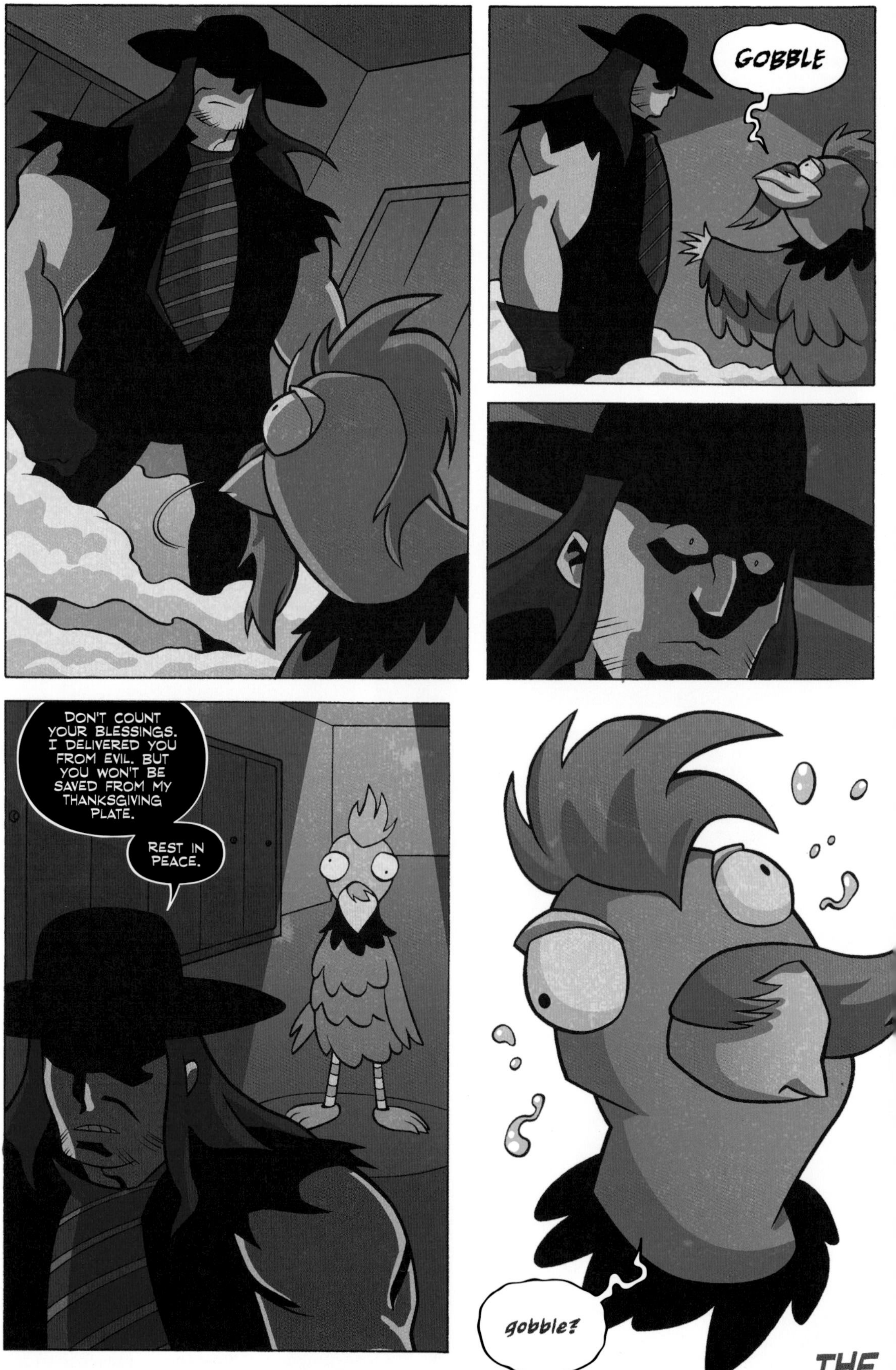
GOBBLE
DON'T COUNT YOUR BLESSINGS. I DELIVERED YOU FROM EVIL. BUT YOU WON'T BE SAVED FROM MY THANKSGIVING PLATE.
REST IN PEACE.
gobble?
THE END

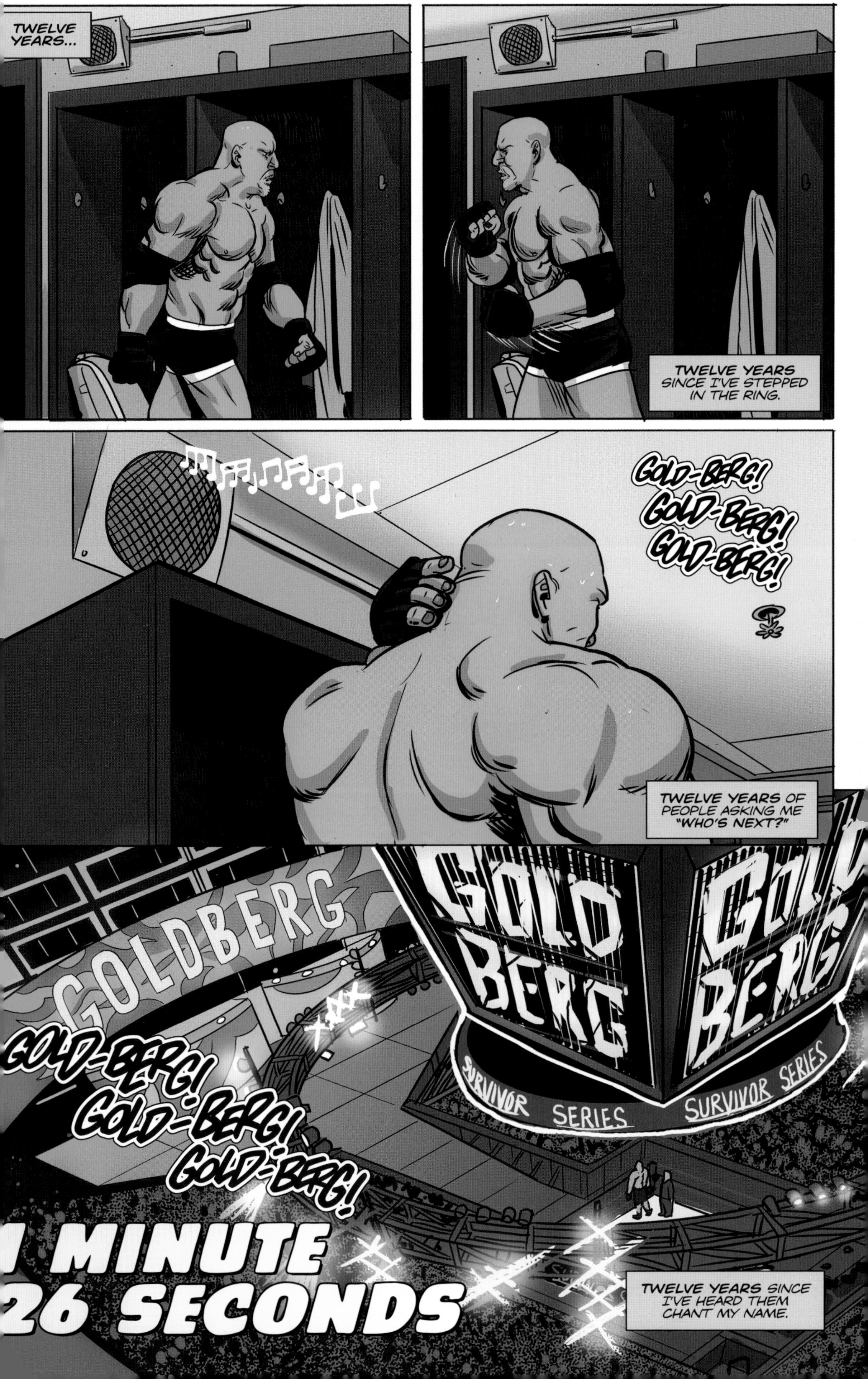
TWELVE YEARS...
TWELVE YEARS SINCE I'VE STEPPED IN THE RING.
GOLD-BERG! GOLD-BERG! GOLD-BERG!
TWELVE YEARS OF PEOPLE ASKING ME "WHO'S NEXT?"
GOLDBERG
GOLDBERG
GOLDBERG
SURVIVOR SERIES
SURVIVOR SERIES
GOLD-BERG! GOLD-BERG! GOLD-BERG!
1 MINUTE 26 SECONDS
TWELVE YEARS SINCE I'VE HEARD THEM CHANT MY NAME.

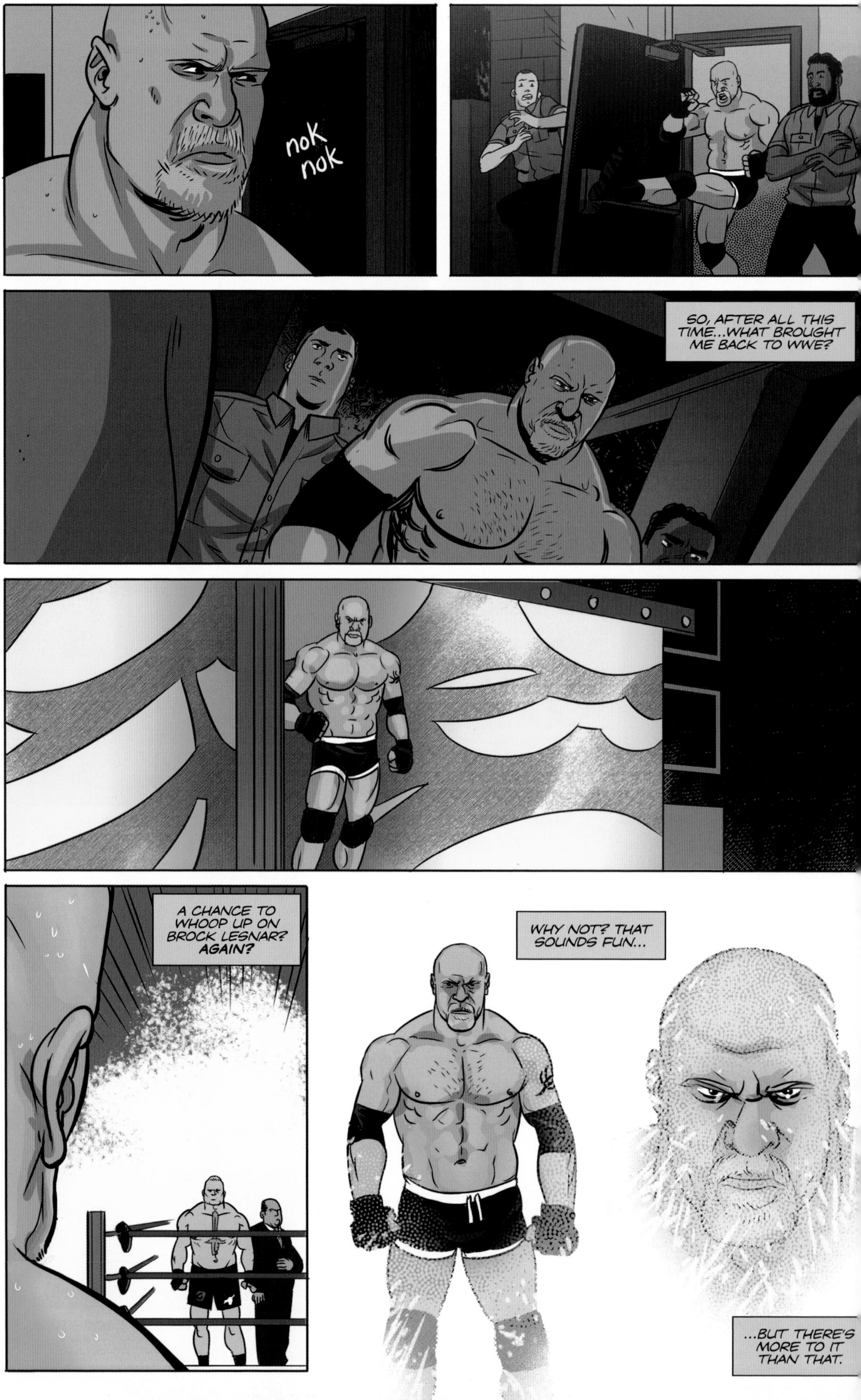
nok nok
SO, AFTER ALL THIS TIME...WHAT BROUGHT ME BACK TO WWE?
A CHANCE TO WHOOP UP ON BROCK LESNAR? AGAIN?
WHY NOT? THAT SOUNDS FUN...
...BUT THERE'S MORE TO IT THAN THAT.

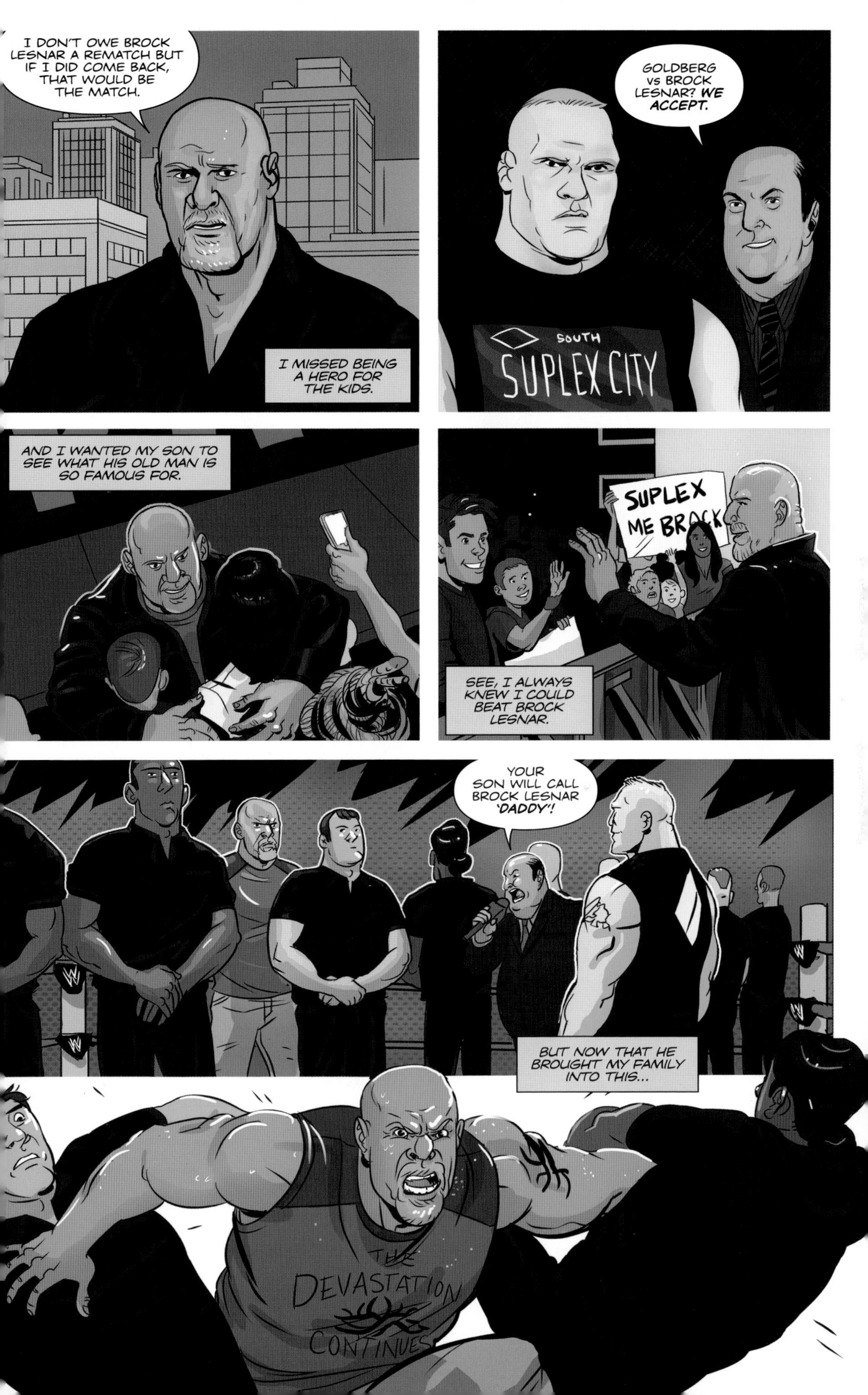
I DON'T OWE BROCK LESNAR A REMATCH BUT IF I DID COME BACK, THAT WOULD BE THE MATCH.
I MISSED BEING A HERO FOR THE KIDS.
GOLDBERG vs BROCK LESNAR? WE ACCEPT.
SOUTH
SUPLEX CITY
AND I WANTED MY SON TO SEE WHAT HIS OLD MAN IS SO FAMOUS FOR.
SUPLEX ME BROCK
SEE, I ALWAYS KNEW I COULD BEAT BROCK LESNAR.
YOUR SON WILL CALL BROCK LESNAR 'DADDY'!
BUT NOW THAT HE BROUGHT MY FAMILY INTO THIS...
THE DEVASTATION CONTINUES

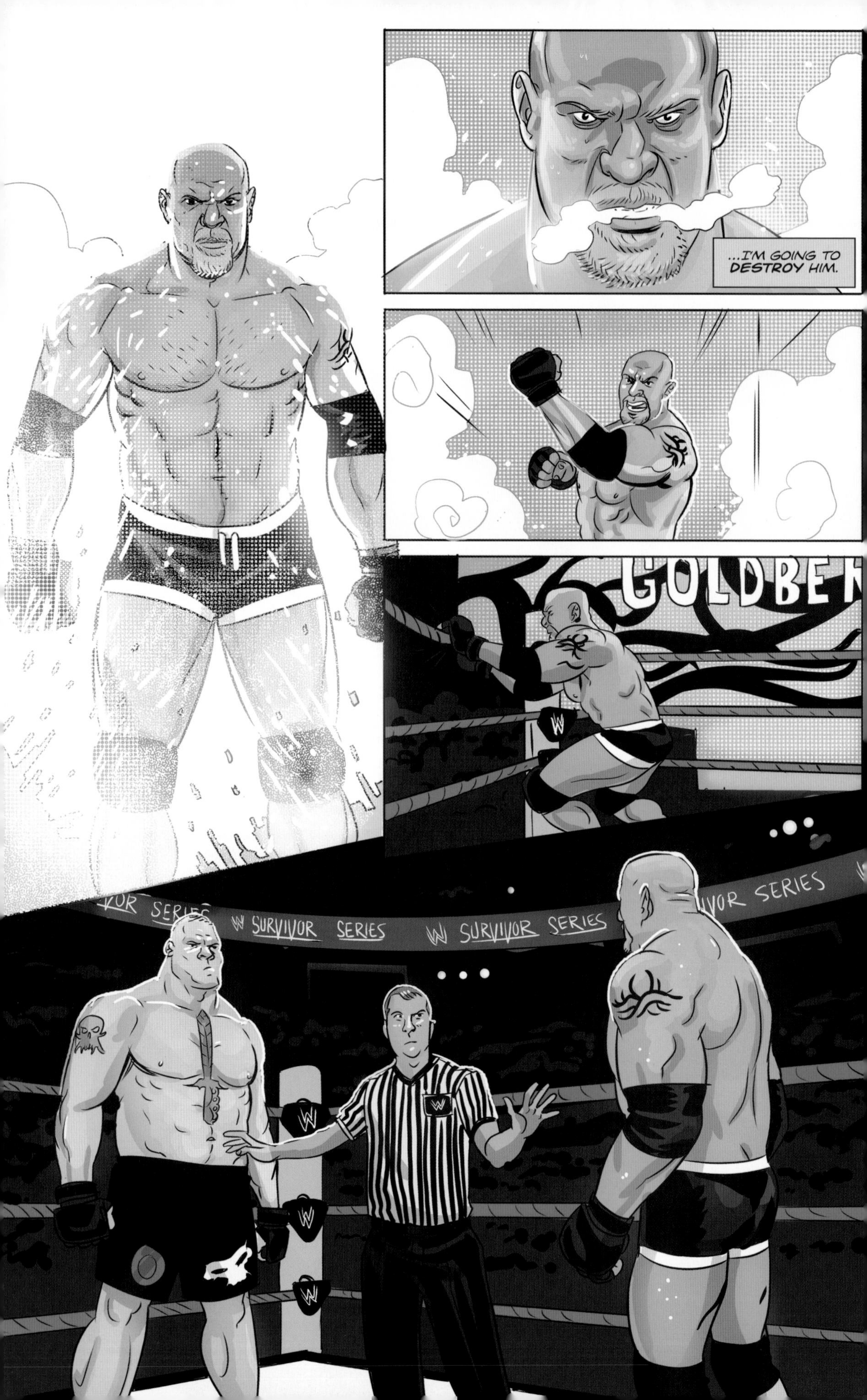
...I'M GOING TO DESTROY HIM.
GOLDBER
VIVOR SERIES
VOR SERIES
SURVIVOR SERIES
SURVIVOR SERIES

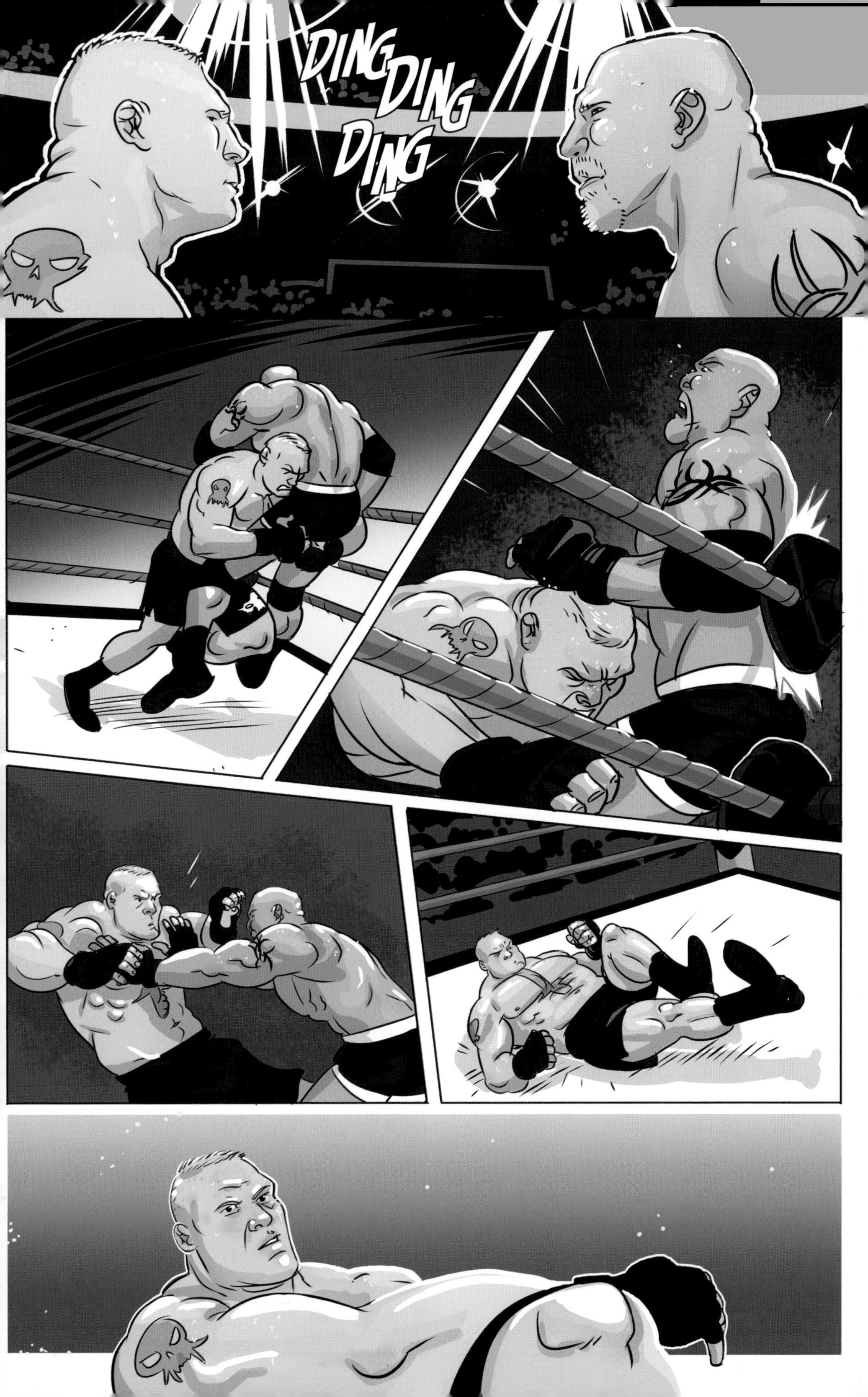
DING DING DING

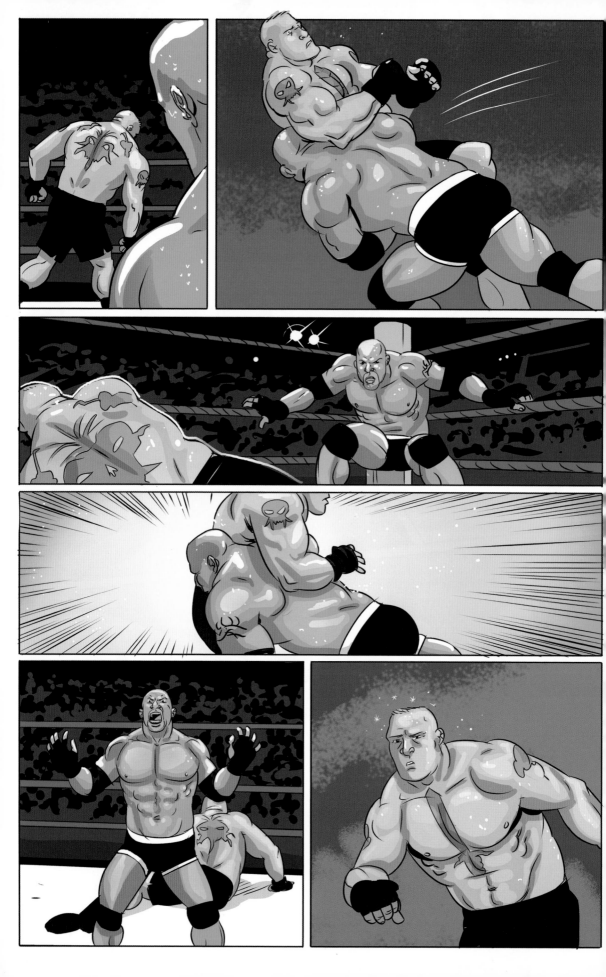

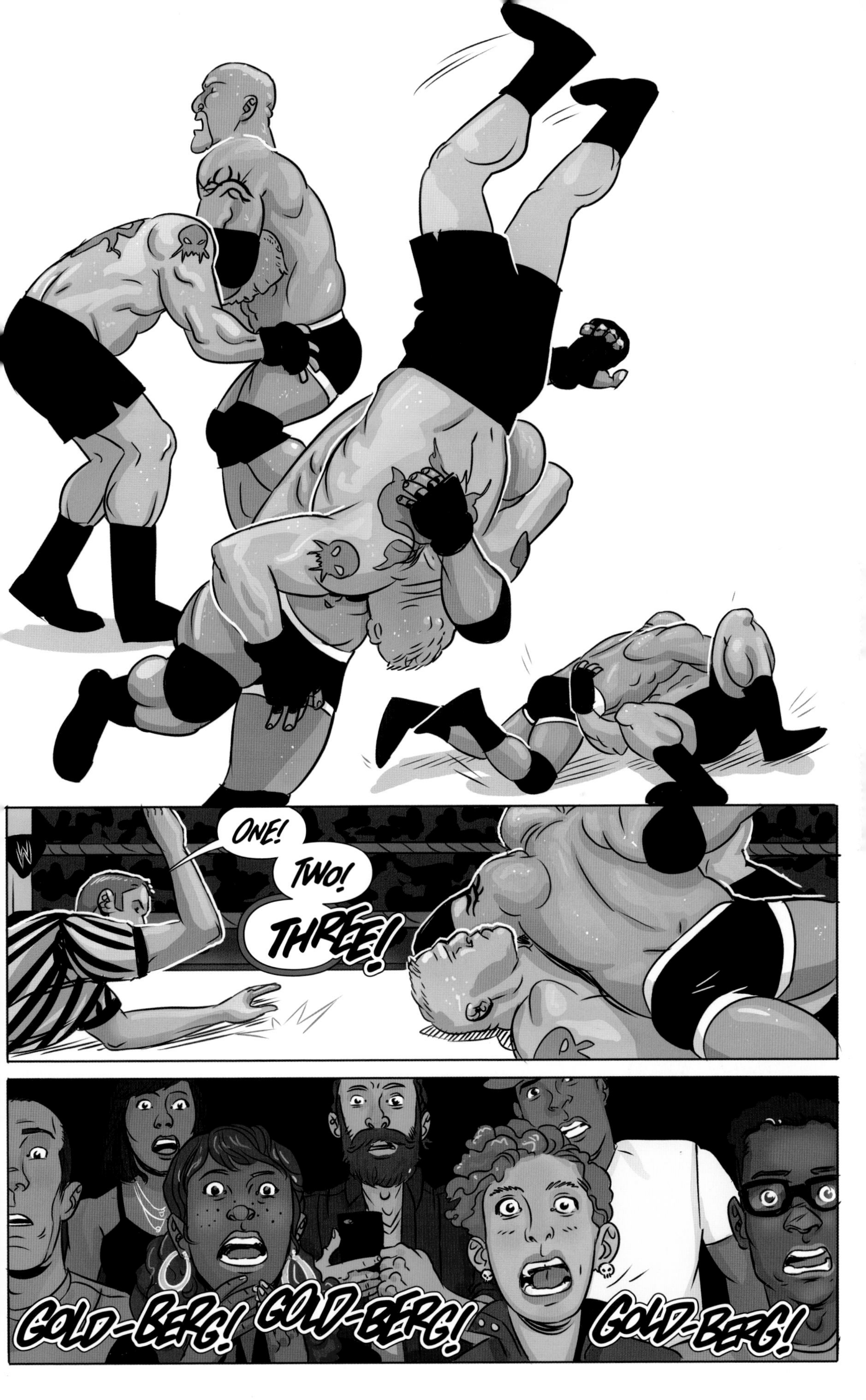
ONE!
TWO!
THREE!
GOLD-BERG!
GOLD-BERG!
GOLD-BERG!

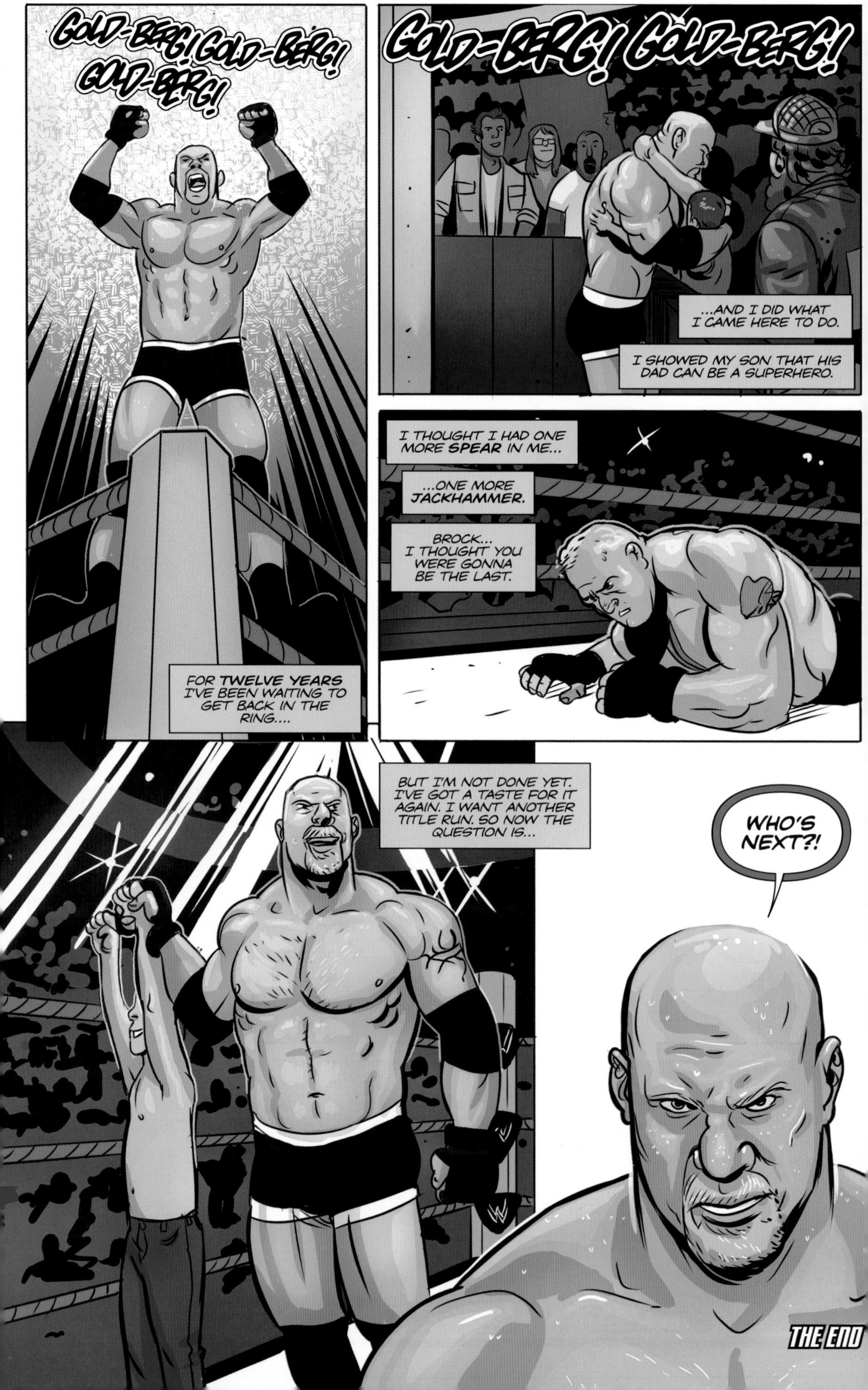
GOLD-BERG! GOLD-BERG!
GOLD-BERG!
FOR TWELVE YEARS I'VE BEEN WAITING TO GET BACK IN THE RING....
GOLD-BERG! GOLD-BERG!
...AND I DID WHAT I CAME HERE TO DO.
I SHOWED MY SON THAT HIS DAD CAN BE A SUPERHERO.
I THOUGHT I HAD ONE MORE SPEAR IN ME...
...ONE MORE JACKHAMMER.
BROCK... I THOUGHT YOU WERE GONNA BE THE LAST.
BUT I'M NOT DONE YET. I'VE GOT A TASTE FOR IT AGAIN. I WANT ANOTHER TITLE RUN. SO NOW THE QUESTION IS...
WHO'S NEXT?!
THE END

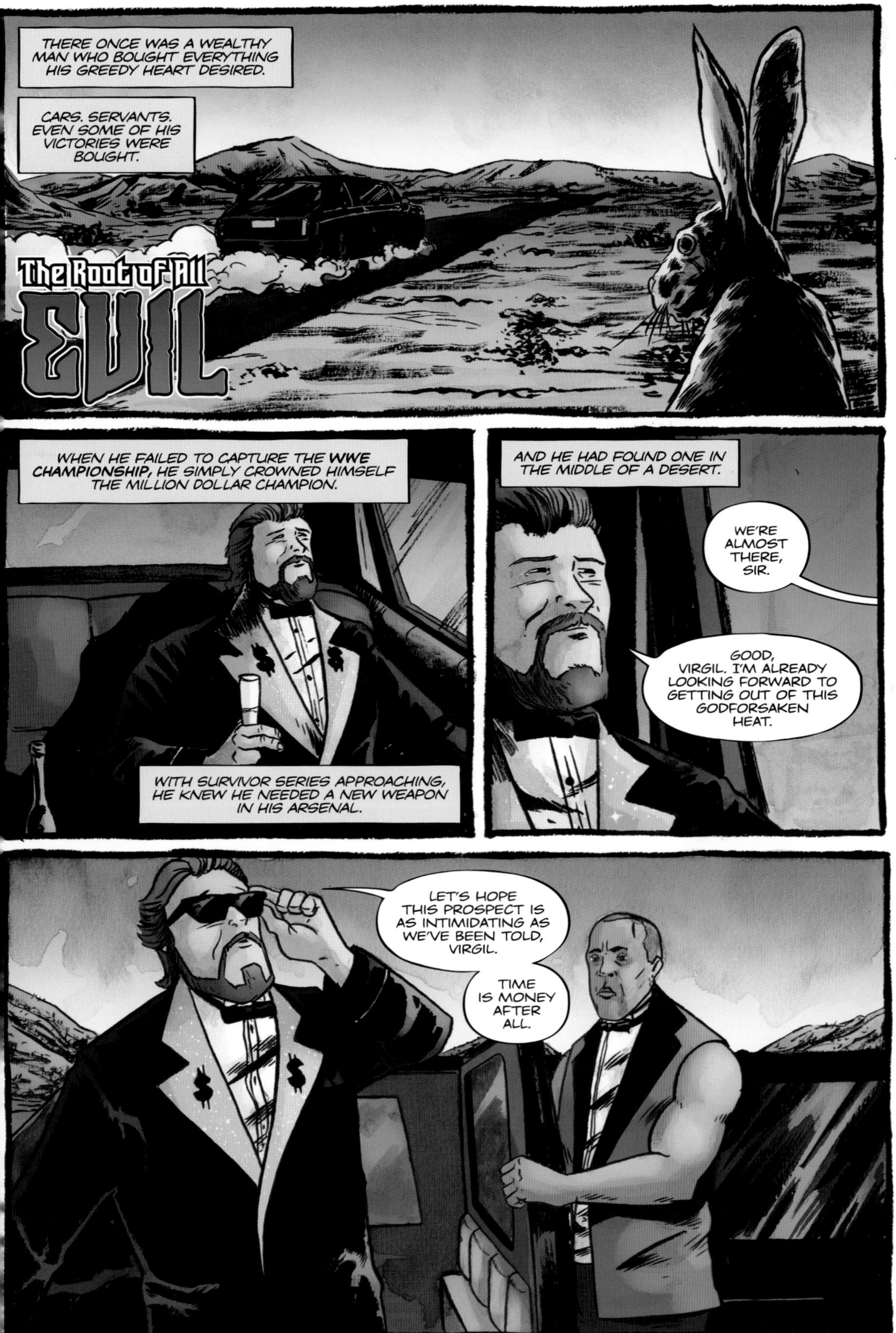
THERE ONCE WAS A WEALTHY MAN WHO BOUGHT EVERYTHING HIS GREEDY HEART DESIRED.
CARS. SERVANTS. EVEN SOME OF HIS VICTORIES WERE BOUGHT.
The Root of All EVIL
WHEN HE FAILED TO CAPTURE THE **WWE CHAMPIONSHIP,** HE SIMPLY CROWNED HIMSELF THE MILLION DOLLAR CHAMPION.
WITH SURVIVOR SERIES APPROACHING, HE KNEW HE NEEDED A NEW WEAPON IN HIS ARSENAL.
AND HE HAD FOUND ONE IN THE MIDDLE OF A DESERT.
WE'RE ALMOST THERE, SIR.
GOOD, VIRGIL. I'M ALREADY LOOKING FORWARD TO GETTING OUT OF THIS GODFORSAKEN HEAT.
LET'S HOPE THIS PROSPECT IS AS INTIMIDATING AS WE'VE BEEN TOLD, VIRGIL.
TIME IS MONEY AFTER ALL.

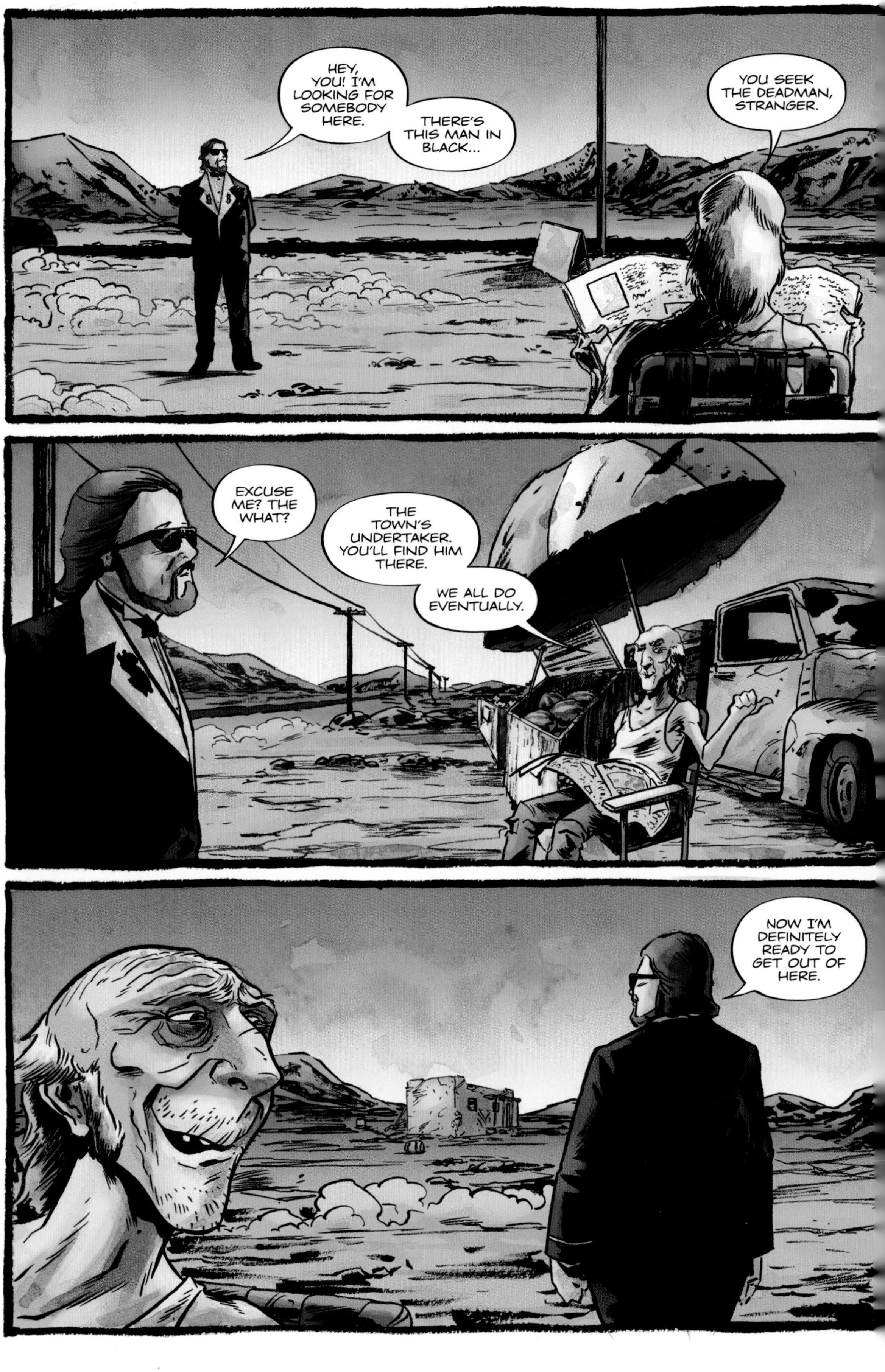
HEY, YOU! I'M LOOKING FOR SOMEBODY HERE.
THERE'S THIS MAN IN BLACK...
YOU SEEK THE DEADMAN, STRANGER.
EXCUSE ME? THE WHAT?
THE TOWN'S UNDERTAKER. YOU'LL FIND HIM THERE.
WE ALL DO EVENTUALLY.
NOW I'M DEFINITELY READY TO GET OUT OF HERE.

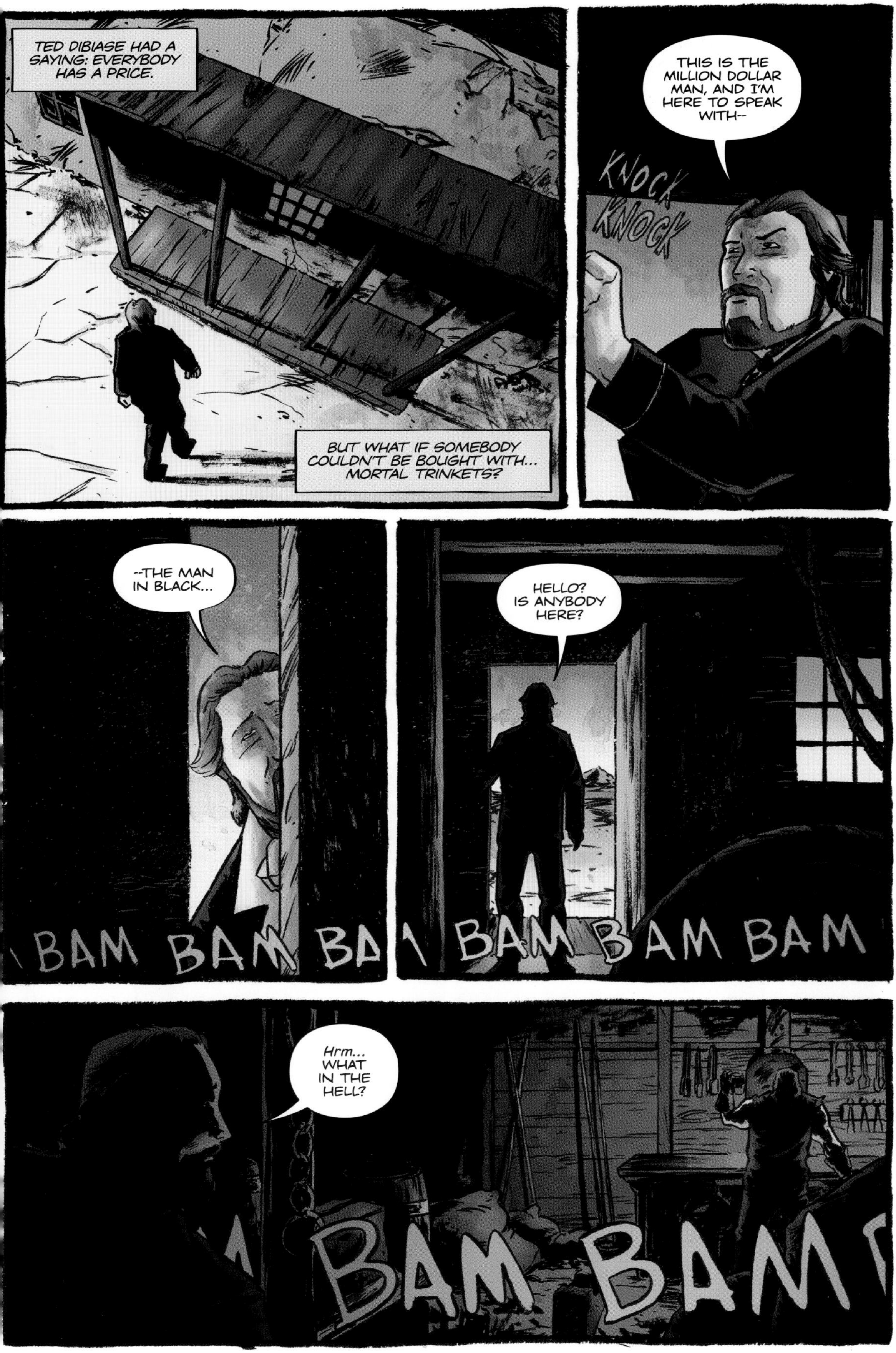
TED DIBIASE HAD A SAYING: EVERYBODY HAS A PRICE.
BUT WHAT IF SOMEBODY COULDN'T BE BOUGHT WITH... MORTAL TRINKETS?
THIS IS THE MILLION DOLLAR MAN, AND I'M HERE TO SPEAK WITH--
KNOCK KNOCK
--THE MAN IN BLACK...
HELLO? IS ANYBODY HERE?
BAM BAM BA BAM BAM BAM
Hrm... WHAT IN THE HELL?
BAM BAM

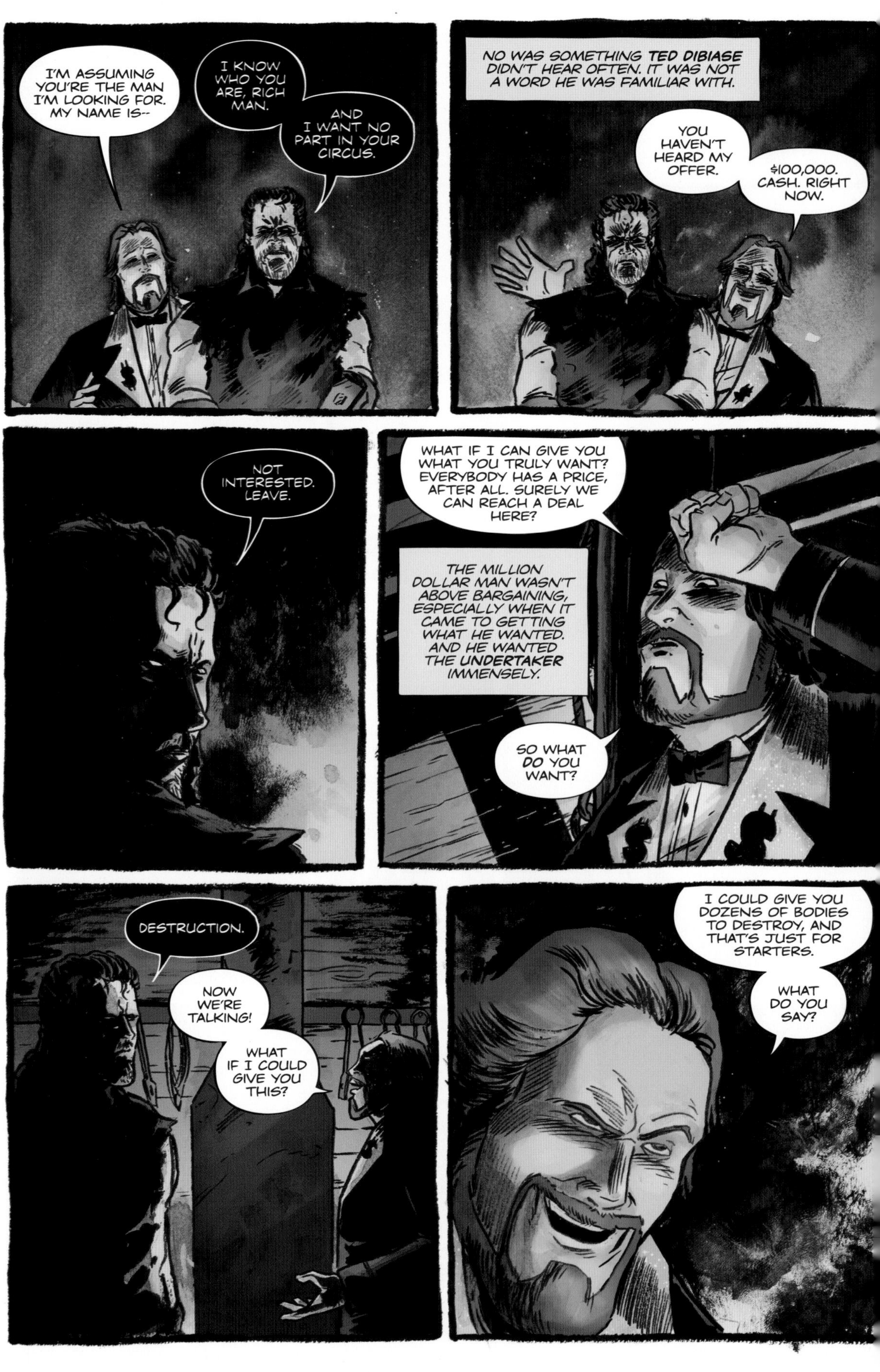

I'M ASSUMING YOU'RE THE MAN I'M LOOKING FOR. MY NAME IS--
I KNOW WHO YOU ARE, RICH MAN.
AND I WANT NO PART IN YOUR CIRCUS.
NO WAS SOMETHING TED DIBIASE DIDN'T HEAR OFTEN. IT WAS NOT A WORD HE WAS FAMILIAR WITH.
YOU HAVEN'T HEARD MY OFFER.
$100,000. CASH. RIGHT NOW.
NOT INTERESTED. LEAVE.
WHAT IF I CAN GIVE YOU WHAT YOU TRULY WANT? EVERYBODY HAS A PRICE, AFTER ALL. SURELY WE CAN REACH A DEAL HERE?
THE MILLION DOLLAR MAN WASN'T ABOVE BARGAINING, ESPECIALLY WHEN IT CAME TO GETTING WHAT HE WANTED. AND HE WANTED THE UNDERTAKER IMMENSELY.
SO WHAT DO YOU WANT?
DESTRUCTION.
NOW WE'RE TALKING!
WHAT IF I COULD GIVE YOU THIS?
I COULD GIVE YOU DOZENS OF BODIES TO DESTROY, AND THAT'S JUST FOR STARTERS.
WHAT DO YOU SAY?

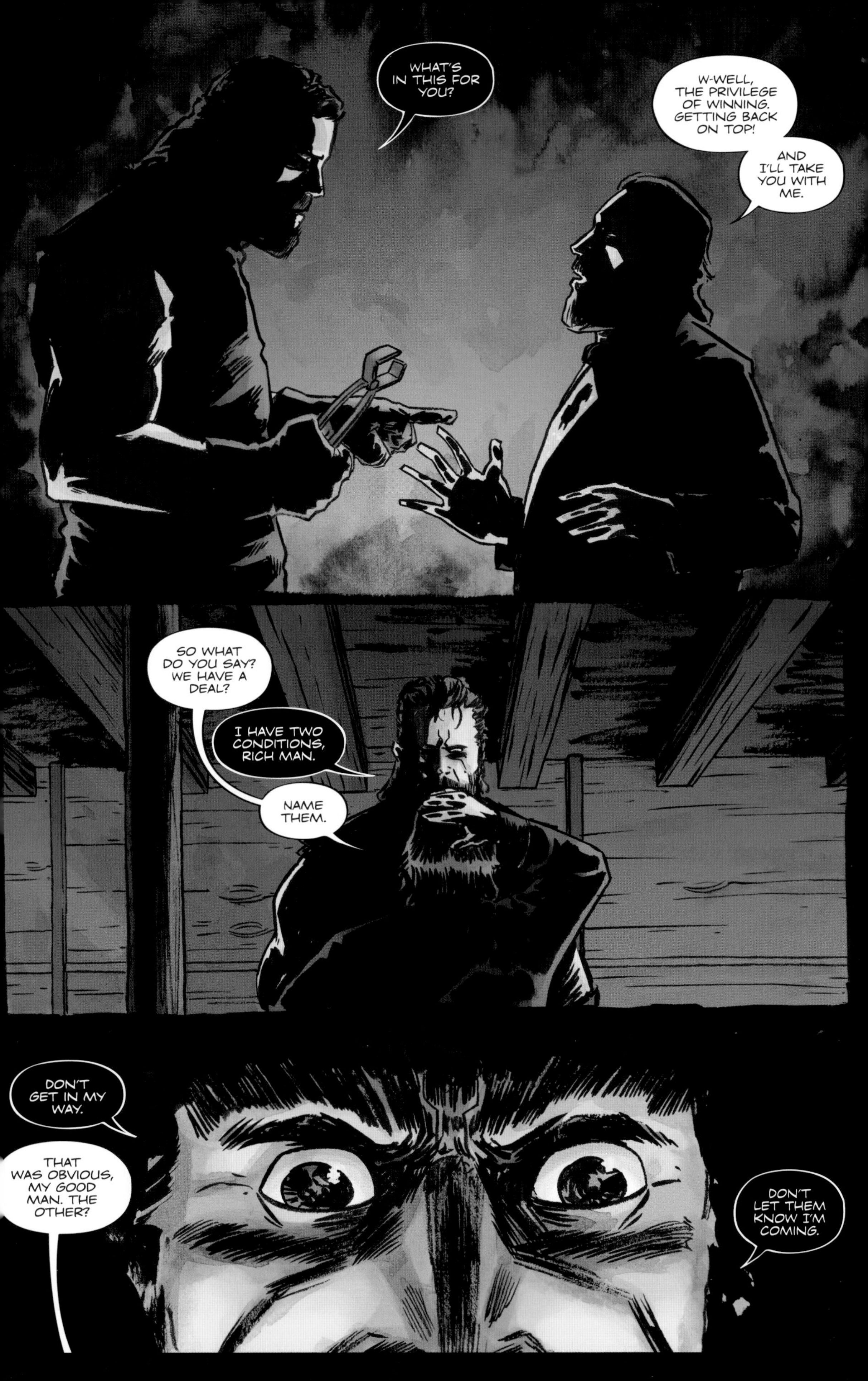
WHAT'S IN THIS FOR YOU?
W-WELL, THE PRIVILEGE OF WINNING. GETTING BACK ON TOP!
AND I'LL TAKE YOU WITH ME.
SO WHAT DO YOU SAY? WE HAVE A DEAL?
I HAVE TWO CONDITIONS, RICH MAN.
NAME THEM.
DON'T GET IN MY WAY.
THAT WAS OBVIOUS, MY GOOD MAN. THE OTHER?
DON'T LET THEM KNOW I'M COMING.

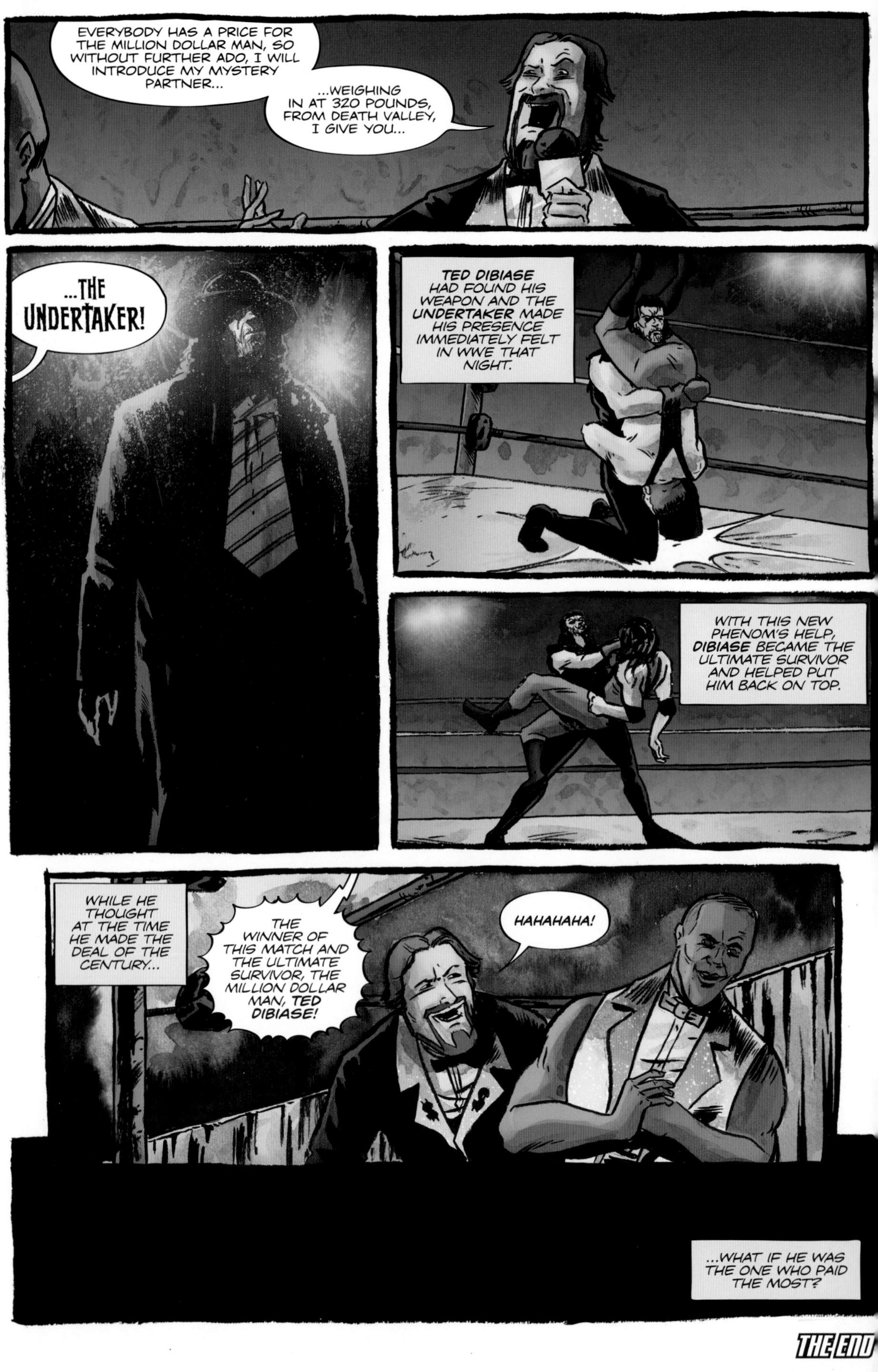
EVERYBODY HAS A PRICE FOR THE MILLION DOLLAR MAN, SO WITHOUT FURTHER ADO, I WILL INTRODUCE MY MYSTERY PARTNER...
...WEIGHING IN AT 320 POUNDS, FROM DEATH VALLEY, I GIVE YOU...
...THE UNDERTAKER!
TED DIBIASE HAD FOUND HIS WEAPON AND THE UNDERTAKER MADE HIS PRESENCE IMMEDIATELY FELT IN WWE THAT NIGHT.
WITH THIS NEW PHENOM'S HELP, DIBIASE BECAME THE ULTIMATE SURVIVOR AND HELPED PUT HIM BACK ON TOP.
WHILE HE THOUGHT AT THE TIME HE MADE THE DEAL OF THE CENTURY...
THE WINNER OF THIS MATCH AND THE ULTIMATE SURVIVOR, THE MILLION DOLLAR MAN, TED DIBIASE!
HAHAHAHA!
...WHAT IF HE WAS THE ONE WHO PAID THE MOST?
THE END

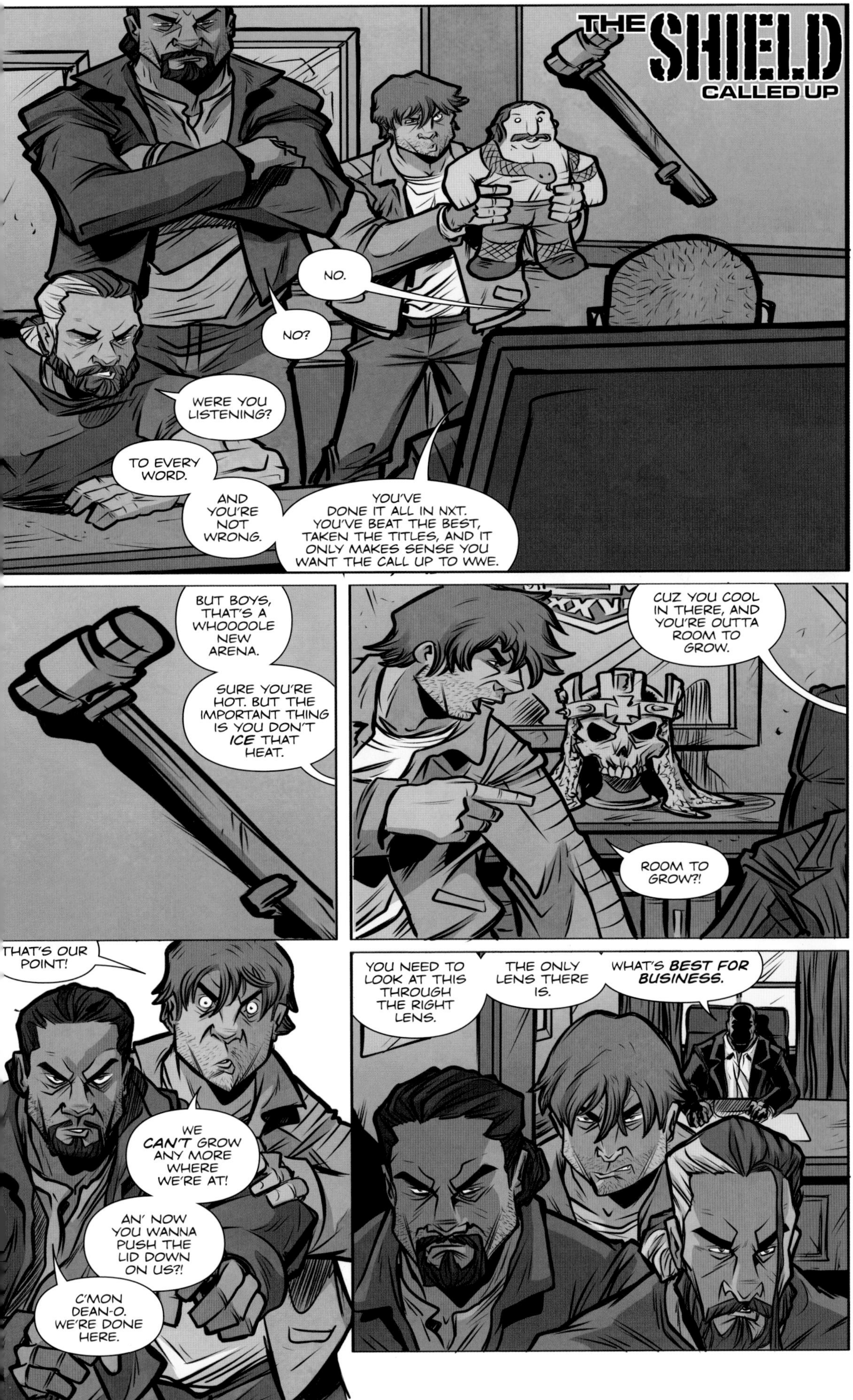
THE SHIELD CALLED UP
NO.
NO?
WERE YOU LISTENING?
TO EVERY WORD.
AND YOU'RE NOT WRONG.
YOU'VE DONE IT ALL IN NXT. YOU'VE BEAT THE BEST, TAKEN THE TITLES, AND IT ONLY MAKES SENSE YOU WANT THE CALL UP TO WWE.
BUT BOYS, THAT'S A WHOOOOLE NEW ARENA.
SURE YOU'RE HOT. BUT THE IMPORTANT THING IS YOU DON'T *ICE* THAT HEAT.
CUZ YOU COOL IN THERE, AND YOU'RE OUTTA ROOM TO GROW.
ROOM TO GROW?!
THAT'S OUR POINT!
WE *CAN'T* GROW ANY MORE WHERE WE'RE AT!
AN' NOW YOU WANNA PUSH THE LID DOWN ON US?!
C'MON DEAN-O. WE'RE DONE HERE.
YOU NEED TO LOOK AT THIS THROUGH THE RIGHT LENS.
THE ONLY LENS THERE IS.
WHAT'S **BEST FOR BUSINESS.**

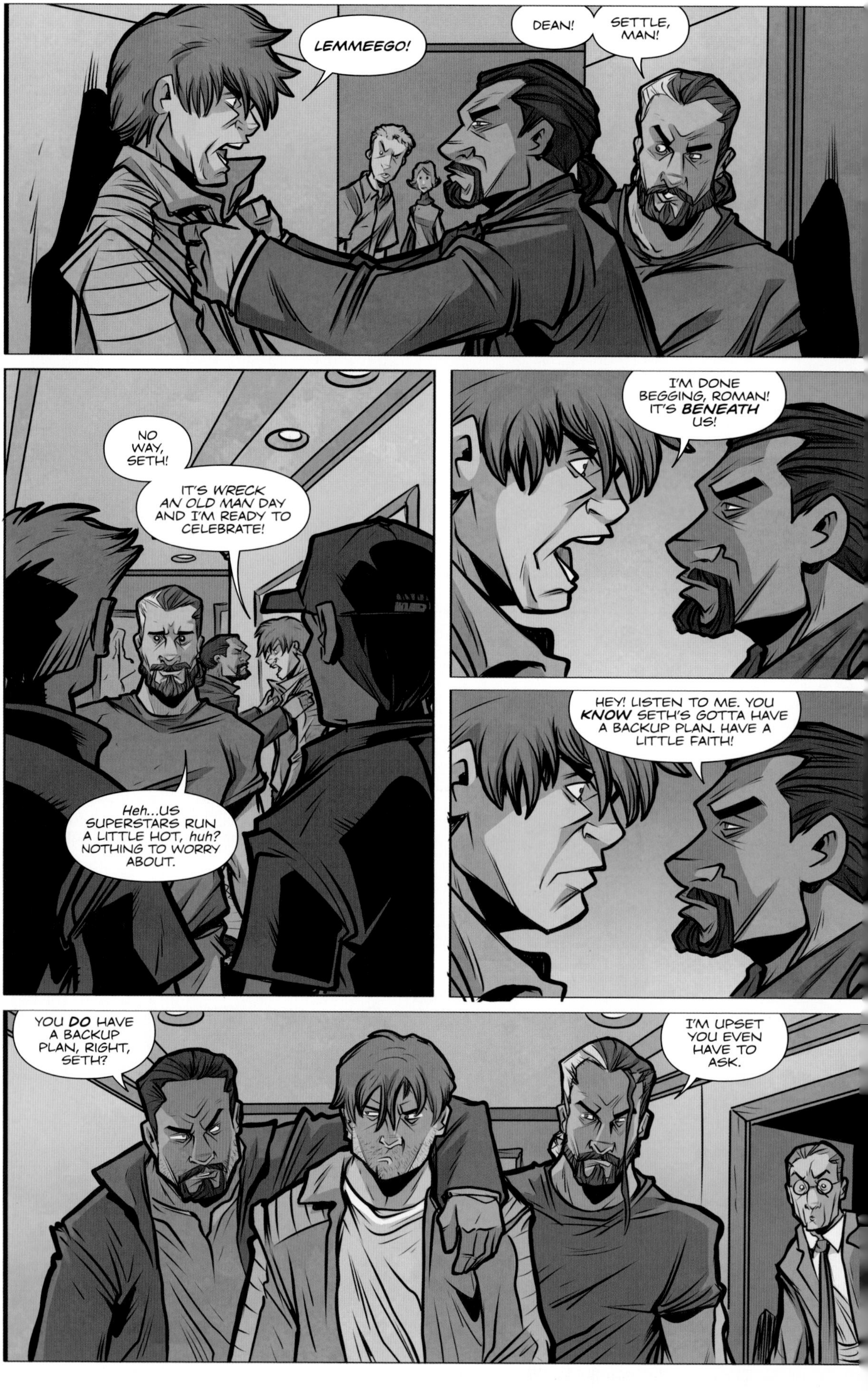
LEMMEEGO!
DEAN!
SETTLE, MAN!
NO WAY, SETH!
IT'S *WRECK AN OLD MAN DAY* AND I'M READY TO CELEBRATE!
*Heh*...US SUPERSTARS RUN A LITTLE HOT, *huh*? NOTHING TO WORRY ABOUT.
I'M DONE BEGGING, ROMAN! IT'S ***BENEATH*** US!
HEY! LISTEN TO ME. YOU ***KNOW*** SETH'S GOTTA HAVE A BACKUP PLAN. HAVE A LITTLE FAITH!
YOU ***DO*** HAVE A BACKUP PLAN, RIGHT, SETH?
I'M UPSET YOU EVEN HAVE TO ASK.

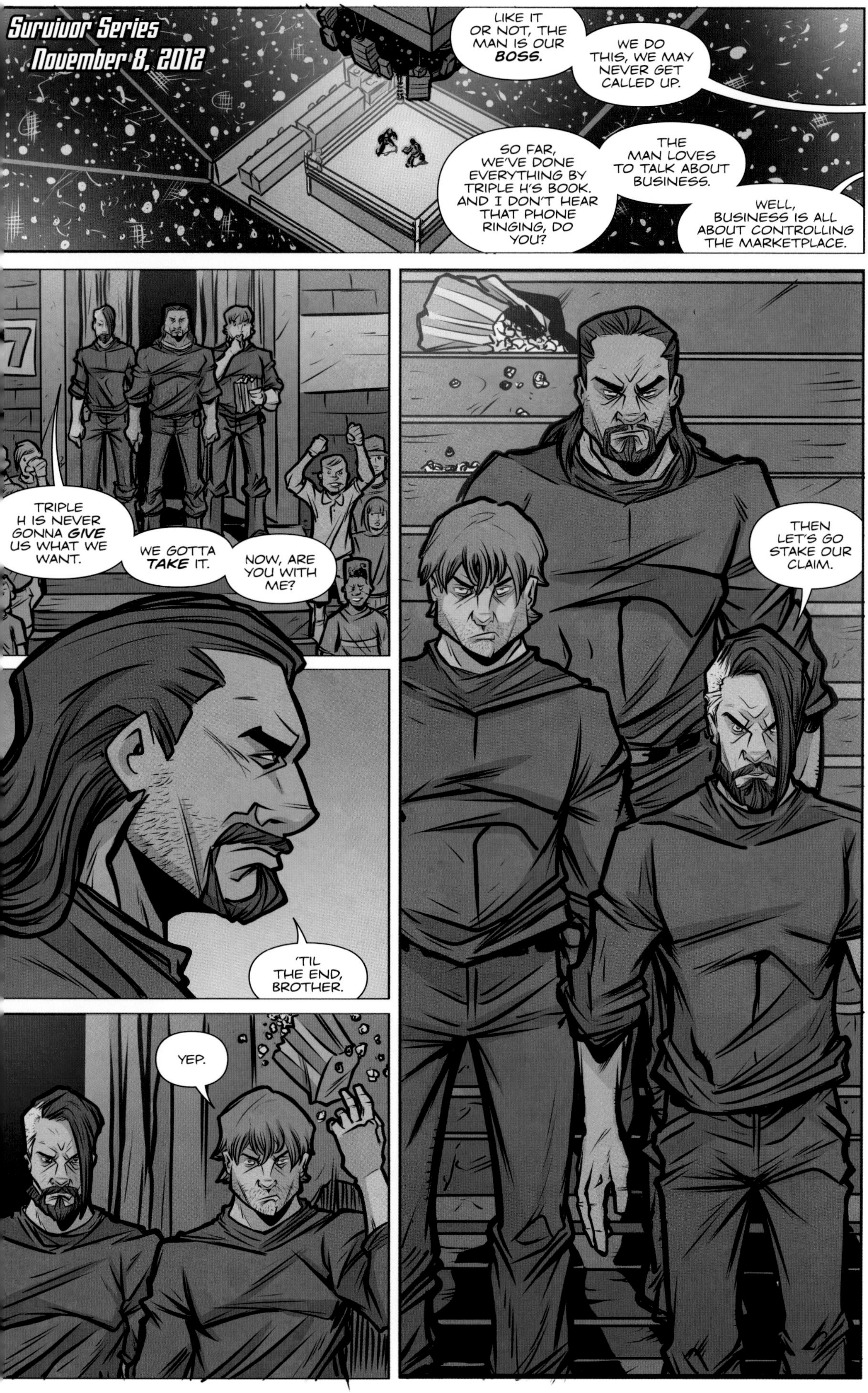
Survivor Series
November 8, 2012
LIKE IT OR NOT, THE MAN IS OUR BOSS.
WE DO THIS, WE MAY NEVER GET CALLED UP.
SO FAR, WE'VE DONE EVERYTHING BY TRIPLE H'S BOOK. AND I DON'T HEAR THAT PHONE RINGING, DO YOU?
THE MAN LOVES TO TALK ABOUT BUSINESS.
WELL, BUSINESS IS ALL ABOUT CONTROLLING THE MARKETPLACE.
7
TRIPLE H IS NEVER GONNA GIVE US WHAT WE WANT.
WE GOTTA TAKE IT.
NOW, ARE YOU WITH ME?
'TIL THE END, BROTHER.
YEP.
THEN LET'S GO STAKE OUR CLAIM.

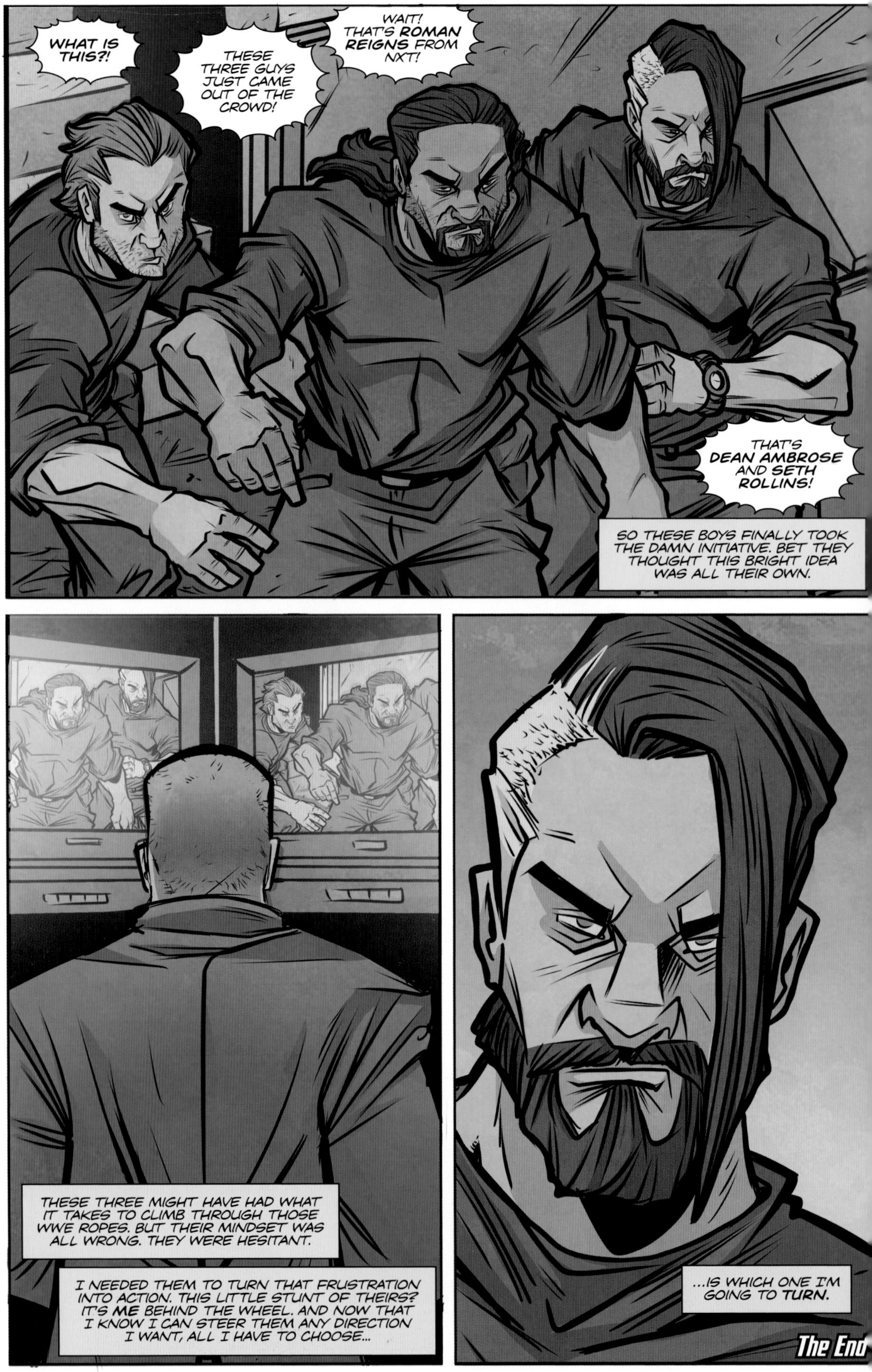
WHAT IS THIS?!
THESE THREE GUYS JUST CAME OUT OF THE CROWD!
WAIT! THAT'S ROMAN REIGNS FROM NXT!
THAT'S DEAN AMBROSE AND SETH ROLLINS!
SO THESE BOYS FINALLY TOOK THE DAMN INITIATIVE. BET THEY THOUGHT THIS BRIGHT IDEA WAS ALL THEIR OWN.
THESE THREE MIGHT HAVE HAD WHAT IT TAKES TO CLIMB THROUGH THOSE WWE ROPES. BUT THEIR MINDSET WAS ALL WRONG. THEY WERE HESITANT.
I NEEDED THEM TO TURN THAT FRUSTRATION INTO ACTION. THIS LITTLE STUNT OF THEIRS? IT'S ME BEHIND THE WHEEL. AND NOW THAT I KNOW I CAN STEER THEM ANY DIRECTION I WANT, ALL I HAVE TO CHOOSE...
...IS WHICH ONE I'M GOING TO TURN.
The End

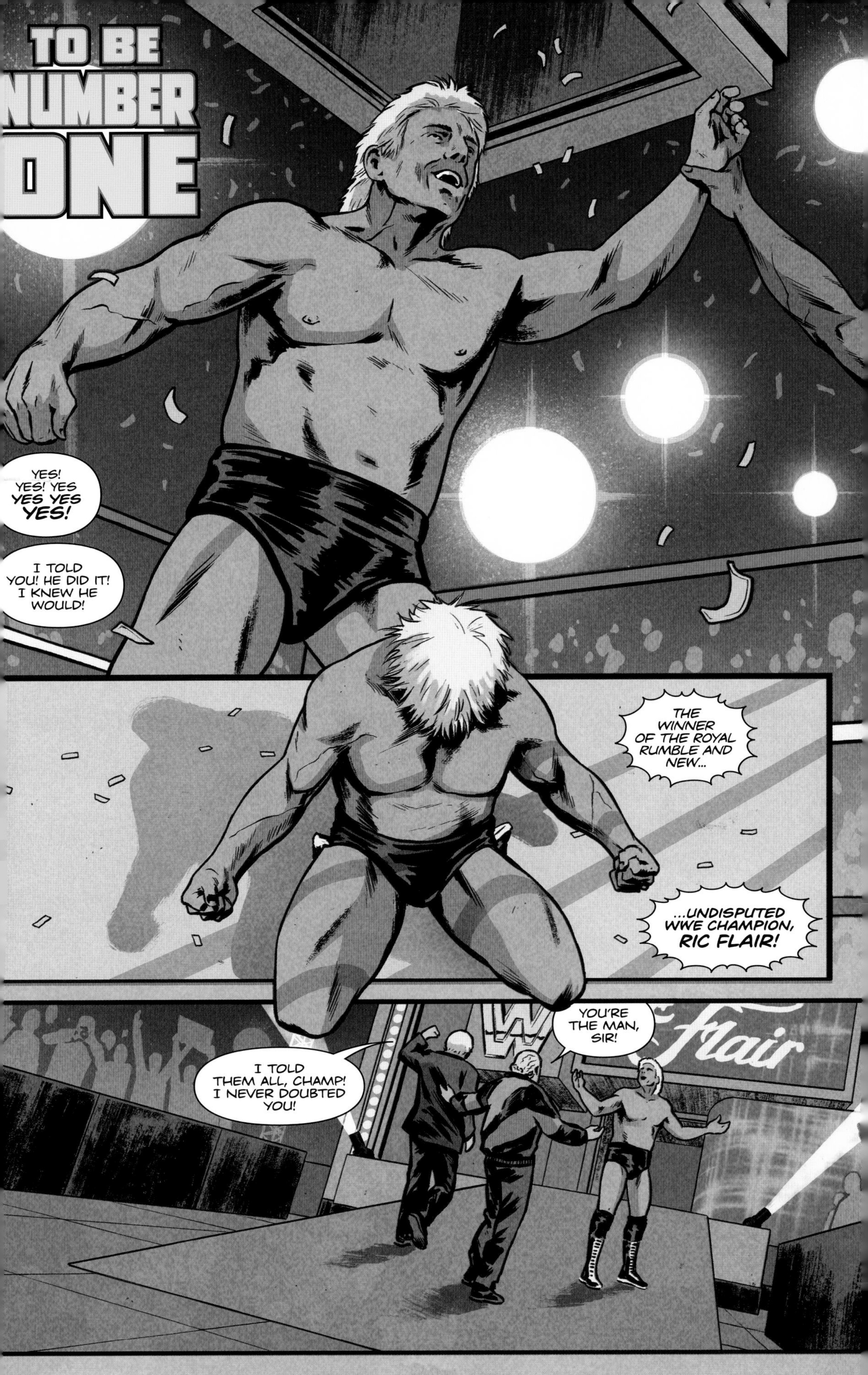
TO BE NUMBER ONE
YES! YES! YES YES YES YES!
I TOLD YOU! HE DID IT! I KNEW HE WOULD!
THE WINNER OF THE ROYAL RUMBLE AND NEW...
...UNDISPUTED WWE CHAMPION, RIC FLAIR!
YOU'RE THE MAN, SIR!
I TOLD THEM ALL, CHAMP! I NEVER DOUBTED YOU!
flair

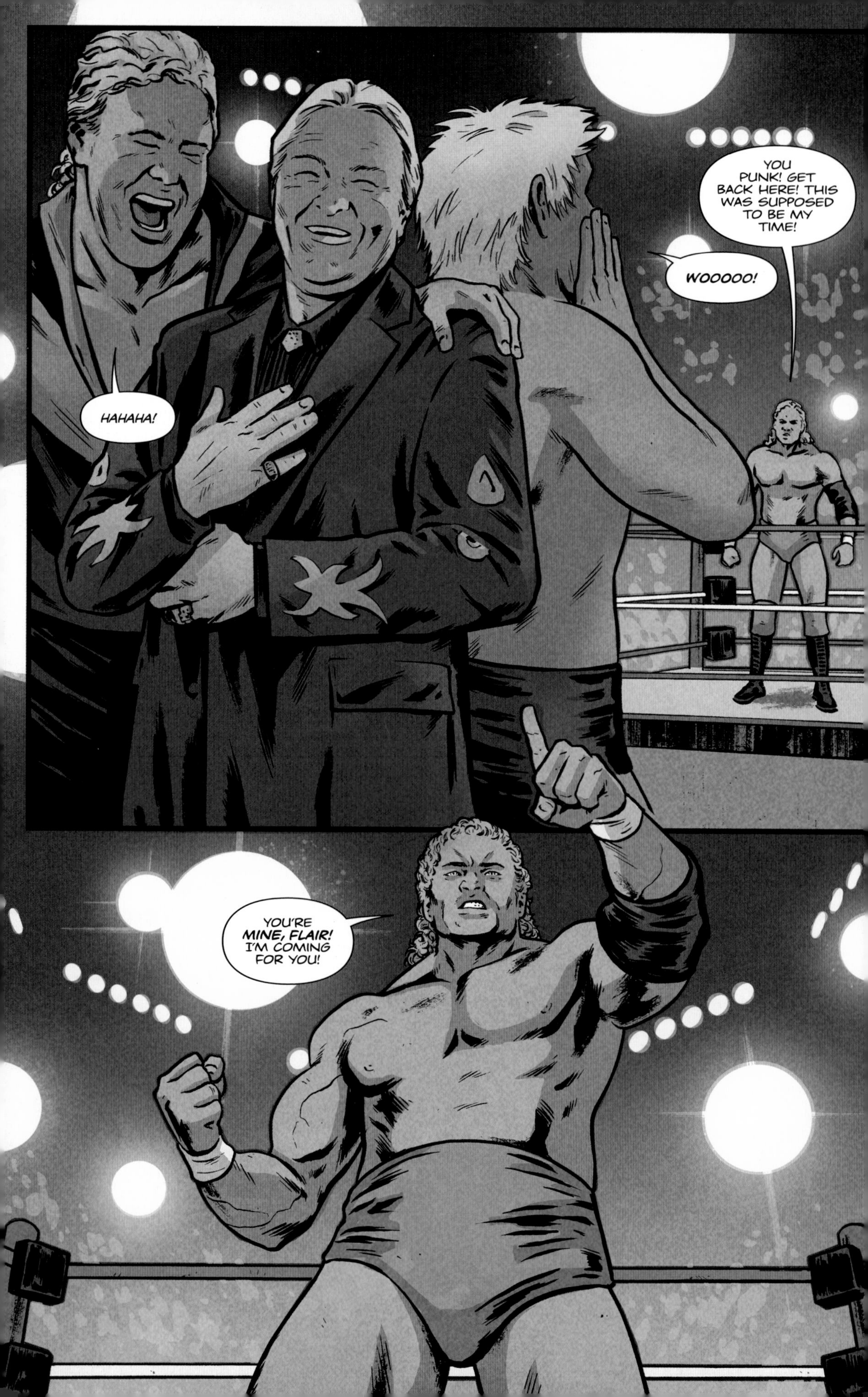
HAHAHA!
YOU PUNK! GET BACK HERE! THIS WAS SUPPOSED TO BE MY TIME!
WOOOOO!
YOU'RE MINE, FLAIR! I'M COMING FOR YOU!

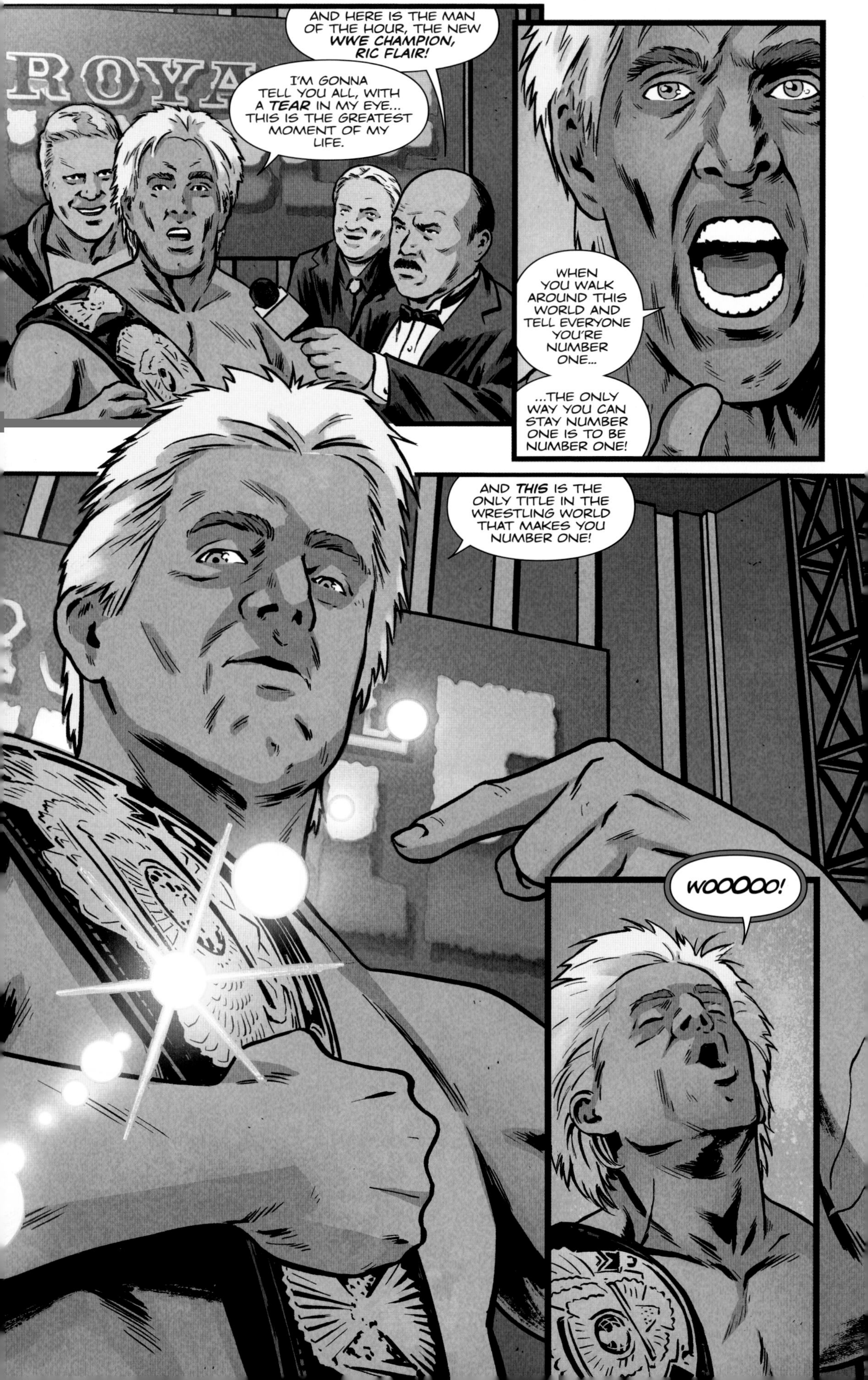
ROYA
AND HERE IS THE MAN OF THE HOUR, THE NEW *WWE CHAMPION, RIC FLAIR!*
I'M GONNA TELL YOU ALL, WITH A *TEAR* IN MY EYE... THIS IS THE GREATEST MOMENT OF MY LIFE.
WHEN YOU WALK AROUND THIS WORLD AND TELL EVERYONE YOU'RE NUMBER ONE...
...THE ONLY WAY YOU CAN STAY NUMBER ONE IS TO BE NUMBER ONE!
AND *THIS* IS THE ONLY TITLE IN THE WRESTLING WORLD THAT MAKES YOU NUMBER ONE!
*WOOOOO!*

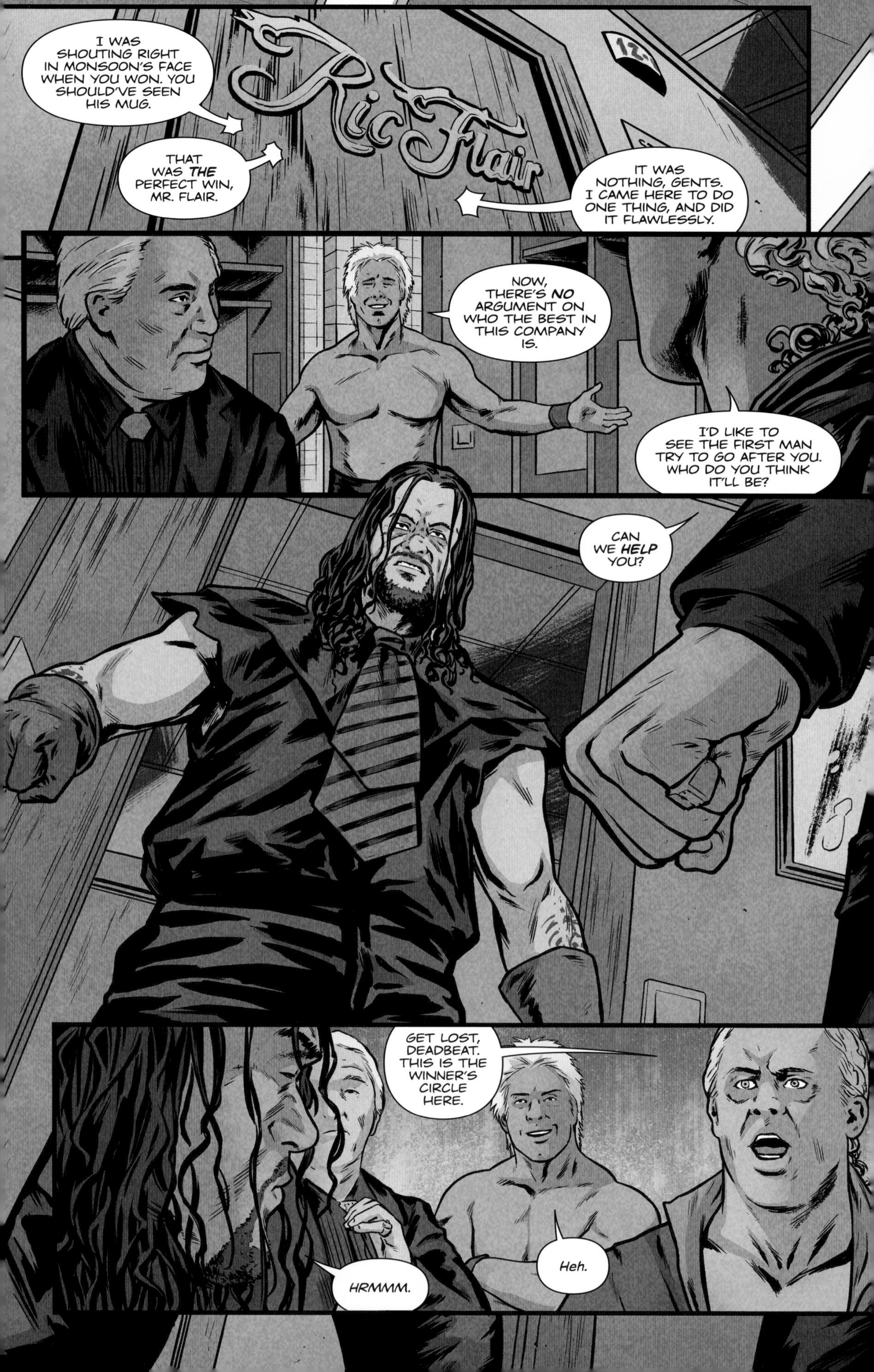

Ric Flair
I WAS SHOUTING RIGHT IN MONSOON'S FACE WHEN YOU WON. YOU SHOULD'VE SEEN HIS MUG.
THAT WAS **THE** PERFECT WIN, MR. FLAIR.
IT WAS NOTHING, GENTS. I CAME HERE TO DO ONE THING, AND DID IT FLAWLESSLY.
NOW, THERE'S **NO** ARGUMENT ON WHO THE BEST IN THIS COMPANY IS.
I'D LIKE TO SEE THE FIRST MAN TRY TO GO AFTER YOU. WHO DO YOU THINK IT'LL BE?
CAN WE ***HELP*** YOU?
GET LOST, DEADBEAT. THIS IS THE WINNER'S CIRCLE HERE.
*HRMMM.*
*Heh.*

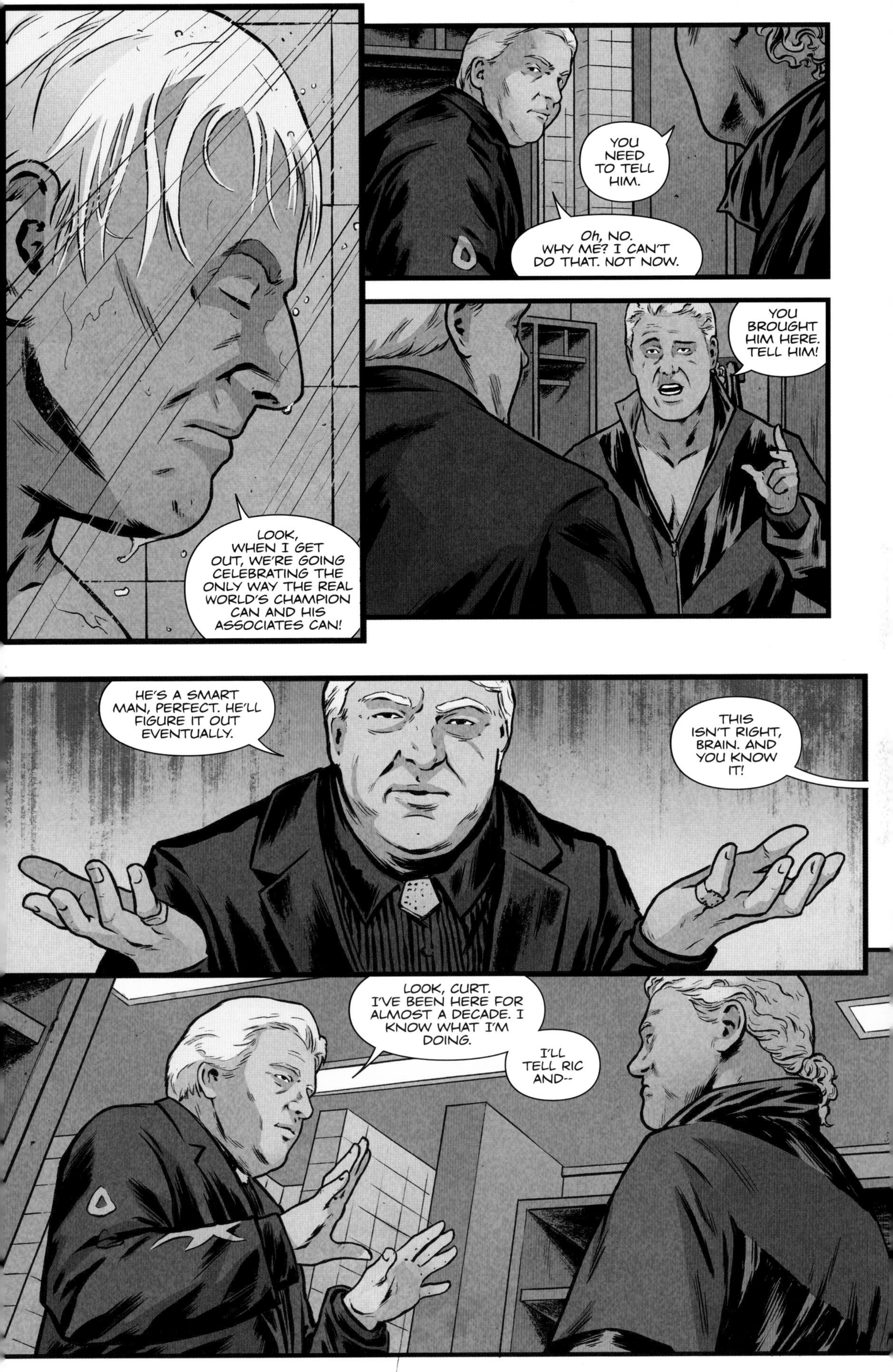
LOOK, WHEN I GET OUT, WE'RE GOING CELEBRATING THE ONLY WAY THE REAL WORLD'S CHAMPION CAN AND HIS ASSOCIATES CAN!
YOU NEED TO TELL HIM.
Oh, NO. WHY ME? I CAN'T DO THAT. NOT NOW.
YOU BROUGHT HIM HERE. TELL HIM!
HE'S A SMART MAN, PERFECT. HE'LL FIGURE IT OUT EVENTUALLY.
THIS ISN'T RIGHT, BRAIN. AND YOU KNOW IT!
LOOK, CURT. I'VE BEEN HERE FOR ALMOST A DECADE. I KNOW WHAT I'M DOING.
I'LL TELL RIC AND--

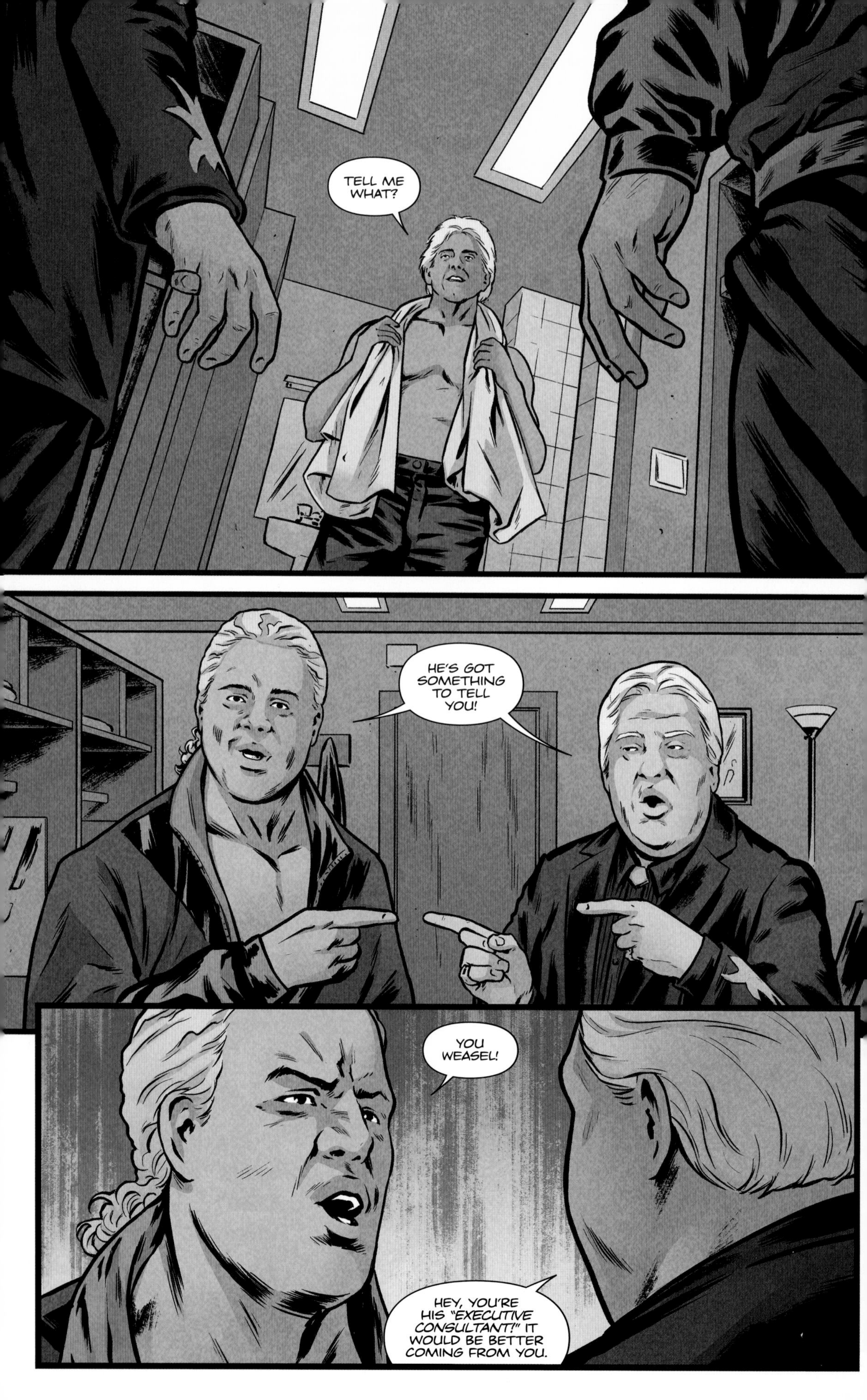
TELL ME WHAT?
HE'S GOT SOMETHING TO TELL YOU!
YOU WEASEL!
HEY, YOU'RE HIS "EXECUTIVE CONSULTANT!" IT WOULD BE BETTER COMING FROM YOU.

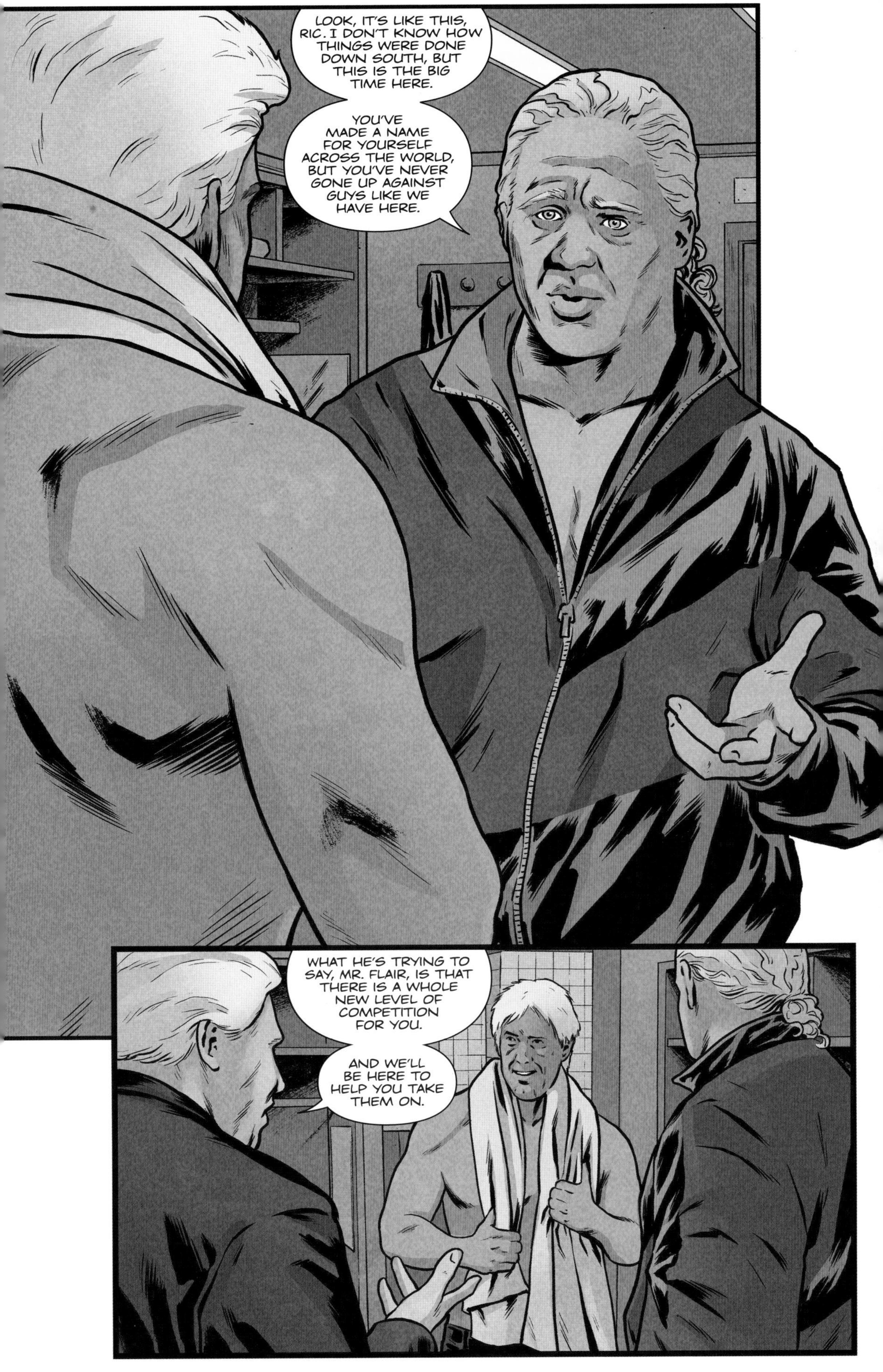
LOOK, IT'S LIKE THIS, RIC. I DON'T KNOW HOW THINGS WERE DONE DOWN SOUTH, BUT THIS IS THE BIG TIME HERE.
YOU'VE MADE A NAME FOR YOURSELF ACROSS THE WORLD, BUT YOU'VE NEVER GONE UP AGAINST GUYS LIKE WE HAVE HERE.
WHAT HE'S TRYING TO SAY, MR. FLAIR, IS THAT THERE IS A WHOLE NEW LEVEL OF COMPETITION FOR YOU.
AND WE'LL BE HERE TO HELP YOU TAKE THEM ON.

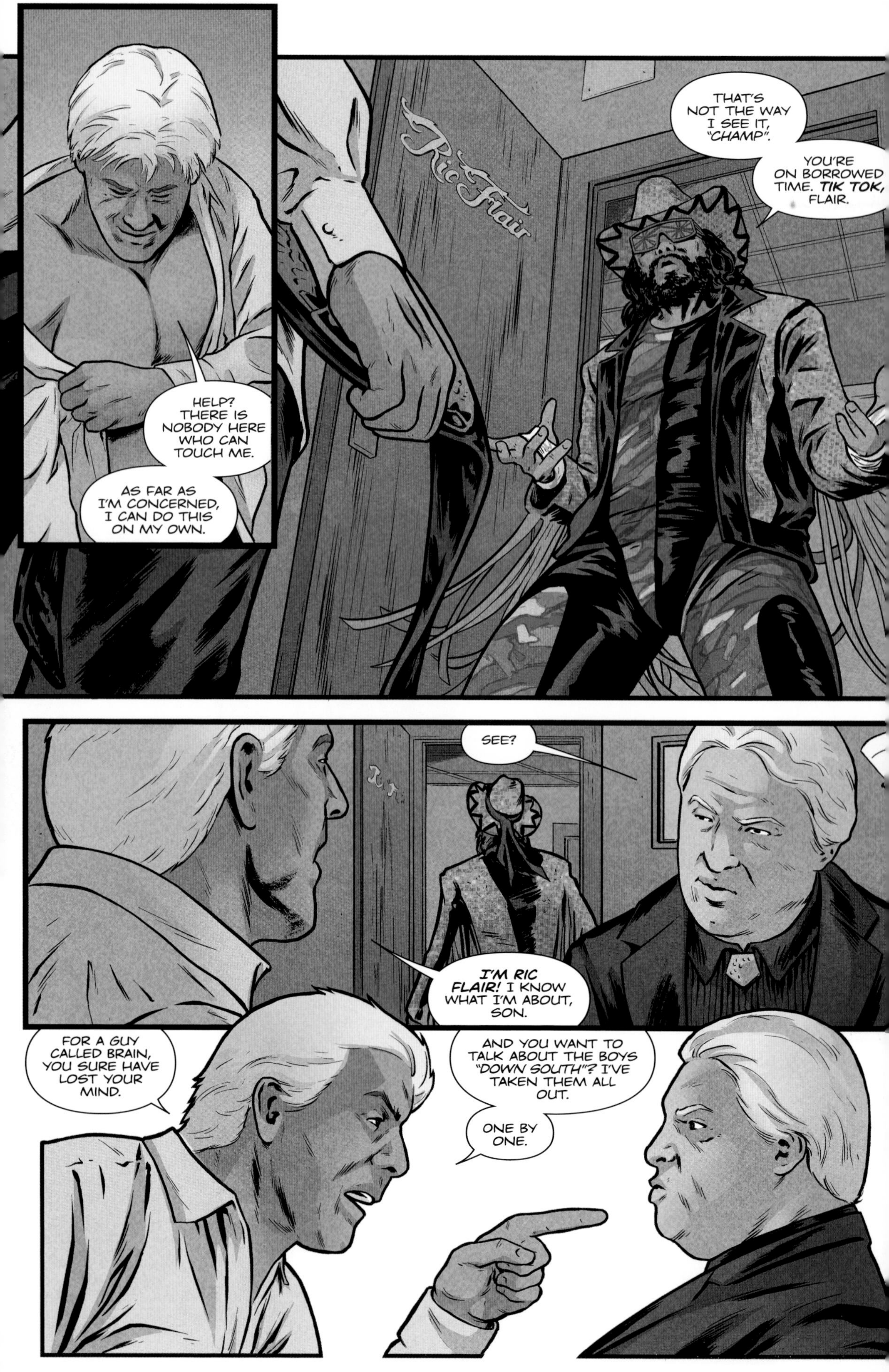
HELP? THERE IS NOBODY HERE WHO CAN TOUCH ME.
AS FAR AS I'M CONCERNED, I CAN DO THIS ON MY OWN.
Ric Flair
THAT'S NOT THE WAY I SEE IT, "CHAMP".
YOU'RE ON BORROWED TIME. TIK TOK, FLAIR.
SEE?
I'M RIC FLAIR! I KNOW WHAT I'M ABOUT, SON.
FOR A GUY CALLED BRAIN, YOU SURE HAVE LOST YOUR MIND.
AND YOU WANT TO TALK ABOUT THE BOYS "DOWN SOUTH"? I'VE TAKEN THEM ALL OUT.
ONE BY ONE.

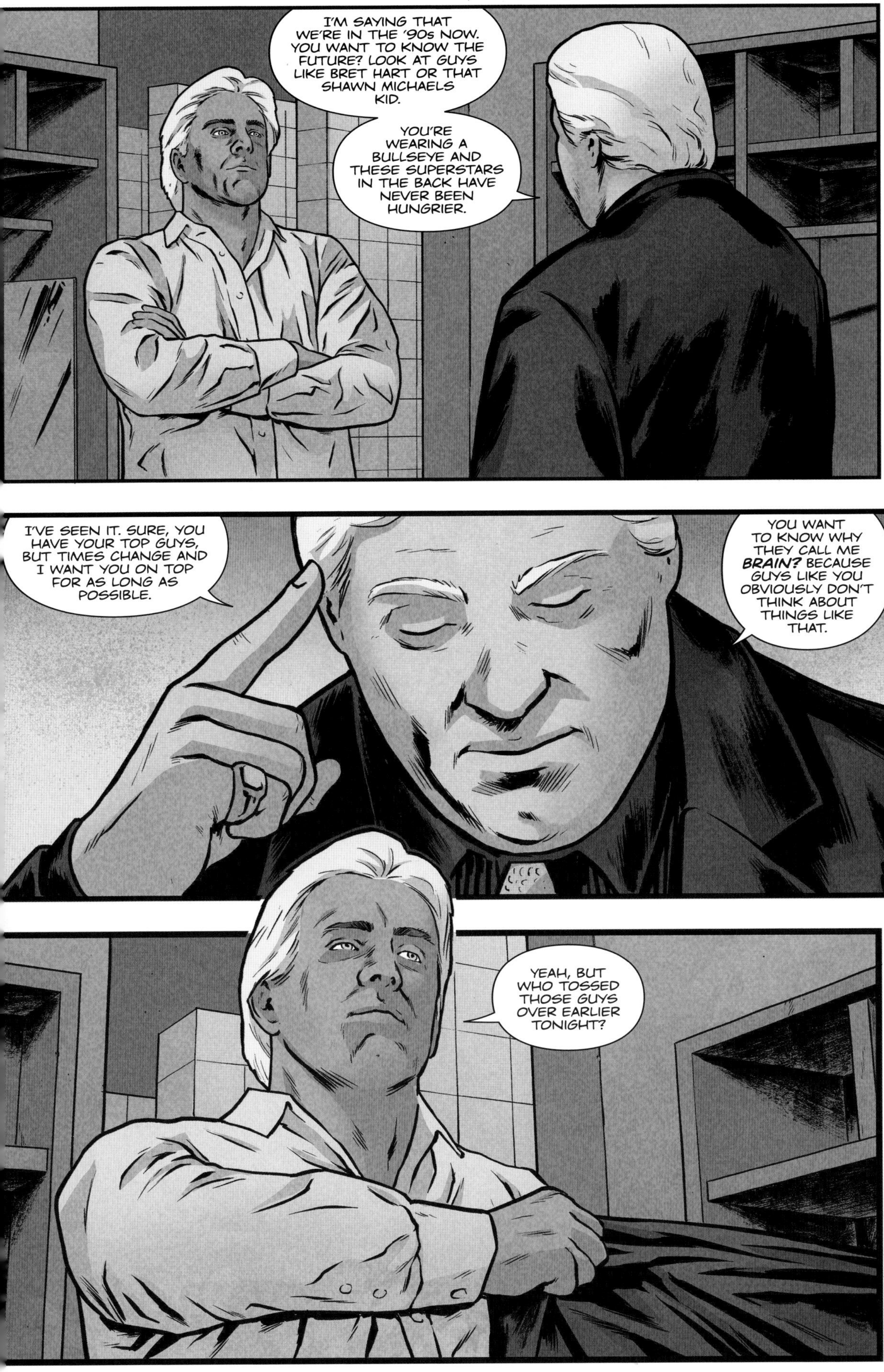
I'M SAYING THAT WE'RE IN THE '90s NOW. YOU WANT TO KNOW THE FUTURE? LOOK AT GUYS LIKE BRET HART OR THAT SHAWN MICHAELS KID.
YOU'RE WEARING A BULLSEYE AND THESE SUPERSTARS IN THE BACK HAVE NEVER BEEN HUNGRIER.
I'VE SEEN IT. SURE, YOU HAVE YOUR TOP GUYS, BUT TIMES CHANGE AND I WANT YOU ON TOP FOR AS LONG AS POSSIBLE.
YOU WANT TO KNOW WHY THEY CALL ME *BRAIN?* BECAUSE GUYS LIKE YOU OBVIOUSLY DON'T THINK ABOUT THINGS LIKE THAT.
YEAH, BUT WHO TOSSED THOSE GUYS OVER EARLIER TONIGHT?

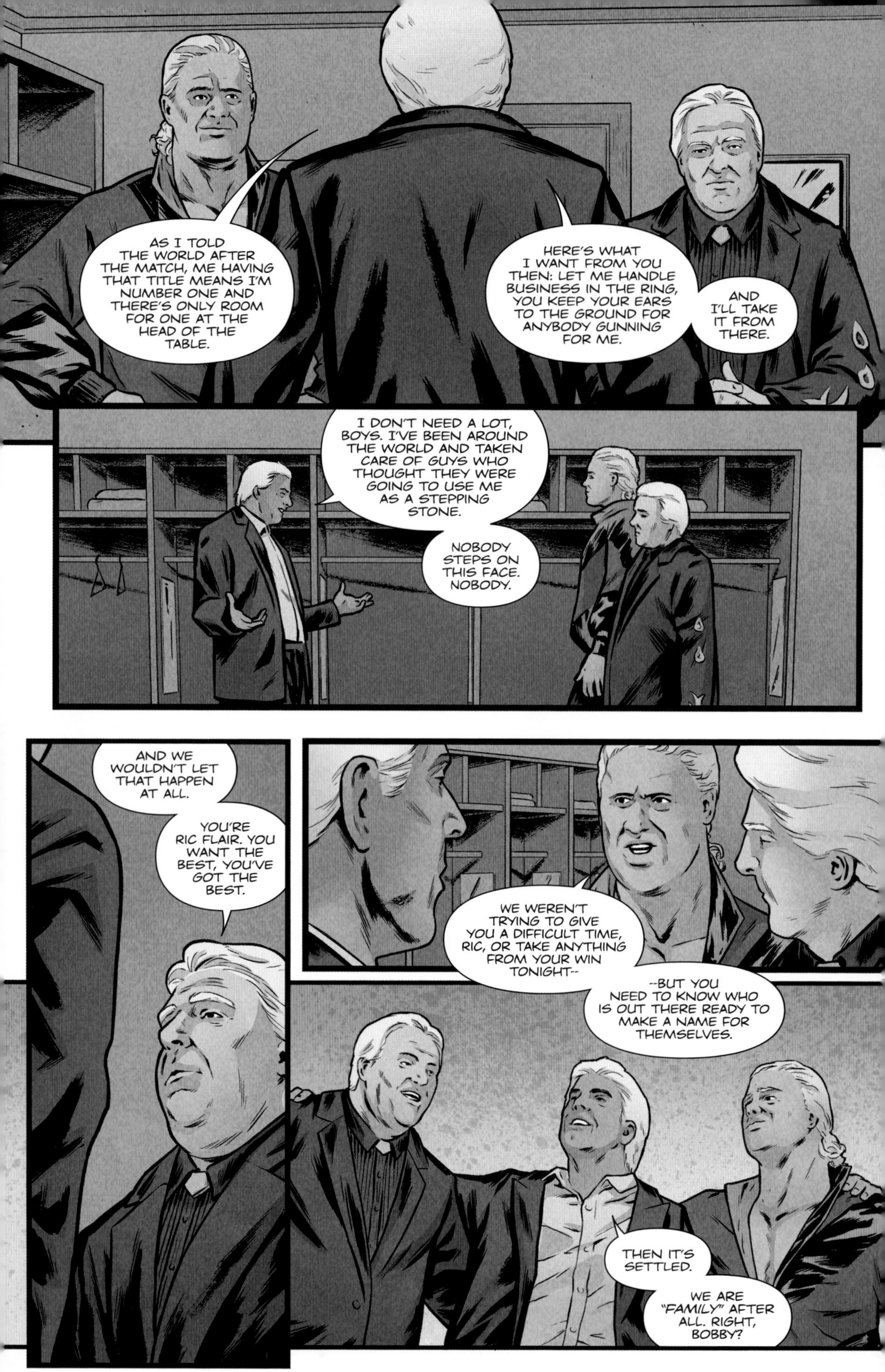
AS I TOLD THE WORLD AFTER THE MATCH, ME HAVING THAT TITLE MEANS I'M NUMBER ONE AND THERE'S ONLY ROOM FOR ONE AT THE HEAD OF THE TABLE.
HERE'S WHAT I WANT FROM YOU THEN: LET ME HANDLE BUSINESS IN THE RING, YOU KEEP YOUR EARS TO THE GROUND FOR ANYBODY GUNNING FOR ME.
AND I'LL TAKE IT FROM THERE.
I DON'T NEED A LOT, BOYS. I'VE BEEN AROUND THE WORLD AND TAKEN CARE OF GUYS WHO THOUGHT THEY WERE GOING TO USE ME AS A STEPPING STONE.
NOBODY STEPS ON THIS FACE. NOBODY.
AND WE WOULDN'T LET THAT HAPPEN AT ALL.
YOU'RE RIC FLAIR. YOU WANT THE BEST, YOU'VE GOT THE BEST.
WE WEREN'T TRYING TO GIVE YOU A DIFFICULT TIME, RIC, OR TAKE ANYTHING FROM YOUR WIN TONIGHT--
--BUT YOU NEED TO KNOW WHO IS OUT THERE READY TO MAKE A NAME FOR THEMSELVES.
THEN IT'S SETTLED.
WE ARE *"FAMILY"* AFTER ALL. RIGHT, BOBBY?

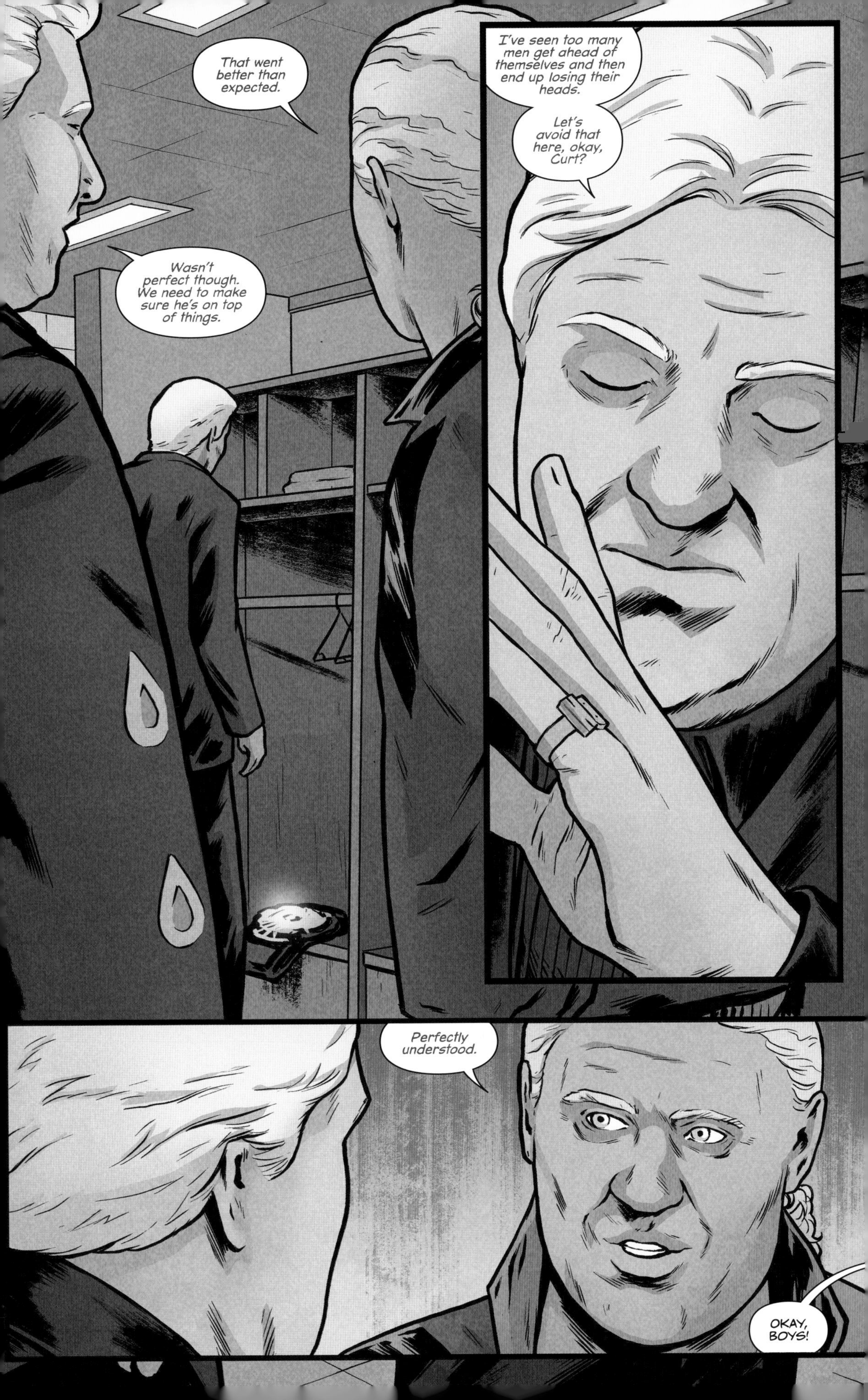

That went better than expected.
Wasn't perfect though. We need to make sure he's on top of things.
I've seen too many men get ahead of themselves and then end up losing their heads.
Let's avoid that here, okay, Curt?
Perfectly understood.
OKAY, BOYS!

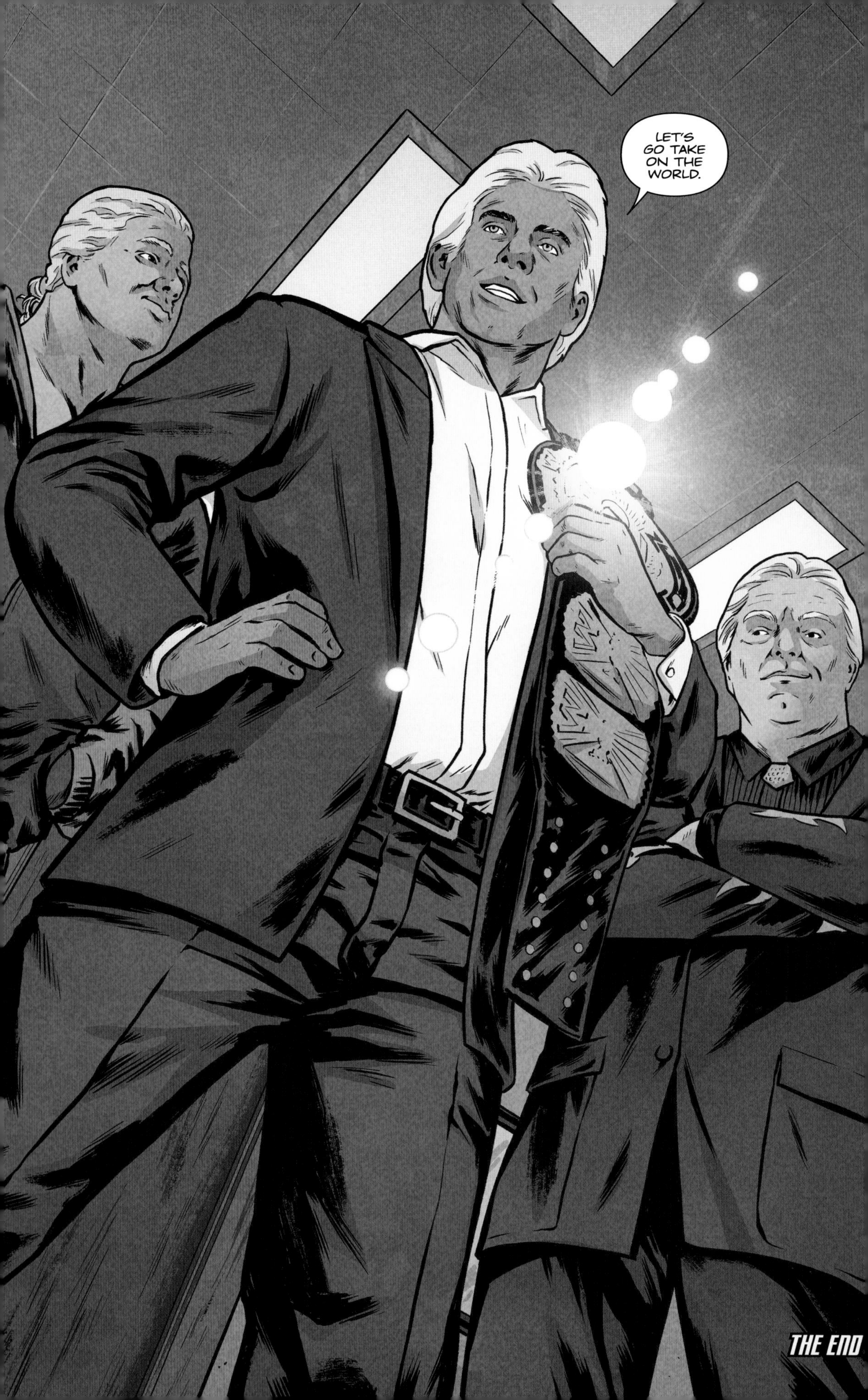
LET'S GO TAKE ON THE WORLD.
THE END

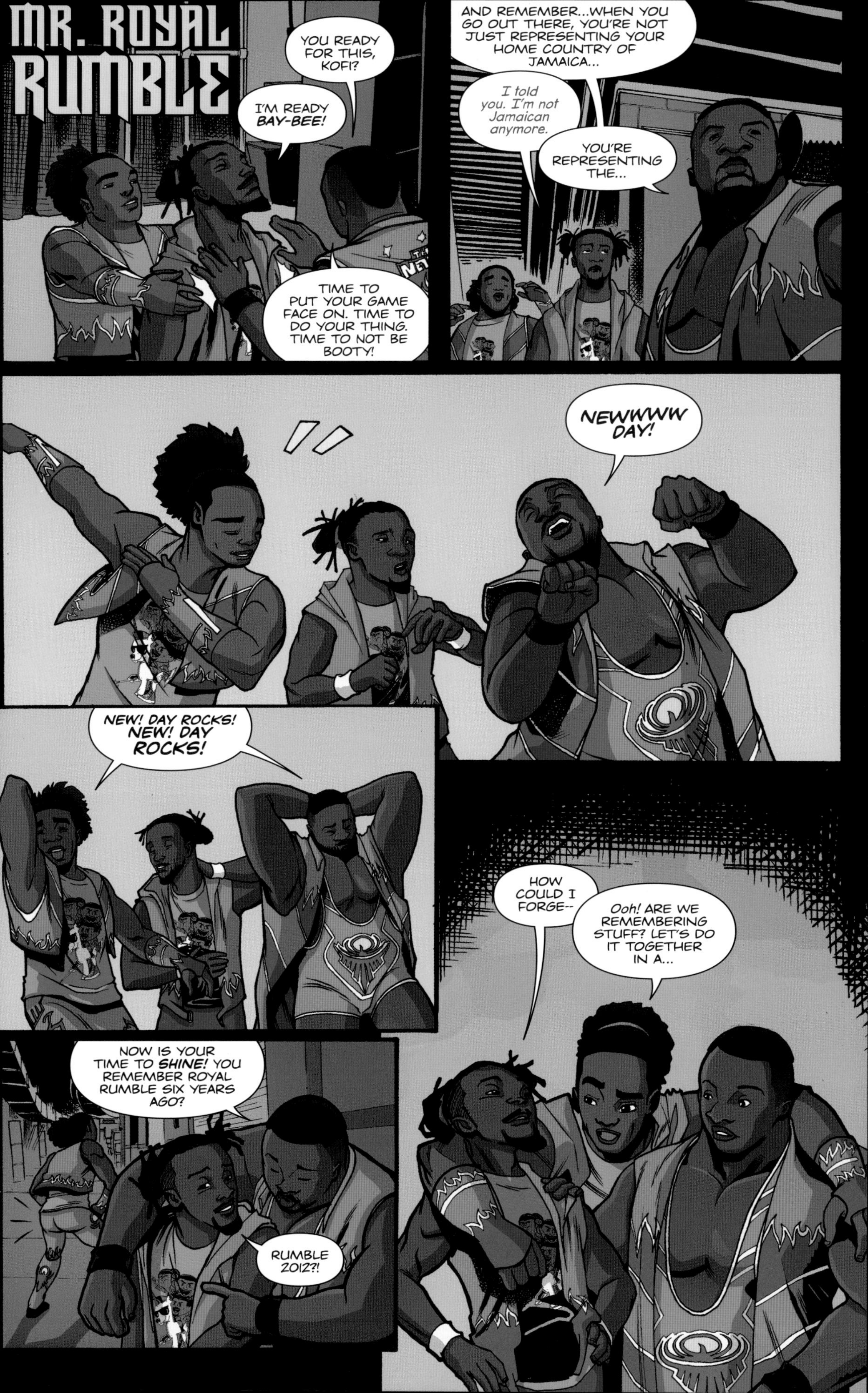
MR. ROYAL RUMBLE
YOU READY FOR THIS, KOFI?
I'M READY BAY-BEE!
TIME TO PUT YOUR GAME FACE ON. TIME TO DO YOUR THING. TIME TO NOT BE BOOTY!
AND REMEMBER...WHEN YOU GO OUT THERE, YOU'RE NOT JUST REPRESENTING YOUR HOME COUNTRY OF JAMAICA...
I told you. I'm not Jamaican anymore.
YOU'RE REPRESENTING THE...
NEWWWW DAY!
NEW! DAY ROCKS! NEW! DAY ROCKS!
HOW COULD I FORGE--
Ooh! ARE WE REMEMBERING STUFF? LET'S DO IT TOGETHER IN A...
NOW IS YOUR TIME TO SHINE! YOU REMEMBER ROYAL RUMBLE SIX YEARS AGO?
RUMBLE 2012?!

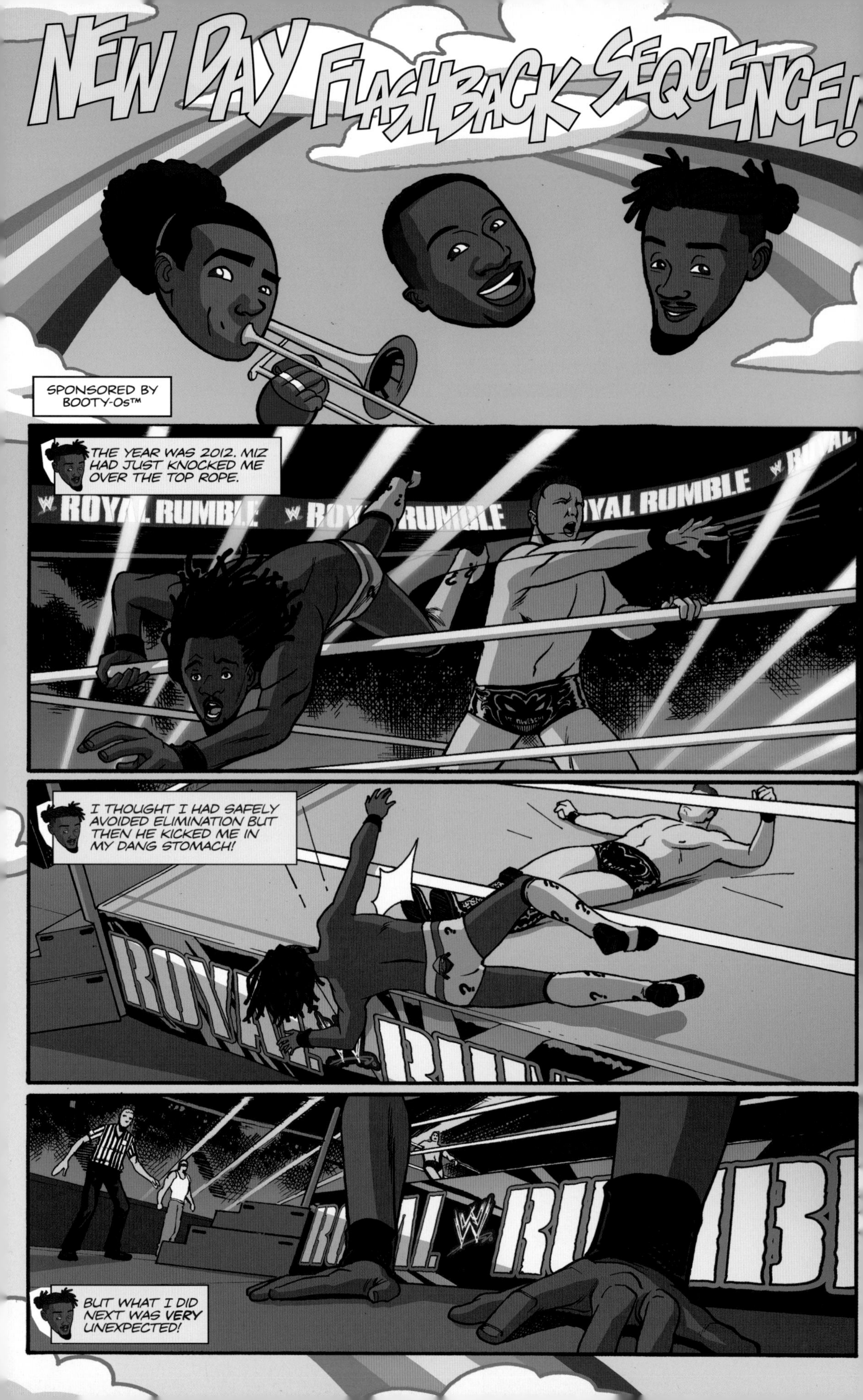
NEW DAY FLASHBACK SEQUENCE!
SPONSORED BY BOOTY-Os™
THE YEAR WAS 2012. MIZ HAD JUST KNOCKED ME OVER THE TOP ROPE.
ROYAL RUMBLE
I THOUGHT I HAD SAFELY AVOIDED ELIMINATION BUT THEN HE KICKED ME IN MY DANG STOMACH!
BUT WHAT I DID NEXT WAS **VERY** UNEXPECTED!

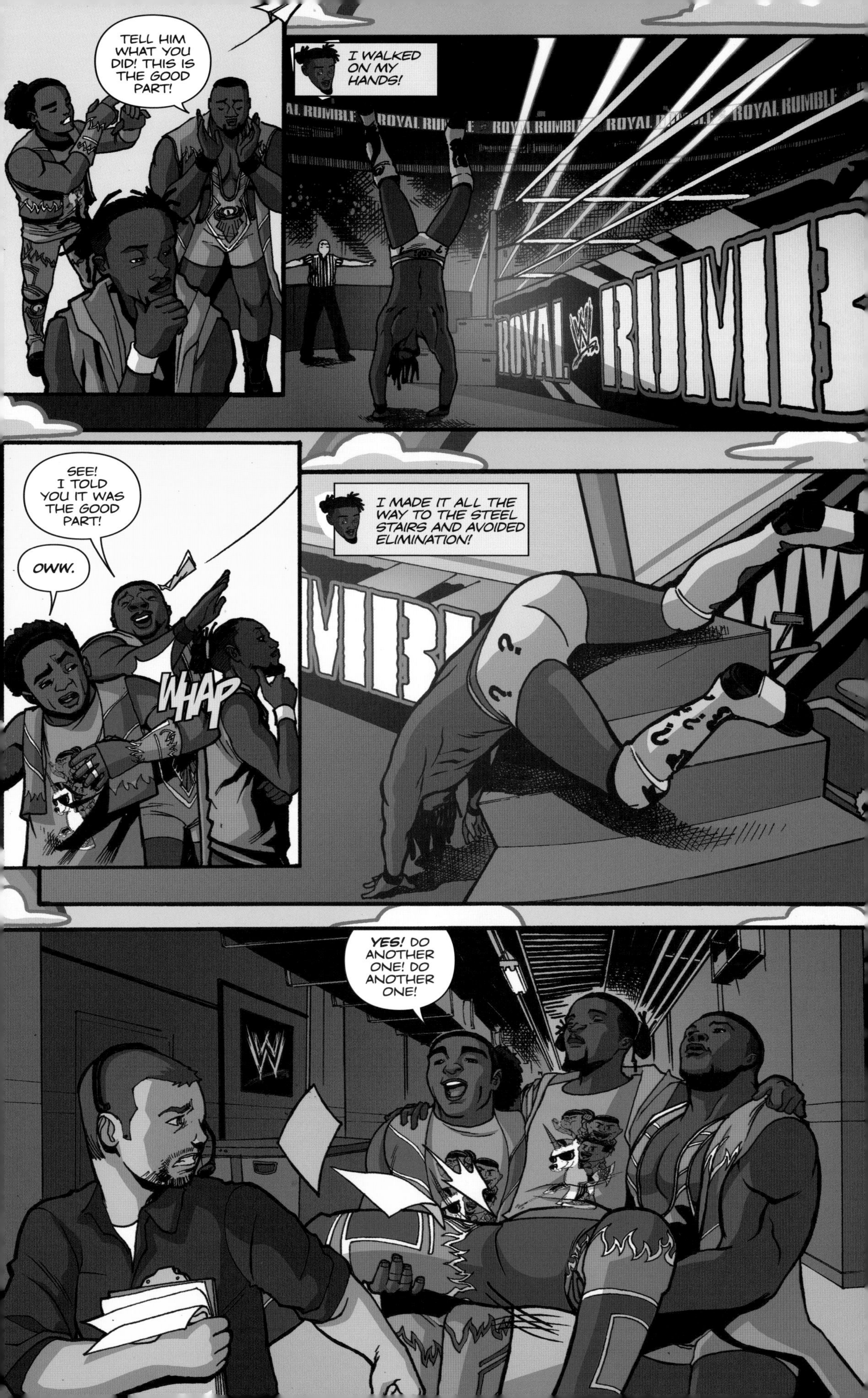
TELL HIM WHAT YOU DID! THIS IS THE GOOD PART!
I WALKED ON MY HANDS!
ROYAL RUMBLE
SEE! I TOLD YOU IT WAS THE GOOD PART!
OWW.
WHAP
I MADE IT ALL THE WAY TO THE STEEL STAIRS AND AVOIDED ELIMINATION!
YES! DO ANOTHER ONE! DO ANOTHER ONE!

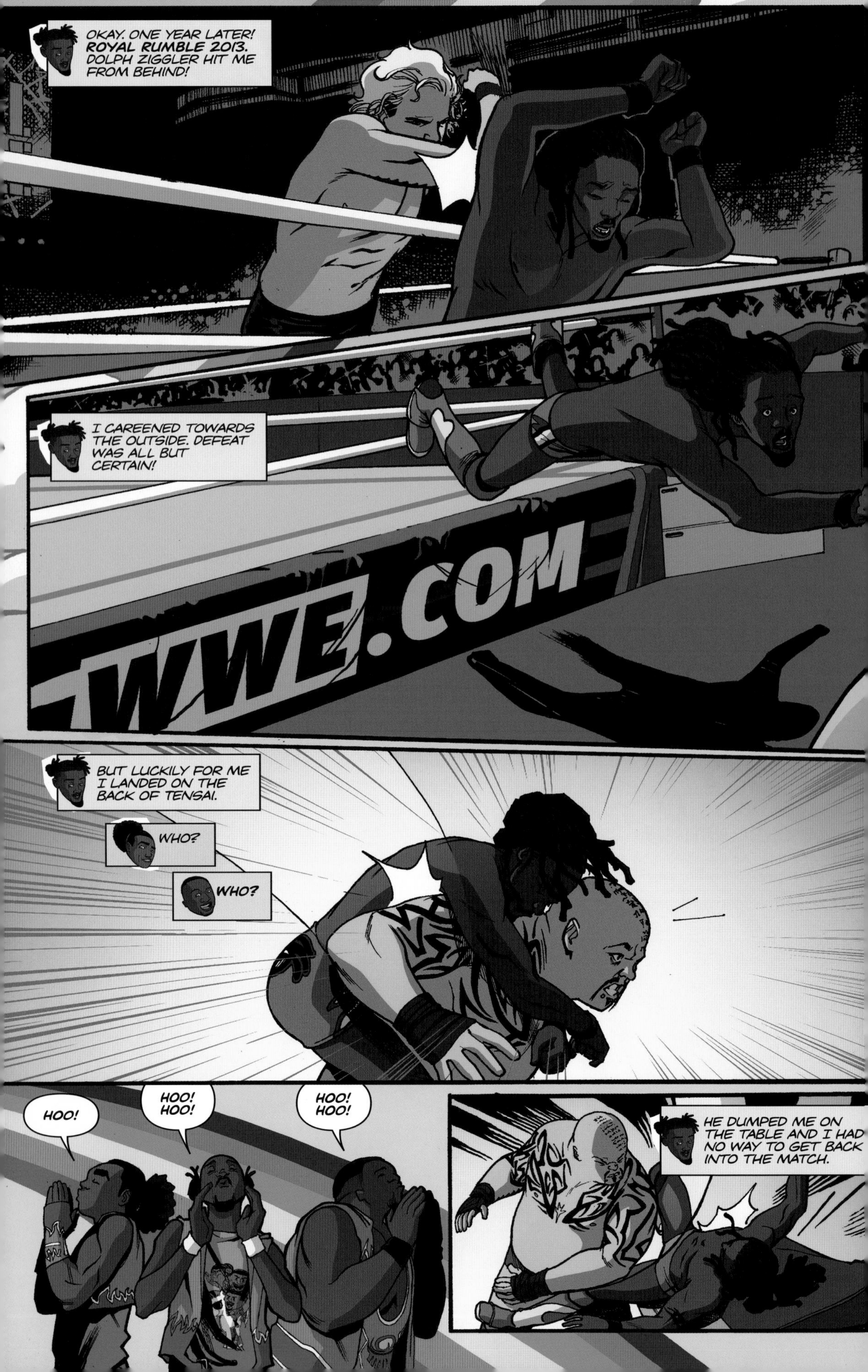
OKAY. ONE YEAR LATER! ROYAL RUMBLE 2013. DOLPH ZIGGLER HIT ME FROM BEHIND!
I CAREENED TOWARDS THE OUTSIDE. DEFEAT WAS ALL BUT CERTAIN!
WWE.COM
BUT LUCKILY FOR ME I LANDED ON THE BACK OF TENSAI.
WHO?
WHO?
HOO!
HOO! HOO!
HOO! HOO!
HE DUMPED ME ON THE TABLE AND I HAD NO WAY TO GET BACK INTO THE MATCH.

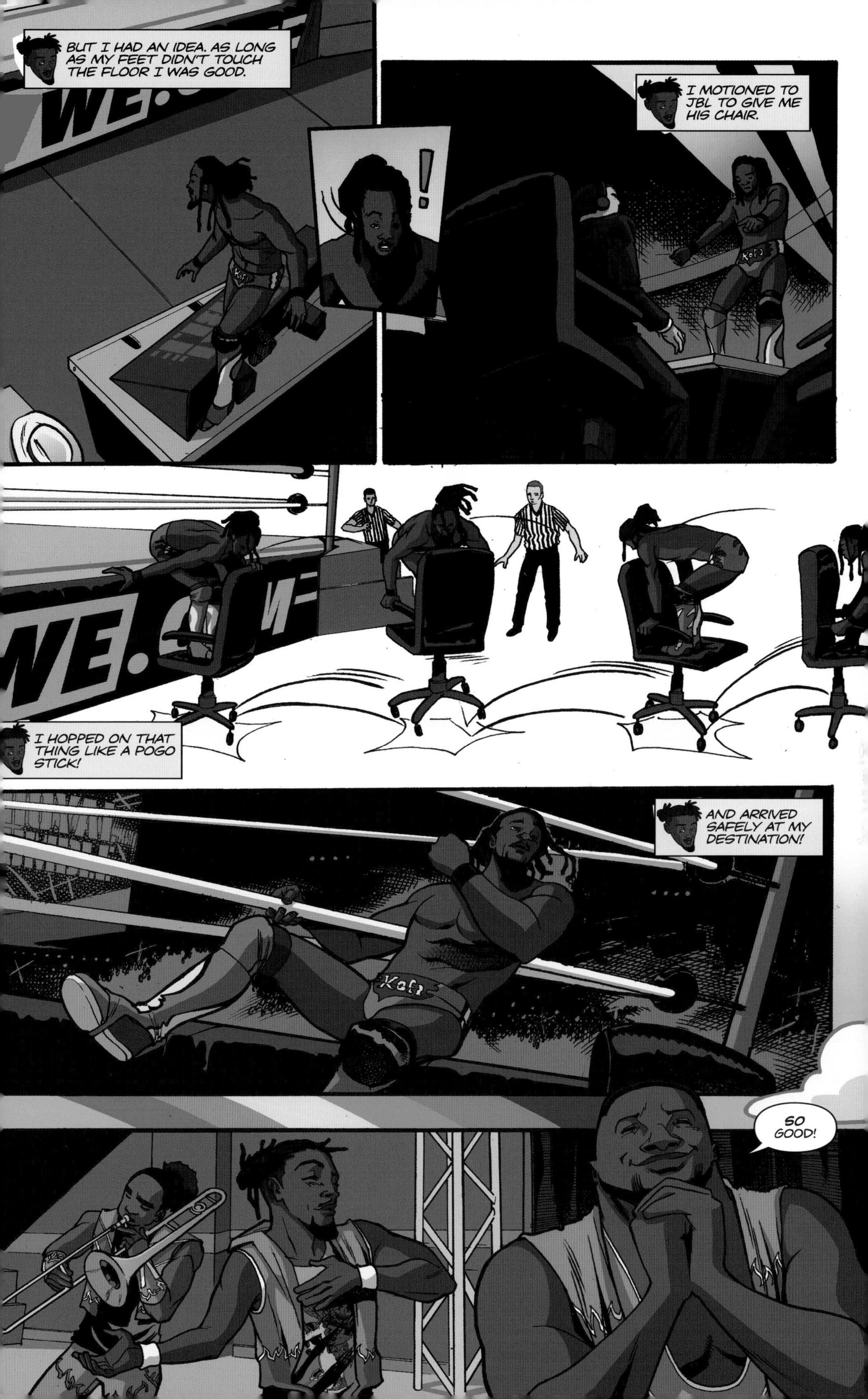
BUT I HAD AN IDEA. AS LONG AS MY FEET DIDN'T TOUCH THE FLOOR I WAS GOOD.
I MOTIONED TO JBL TO GIVE ME HIS CHAIR.
I HOPPED ON THAT THING LIKE A POGO STICK!
AND ARRIVED SAFELY AT MY DESTINATION!
SO GOOD!

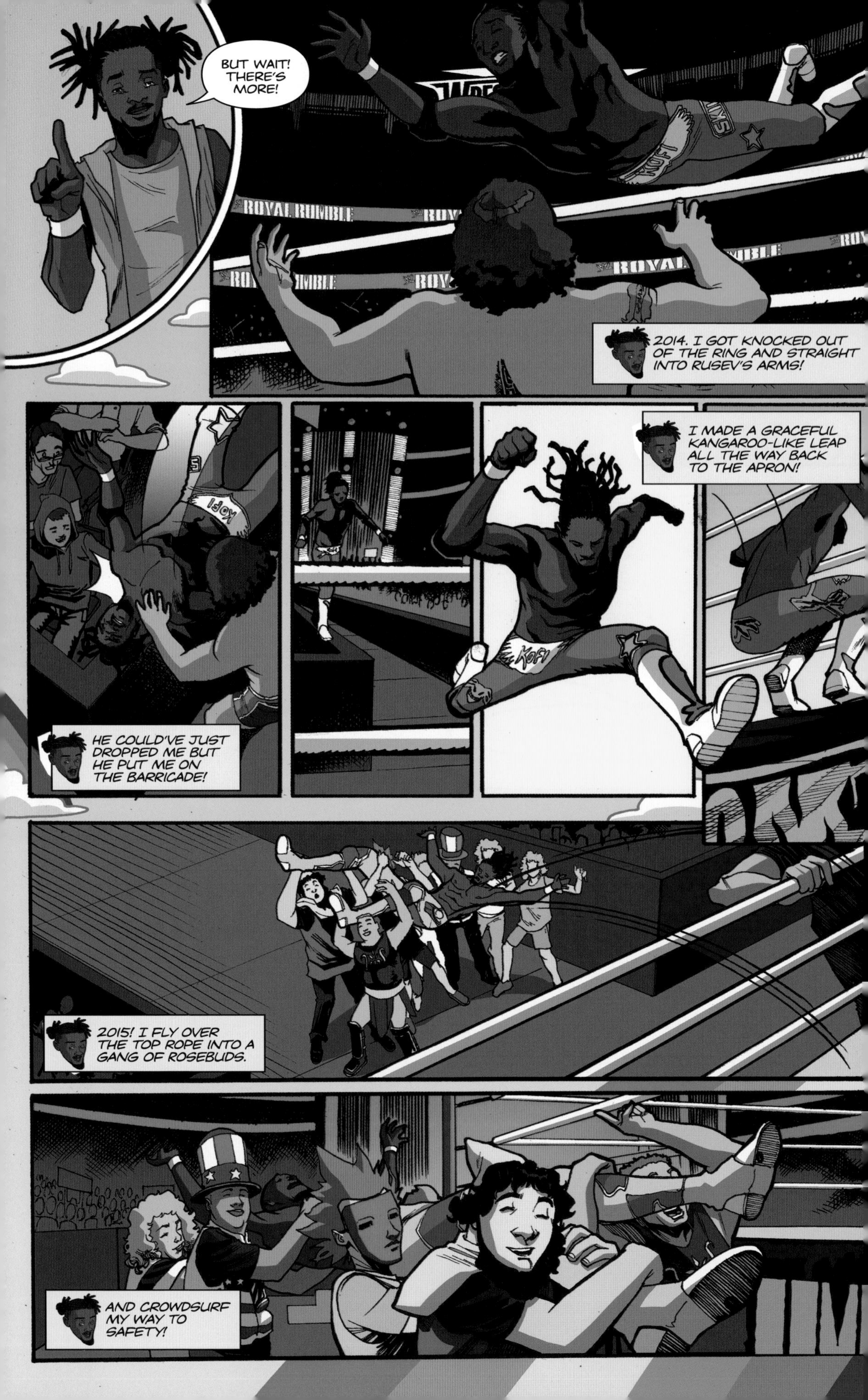
BUT WAIT! THERE'S MORE!
ROYAL RUMBLE
2014. I GOT KNOCKED OUT OF THE RING AND STRAIGHT INTO RUSEV'S ARMS!
KOFI
HE COULD'VE JUST DROPPED ME BUT HE PUT ME ON THE BARRICADE!
I MADE A GRACEFUL KANGAROO-LIKE LEAP ALL THE WAY BACK TO THE APRON!
KOFI
2015! I FLY OVER THE TOP ROPE INTO A GANG OF ROSEBUDS.
AND CROWDSURF MY WAY TO SAFETY!

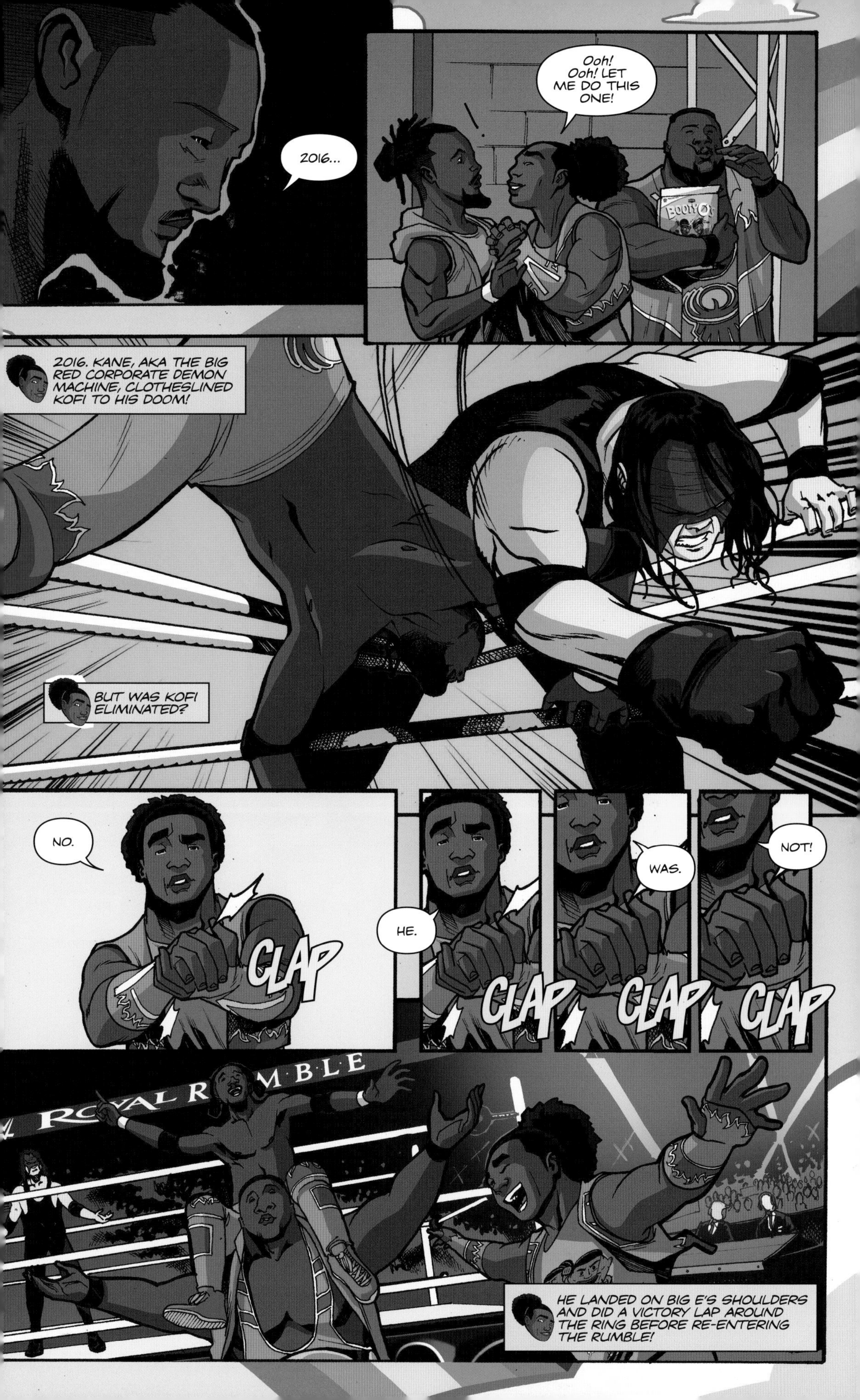
2016...
Ooh! Ooh! LET ME DO THIS ONE!
2016. KANE, AKA THE BIG RED CORPORATE DEMON MACHINE, CLOTHESLINED KOFI TO HIS DOOM!
BUT WAS KOFI ELIMINATED?
NO.
CLAP
HE.
WAS.
NOT!
CLAP
CLAP
CLAP
ROYAL RUMBLE
HE LANDED ON BIG E'S SHOULDERS AND DID A VICTORY LAP AROUND THE RING BEFORE RE-ENTERING THE RUMBLE!

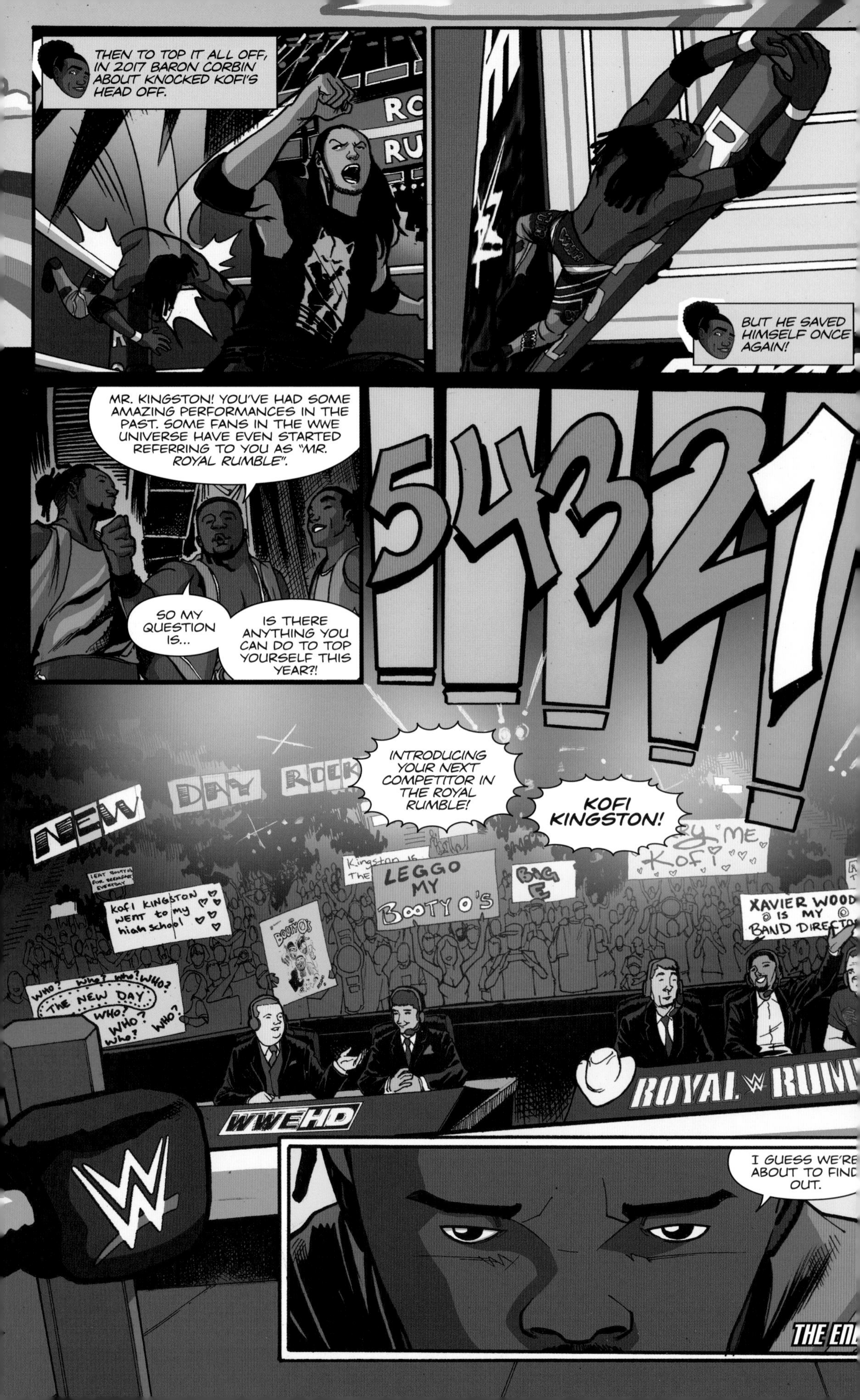
THEN TO TOP IT ALL OFF, IN 2017 BARON CORBIN ABOUT KNOCKED KOFI'S HEAD OFF.
BUT HE SAVED HIMSELF ONCE AGAIN!
MR. KINGSTON! YOU'VE HAD SOME AMAZING PERFORMANCES IN THE PAST. SOME FANS IN THE WWE UNIVERSE HAVE EVEN STARTED REFERRING TO YOU AS "MR. ROYAL RUMBLE".
SO MY QUESTION IS...
IS THERE ANYTHING YOU CAN DO TO TOP YOURSELF THIS YEAR?!
5 4 3 2 1 !
INTRODUCING YOUR NEXT COMPETITOR IN THE ROYAL RUMBLE!
KOFI KINGSTON!
NEW DAY ROCK
NEW
LEGGO MY BOOTY O's
kofi KINGSTON went to my high school
WHO? WHO? WHO? WHO? THE NEW DAY WHO? WHO? WHO? WHO? WHO?
WWEHD
I GUESS WE'RE ABOUT TO FIND OUT.

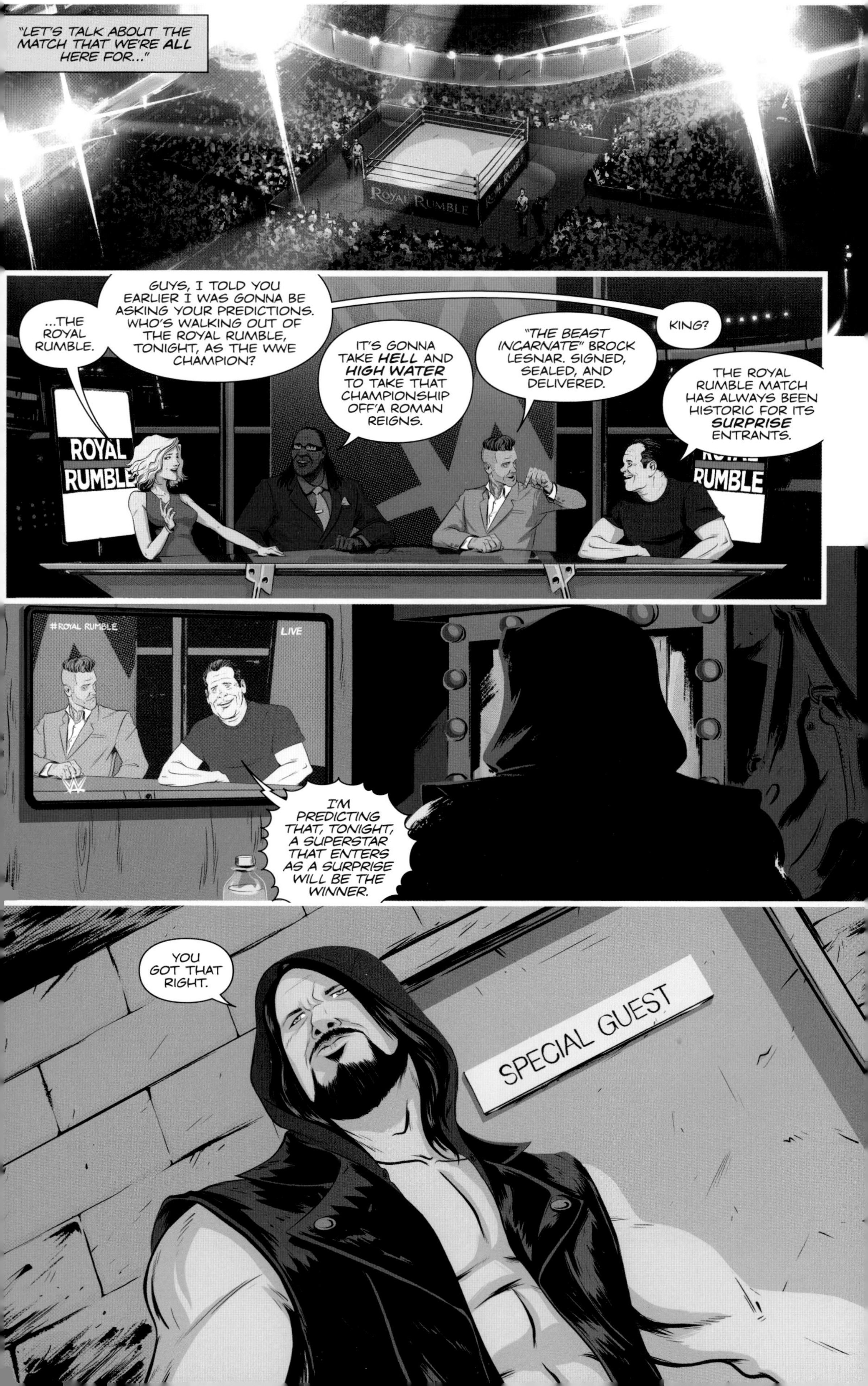
"LET'S TALK ABOUT THE MATCH THAT WE'RE ALL HERE FOR..."
ROYAL RUMBLE
...THE ROYAL RUMBLE.
GUYS, I TOLD YOU EARLIER I WAS GONNA BE ASKING YOUR PREDICTIONS. WHO'S WALKING OUT OF THE ROYAL RUMBLE, TONIGHT, AS THE WWE CHAMPION?
IT'S GONNA TAKE HELL AND HIGH WATER TO TAKE THAT CHAMPIONSHIP OFF'A ROMAN REIGNS.
"THE BEAST INCARNATE" BROCK LESNAR. SIGNED, SEALED, AND DELIVERED.
KING?
THE ROYAL RUMBLE MATCH HAS ALWAYS BEEN HISTORIC FOR ITS SURPRISE ENTRANTS.
ROYAL RUMBLE
RUMBLE
#ROYAL RUMBLE
LIVE
I'M PREDICTING THAT, TONIGHT, A SUPERSTAR THAT ENTERS AS A SURPRISE WILL BE THE WINNER.
YOU GOT THAT RIGHT.
SPECIAL GUEST

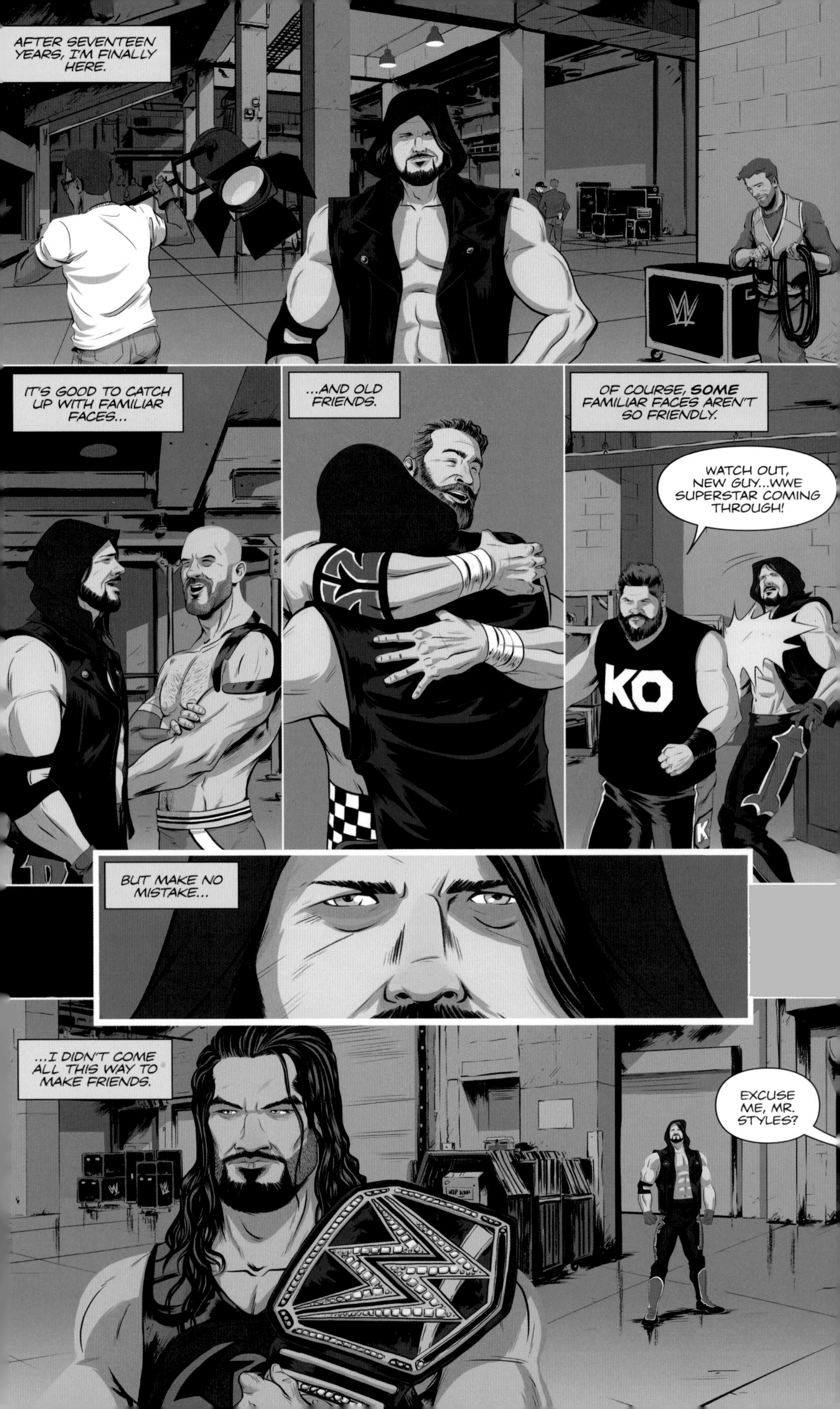
AFTER SEVENTEEN YEARS, I'M FINALLY HERE.
IT'S GOOD TO CATCH UP WITH FAMILIAR FACES...
...AND OLD FRIENDS.
OF COURSE, SOME FAMILIAR FACES AREN'T SO FRIENDLY.
WATCH OUT, NEW GUY...WWE SUPERSTAR COMING THROUGH!
KO
BUT MAKE NO MISTAKE...
...I DIDN'T COME ALL THIS WAY TO MAKE FRIENDS.
EXCUSE ME, MR. STYLES?

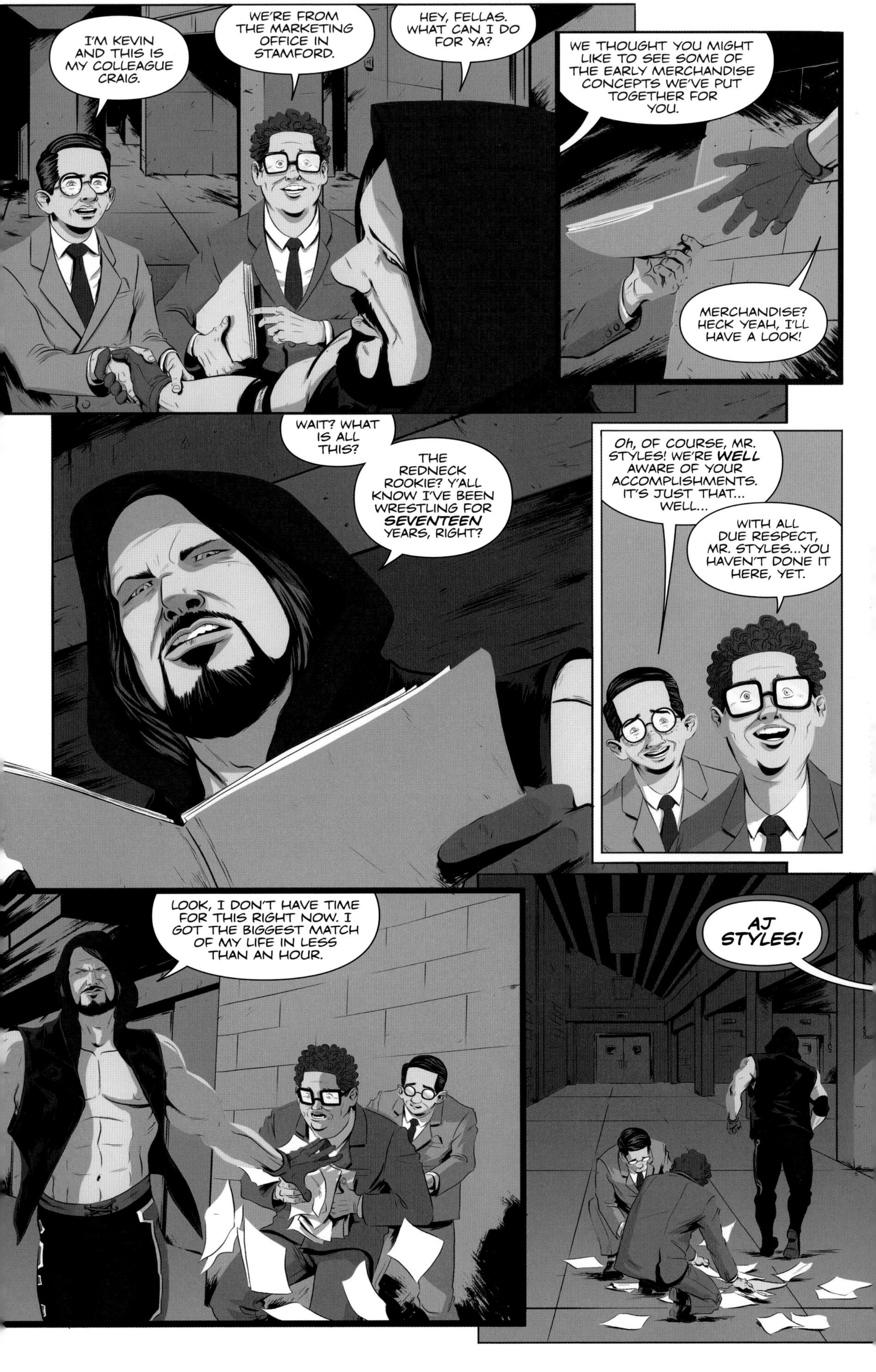

I'M KEVIN AND THIS IS MY COLLEAGUE CRAIG.
WE'RE FROM THE MARKETING OFFICE IN STAMFORD.
HEY, FELLAS. WHAT CAN I DO FOR YA?
WE THOUGHT YOU MIGHT LIKE TO SEE SOME OF THE EARLY MERCHANDISE CONCEPTS WE'VE PUT TOGETHER FOR YOU.
MERCHANDISE? HECK YEAH, I'LL HAVE A LOOK!
WAIT? WHAT IS ALL THIS?
THE REDNECK ROOKIE? Y'ALL KNOW I'VE BEEN WRESTLING FOR ***SEVENTEEN*** YEARS, RIGHT?
*Oh*, OF COURSE, MR. STYLES! WE'RE ***WELL*** AWARE OF YOUR ACCOMPLISHMENTS. IT'S JUST THAT... WELL...
WITH ALL DUE RESPECT, MR. STYLES...YOU HAVEN'T DONE IT HERE, YET.
LOOK, I DON'T HAVE TIME FOR THIS RIGHT NOW. I GOT THE BIGGEST MATCH OF MY LIFE IN LESS THAN AN HOUR.
AJ STYLES!

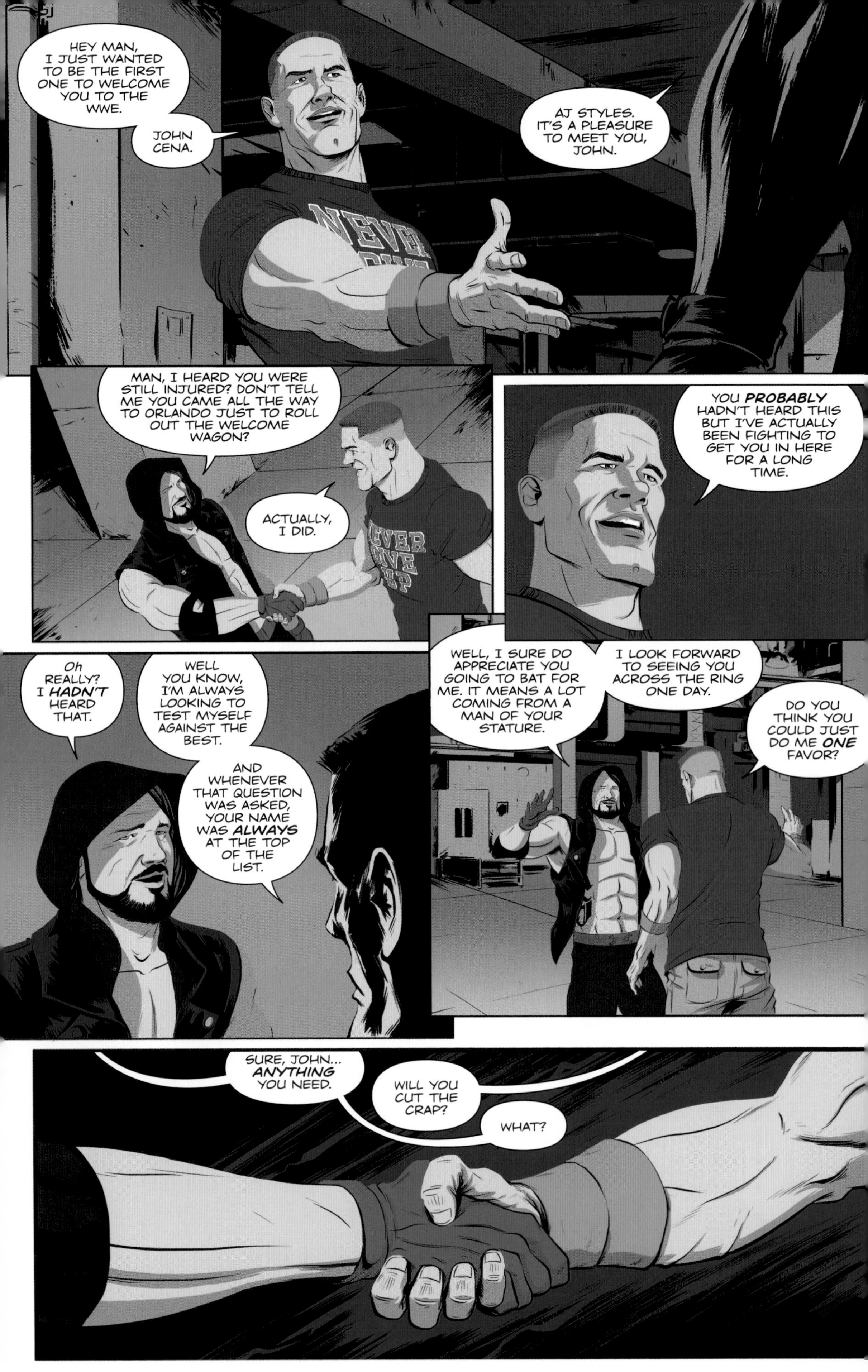
HEY MAN, I JUST WANTED TO BE THE FIRST ONE TO WELCOME YOU TO THE WWE.
JOHN CENA.
AJ STYLES. IT'S A PLEASURE TO MEET YOU, JOHN.
MAN, I HEARD YOU WERE STILL INJURED? DON'T TELL ME YOU CAME ALL THE WAY TO ORLANDO JUST TO ROLL OUT THE WELCOME WAGON?
ACTUALLY, I DID.
NEVER GIVE UP
YOU **PROBABLY** HADN'T HEARD THIS BUT I'VE ACTUALLY BEEN FIGHTING TO GET YOU IN HERE FOR A LONG TIME.
*Oh* REALLY? I ***HADN'T*** HEARD THAT.
WELL YOU KNOW, I'M ALWAYS LOOKING TO TEST MYSELF AGAINST THE BEST.
AND WHENEVER THAT QUESTION WAS ASKED, YOUR NAME WAS ***ALWAYS*** AT THE TOP OF THE LIST.
WELL, I SURE DO APPRECIATE YOU GOING TO BAT FOR ME. IT MEANS A LOT COMING FROM A MAN OF YOUR STATURE.
I LOOK FORWARD TO SEEING YOU ACROSS THE RING ONE DAY.
DO YOU THINK YOU COULD JUST DO ME ***ONE*** FAVOR?
SURE, JOHN... ***ANYTHING*** YOU NEED.
WILL YOU CUT THE CRAP?
WHAT?

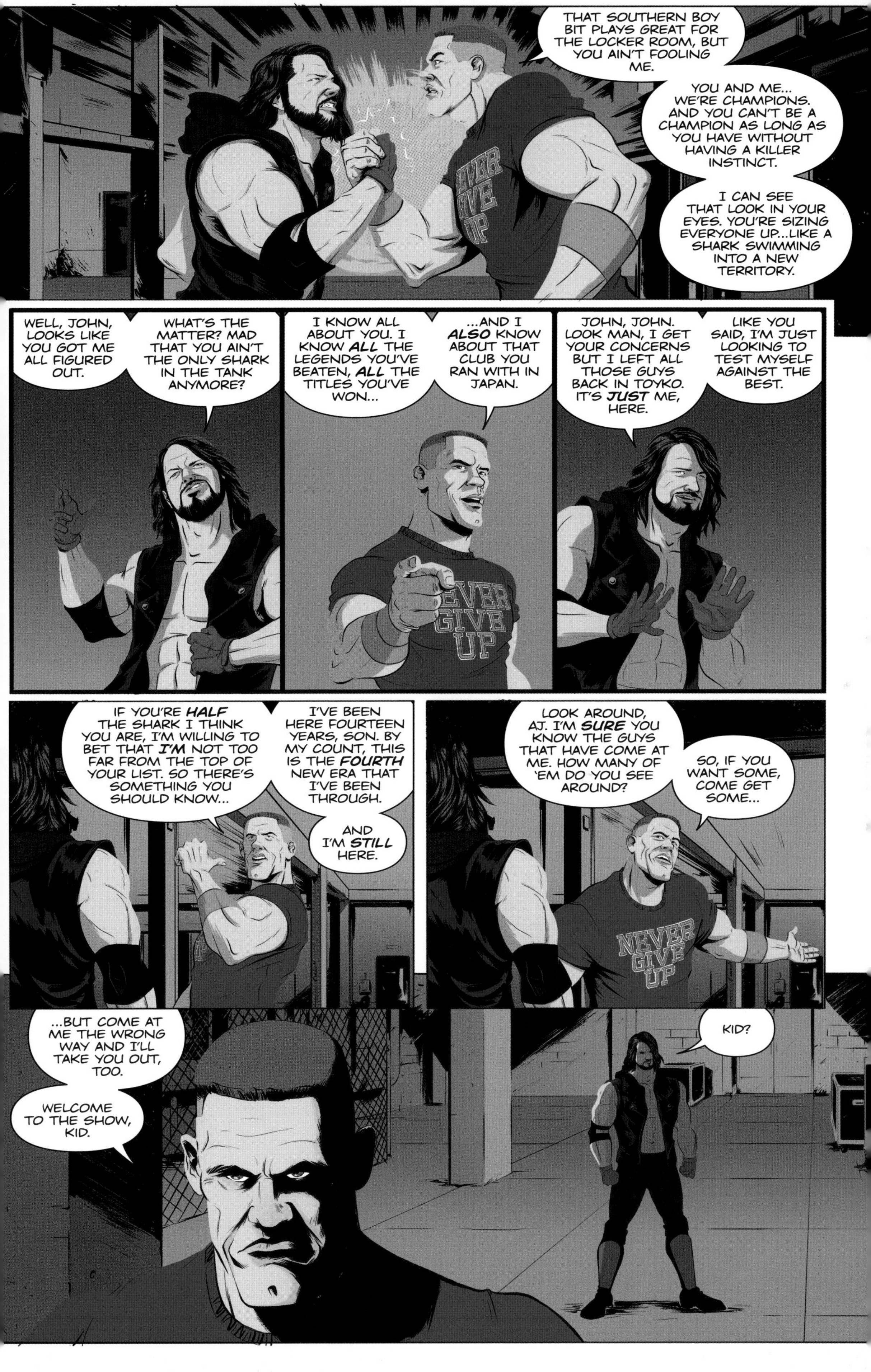
THAT SOUTHERN BOY BIT PLAYS GREAT FOR THE LOCKER ROOM, BUT YOU AIN'T FOOLING ME.
YOU AND ME... WE'RE CHAMPIONS. AND YOU CAN'T BE A CHAMPION AS LONG AS YOU HAVE WITHOUT HAVING A KILLER INSTINCT.
I CAN SEE THAT LOOK IN YOUR EYES. YOU'RE SIZING EVERYONE UP...LIKE A SHARK SWIMMING INTO A NEW TERRITORY.
NEVER GIVE UP
WELL, JOHN, LOOKS LIKE YOU GOT ME ALL FIGURED OUT.
WHAT'S THE MATTER? MAD THAT YOU AIN'T THE ONLY SHARK IN THE TANK ANYMORE?
I KNOW ALL ABOUT YOU. I KNOW **ALL** THE LEGENDS YOU'VE BEATEN, **ALL** THE TITLES YOU'VE WON...
...AND I ***ALSO*** KNOW ABOUT THAT CLUB YOU RAN WITH IN JAPAN.
NEVER GIVE UP
JOHN, JOHN. LOOK MAN, I GET YOUR CONCERNS BUT I LEFT ALL THOSE GUYS BACK IN TOYKO. IT'S ***JUST*** ME, HERE.
LIKE YOU SAID, I'M JUST LOOKING TO TEST MYSELF AGAINST THE BEST.
IF YOU'RE ***HALF*** THE SHARK I THINK YOU ARE, I'M WILLING TO BET THAT ***I'M*** NOT TOO FAR FROM THE TOP OF YOUR LIST. SO THERE'S SOMETHING YOU SHOULD KNOW...
I'VE BEEN HERE FOURTEEN YEARS, SON. BY MY COUNT, THIS IS THE ***FOURTH*** NEW ERA THAT I'VE BEEN THROUGH.
AND I'M ***STILL*** HERE.
LOOK AROUND, AJ. I'M ***SURE*** YOU KNOW THE GUYS THAT HAVE COME AT ME. HOW MANY OF 'EM DO YOU SEE AROUND?
SO, IF YOU WANT SOME, COME GET SOME...
NEVER GIVE UP
...BUT COME AT ME THE WRONG WAY AND I'LL TAKE YOU OUT, TOO.
WELCOME TO THE SHOW, KID.
KID?

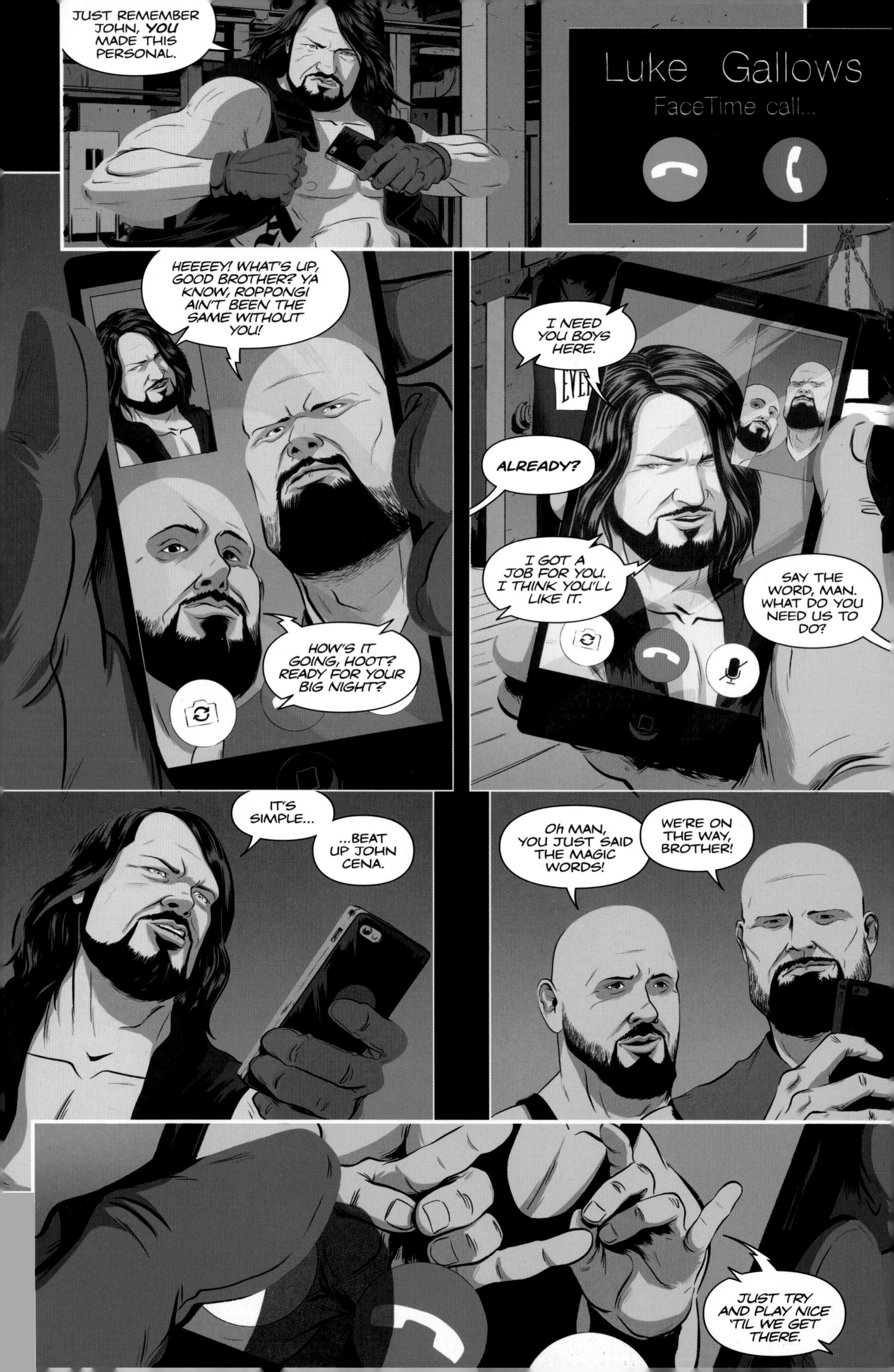
JUST REMEMBER JOHN, ***YOU*** MADE THIS PERSONAL.
Luke Gallows
FaceTime call...
HEEEEY! WHAT'S UP, GOOD BROTHER? YA KNOW, ROPPONGI AIN'T BEEN THE SAME WITHOUT YOU!
HOW'S IT GOING, HOOT? READY FOR YOUR BIG NIGHT?
I NEED YOU BOYS HERE.
***ALREADY?***
I GOT A JOB FOR YOU. I THINK YOU'LL LIKE IT.
SAY THE WORD, MAN. WHAT DO YOU NEED US TO DO?
IT'S SIMPLE...
...BEAT UP JOHN CENA.
*Oh* MAN, YOU JUST SAID THE MAGIC WORDS!
WE'RE ON THE WAY, BROTHER!
JUST TRY AND PLAY NICE 'TIL WE GET THERE.

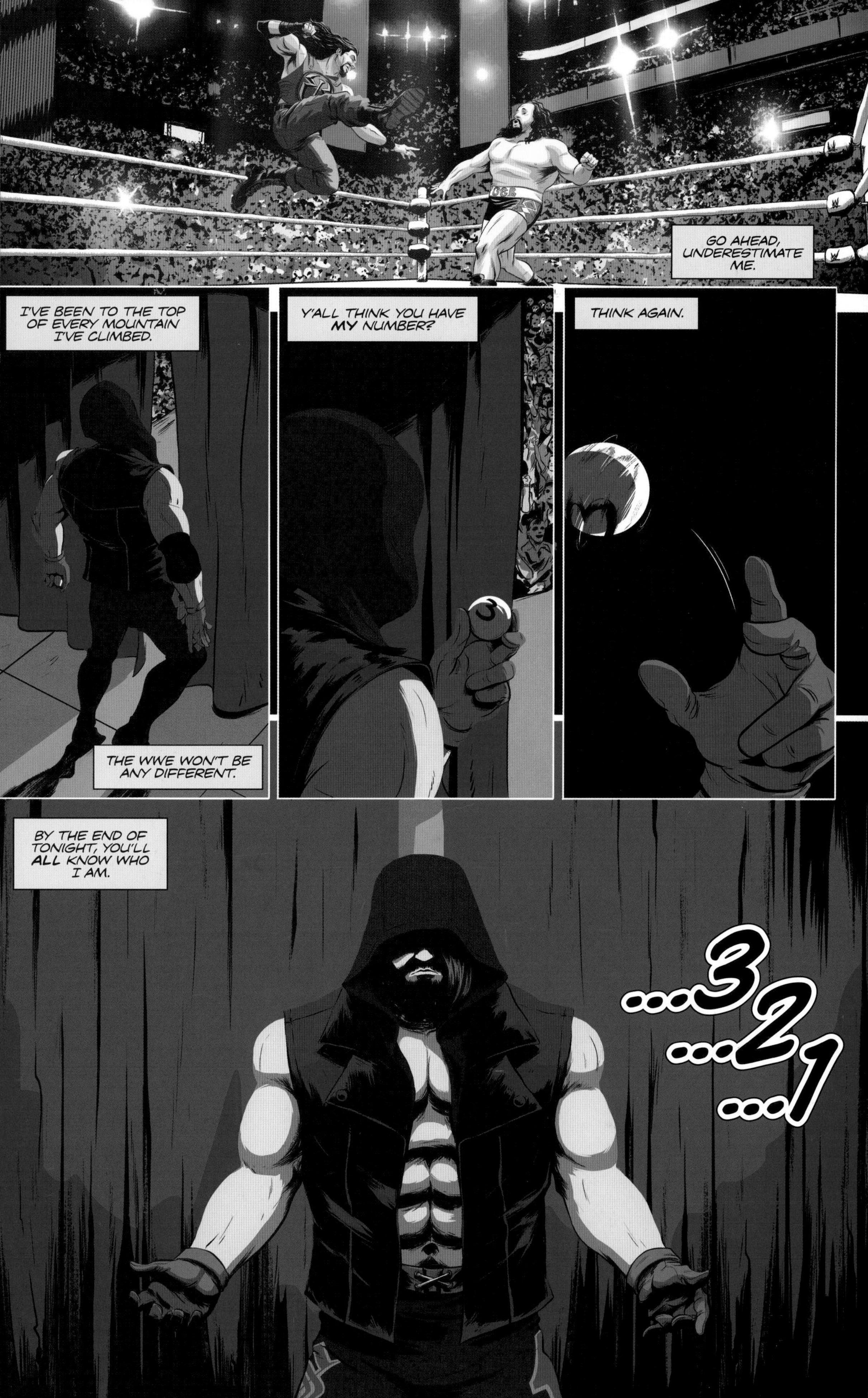
GO AHEAD, UNDERESTIMATE ME.
I'VE BEEN TO THE TOP OF EVERY MOUNTAIN I'VE CLIMBED.
THE WWE WON'T BE ANY DIFFERENT.
Y'ALL THINK YOU HAVE MY NUMBER?
THINK AGAIN.
BY THE END OF TONIGHT, YOU'LL ALL KNOW WHO I AM.
...3
...2
...1

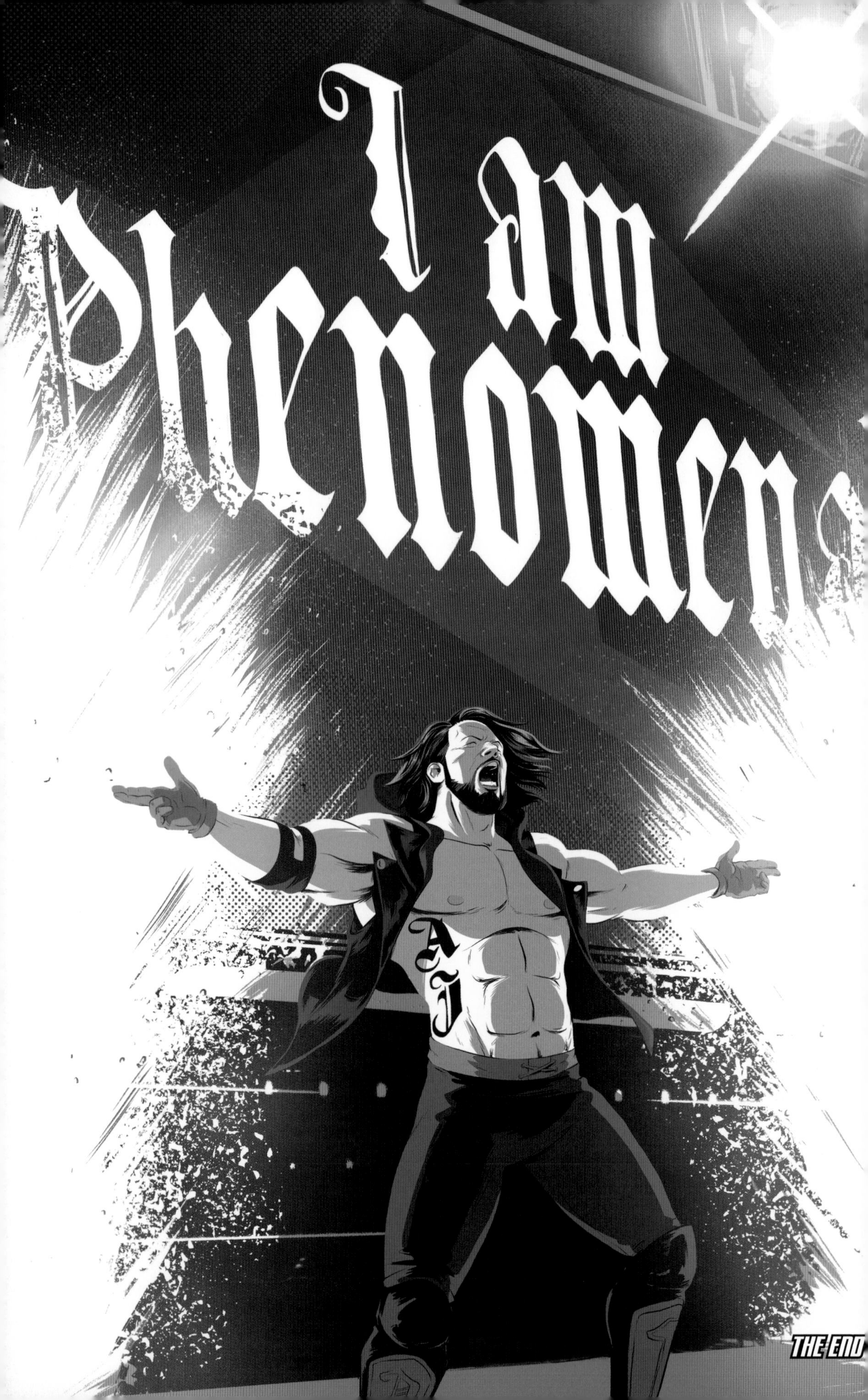
I am Phenomen
AJ
THE END

# YOU CAN HATE ME NOW

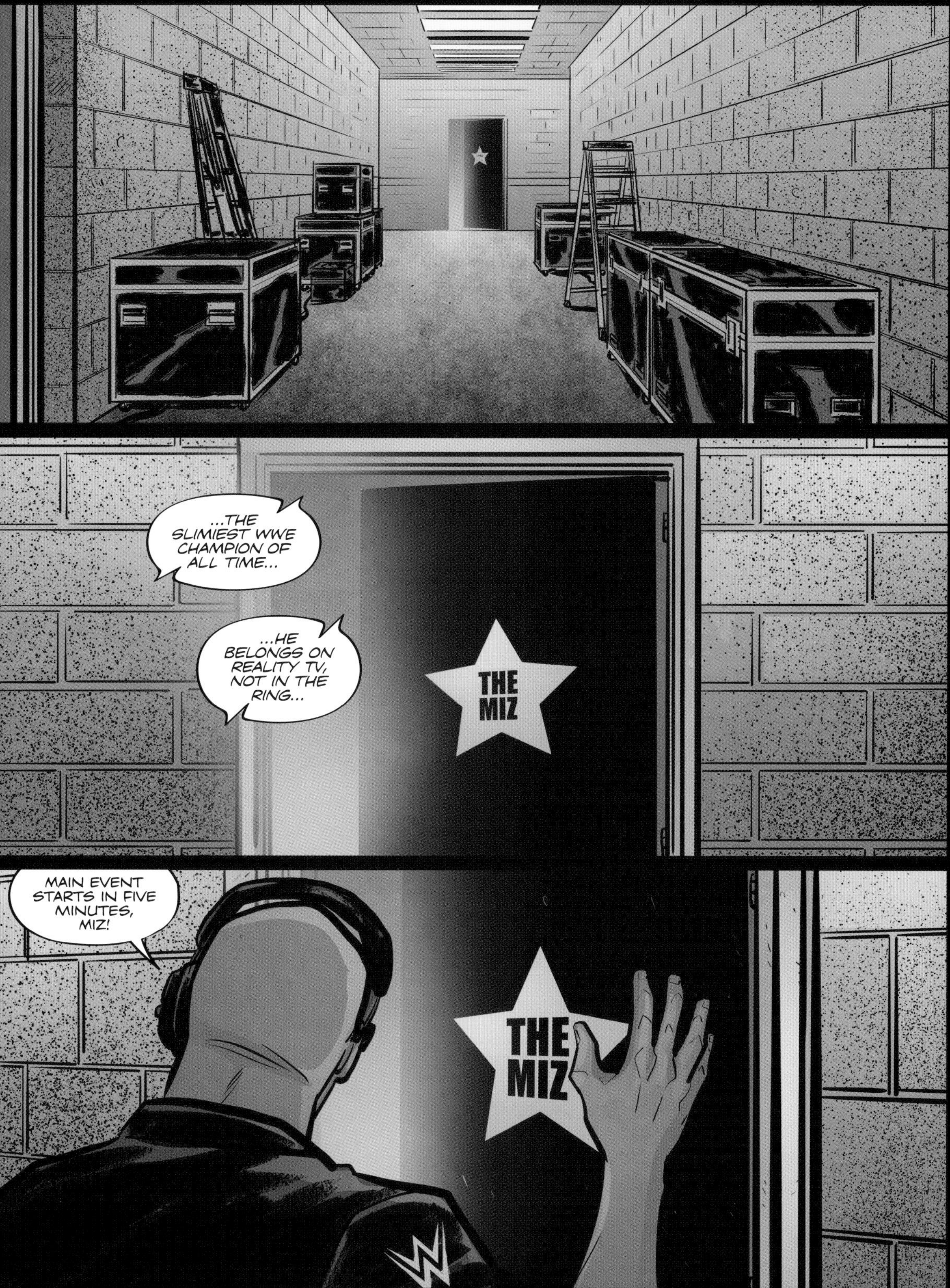
...THE SLIMIEST WWE CHAMPION OF ALL TIME...
...HE BELONGS ON REALITY TV, NOT IN THE RING...
THE MIZ
MAIN EVENT STARTS IN FIVE MINUTES, MIZ!
THE MIZ

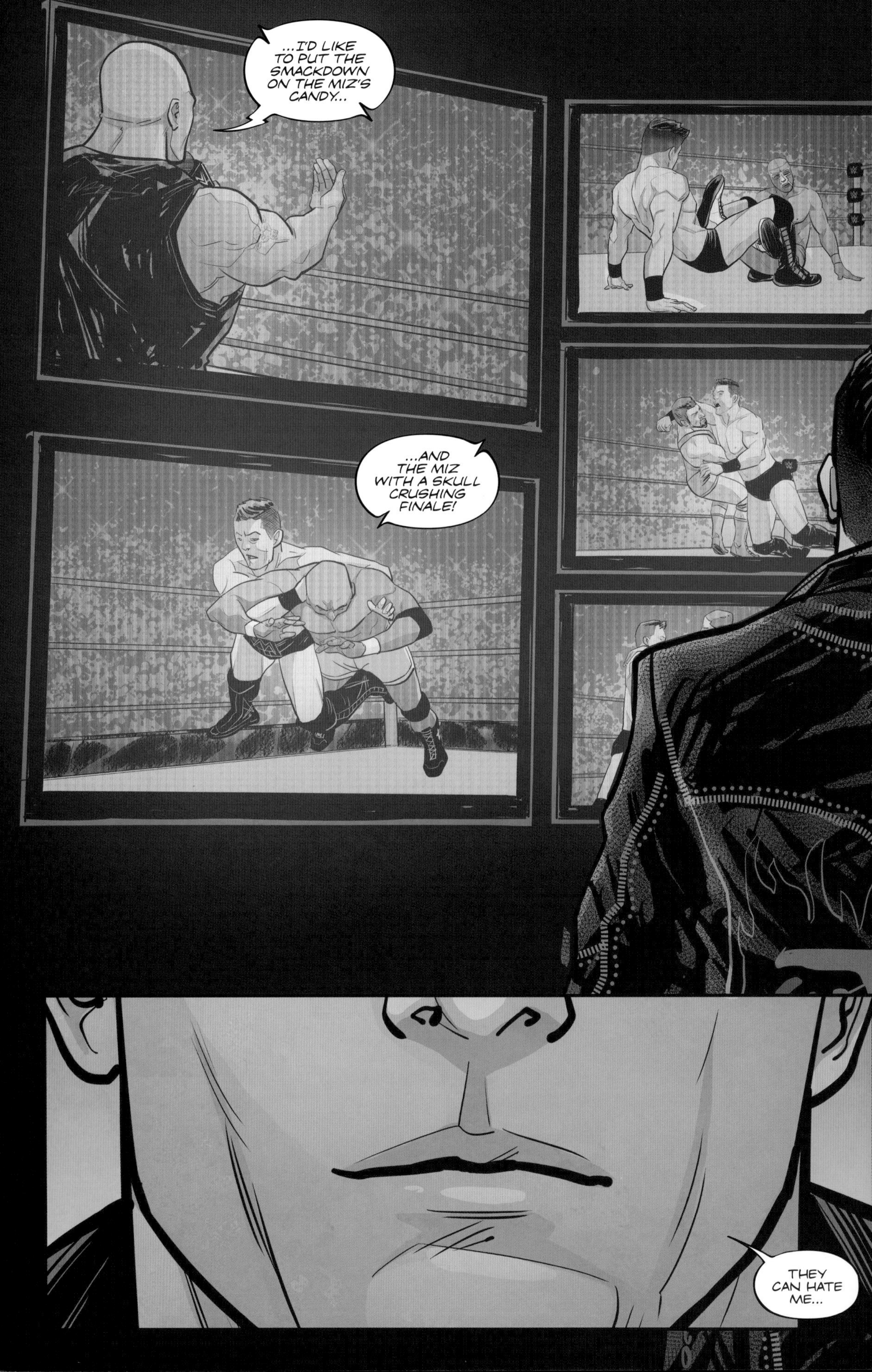
...I'D LIKE TO PUT THE SMACKDOWN ON THE MIZ'S CANDY...
...AND THE MIZ WITH A SKULL CRUSHING FINALE!
THEY CAN HATE ME...

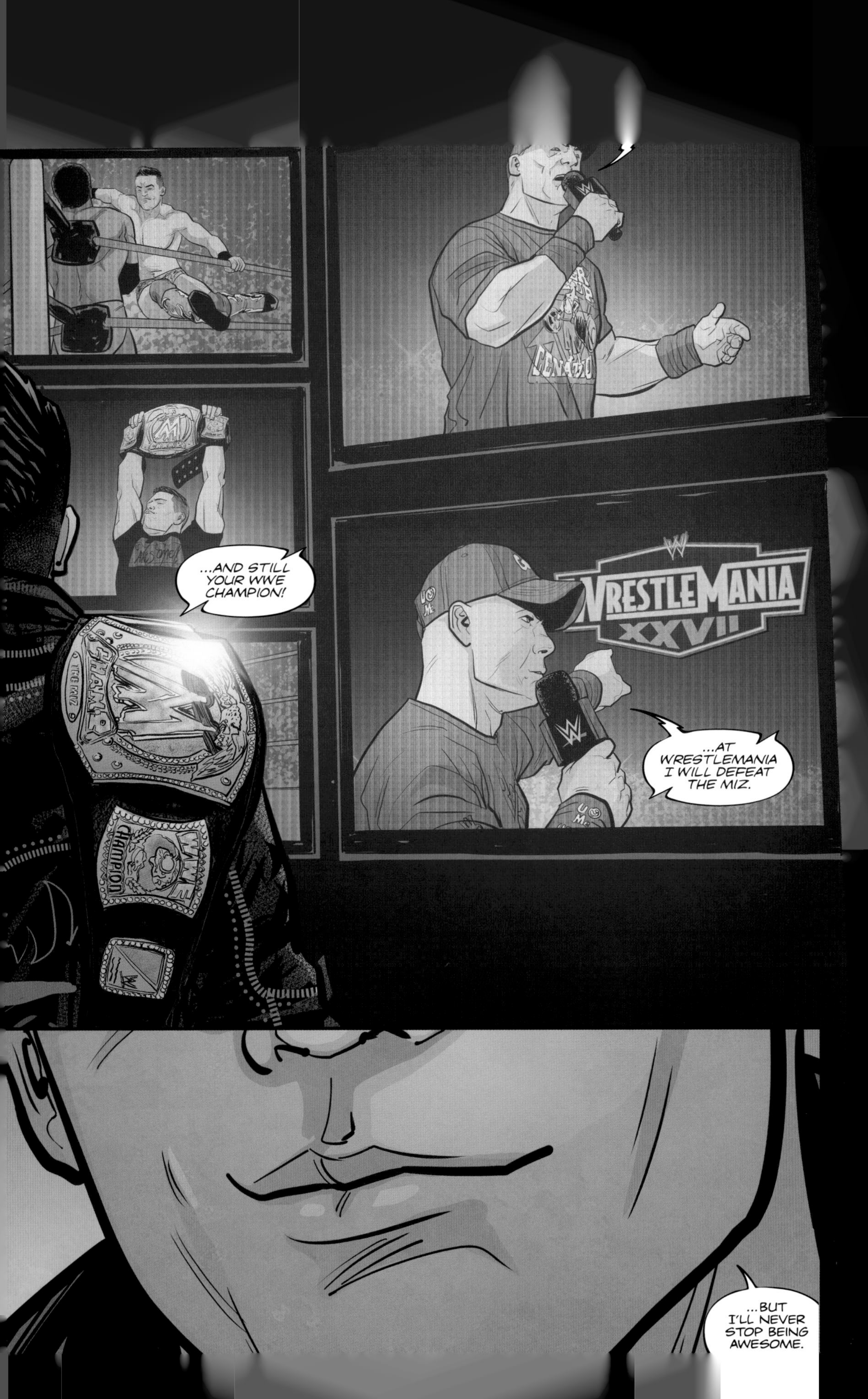

...AND STILL YOUR WWE CHAMPION!
WRESTLEMANIA XXVII
...AT WRESTLEMANIA I WILL DEFEAT THE MIZ.
...BUT I'LL NEVER STOP BEING AWESOME.

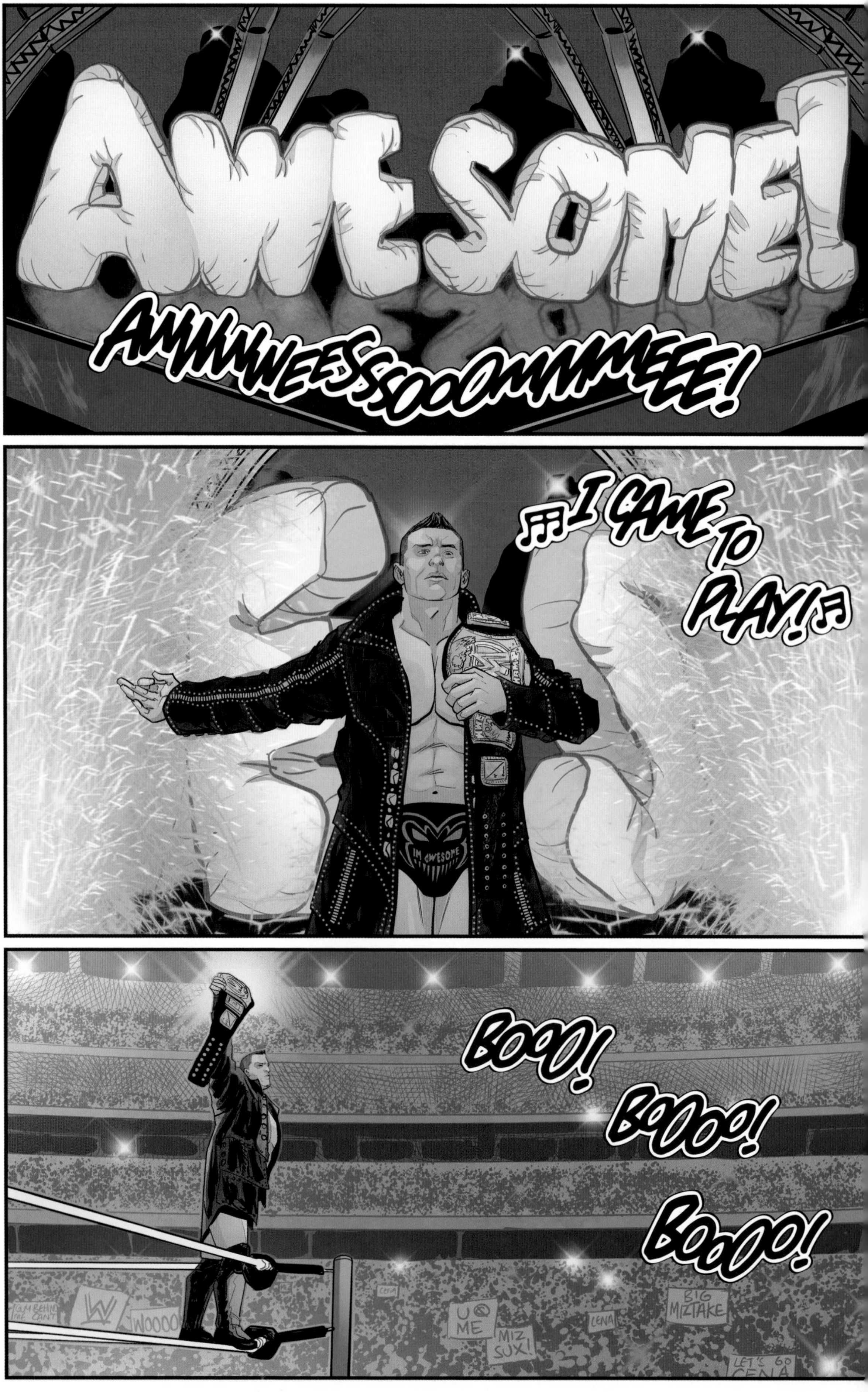
AWESOME!
AWWWWEESSOOOMMMEEE!
I CAME TO PLAY!
IM AWESOME
BOOO!
BOOOO!
BOOOO!
WOOOO
CENA
U ME
MIZ SUX!
CENA
BIG MIZTAKE
LET'S GO CENA

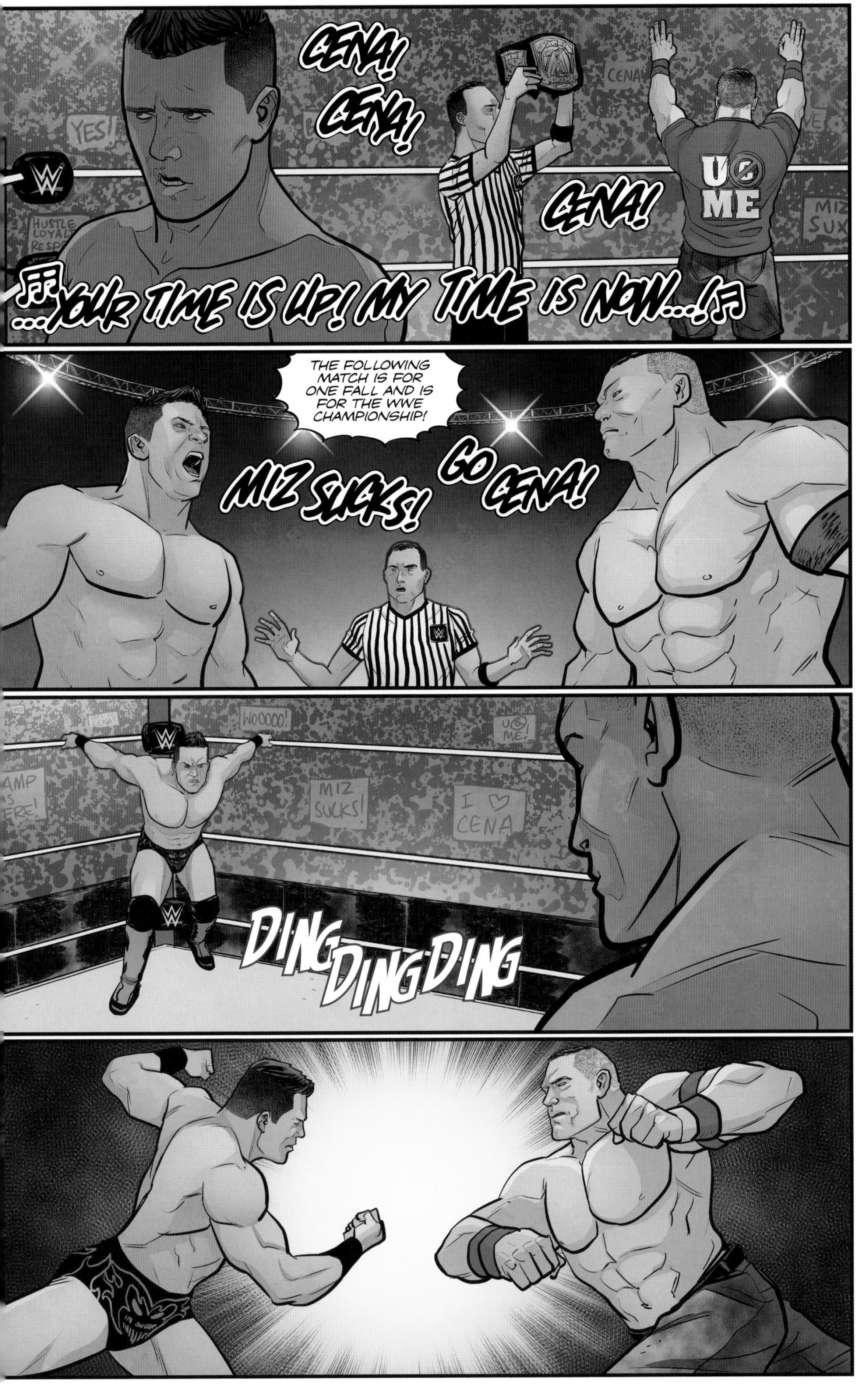
CENA!
CENA!
CENA!
YES!
MIZ SUX
U C ME
...YOUR TIME IS UP! MY TIME IS NOW...!
THE FOLLOWING MATCH IS FOR ONE FALL AND IS FOR THE WWE CHAMPIONSHIP!
MIZ SUCKS!
GO CENA!
WOOOO!
MIZ SUCKS!
I ♥ CENA
DING DING DING

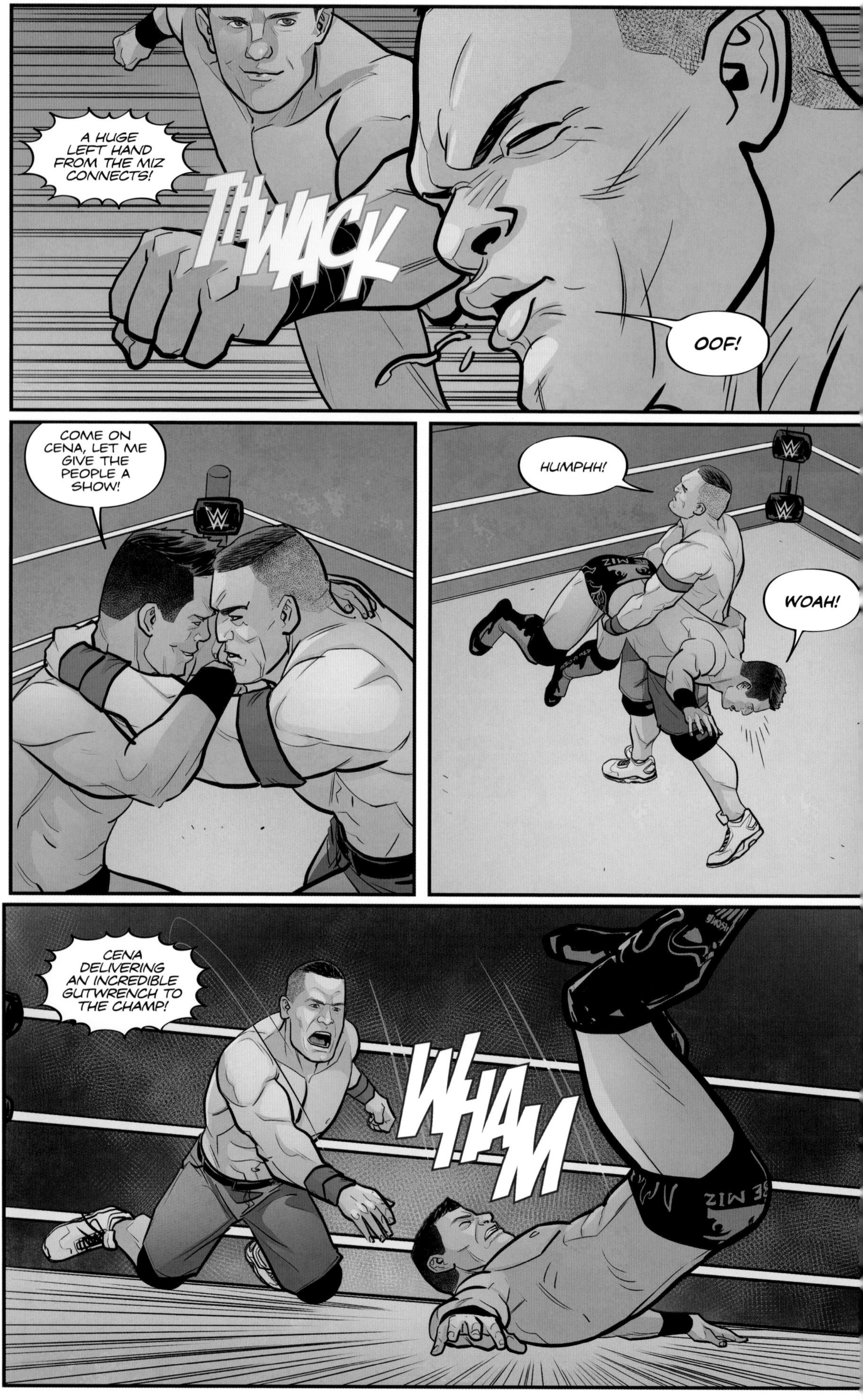
A HUGE LEFT HAND FROM THE MIZ CONNECTS!
THWACK
OOF!
COME ON CENA, LET ME GIVE THE PEOPLE A SHOW!
HUMPHH!
WOAH!
CENA DELIVERING AN INCREDIBLE GUTWRENCH TO THE CHAMP!
WHAM

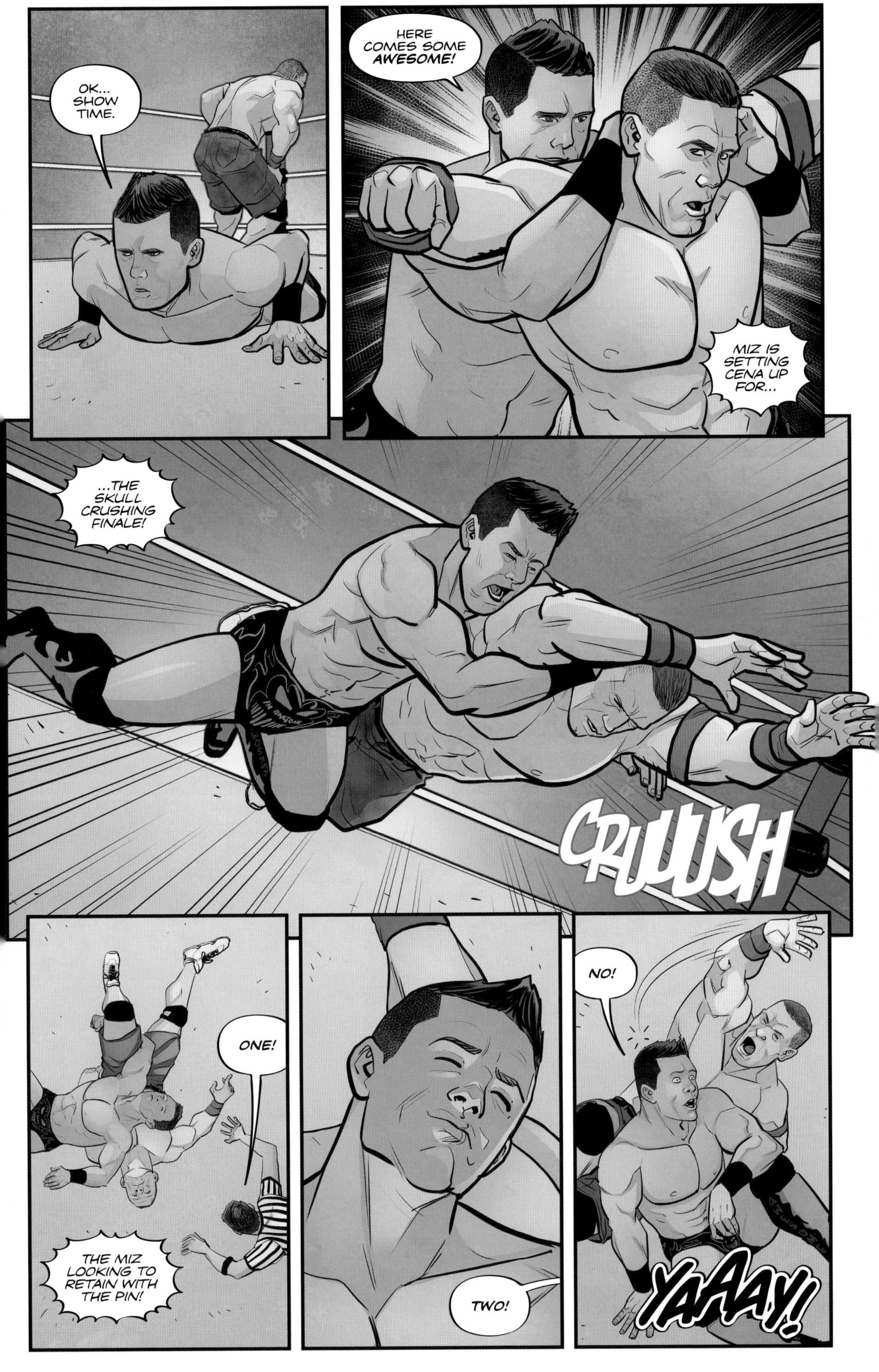
OK... SHOW TIME.
HERE COMES SOME AWESOME!
MIZ IS SETTING CENA UP FOR...
...THE SKULL CRUSHING FINALE!
CRUUUSH
ONE!
THE MIZ LOOKING TO RETAIN WITH THE PIN!
TWO!
NO!
YAAAY!

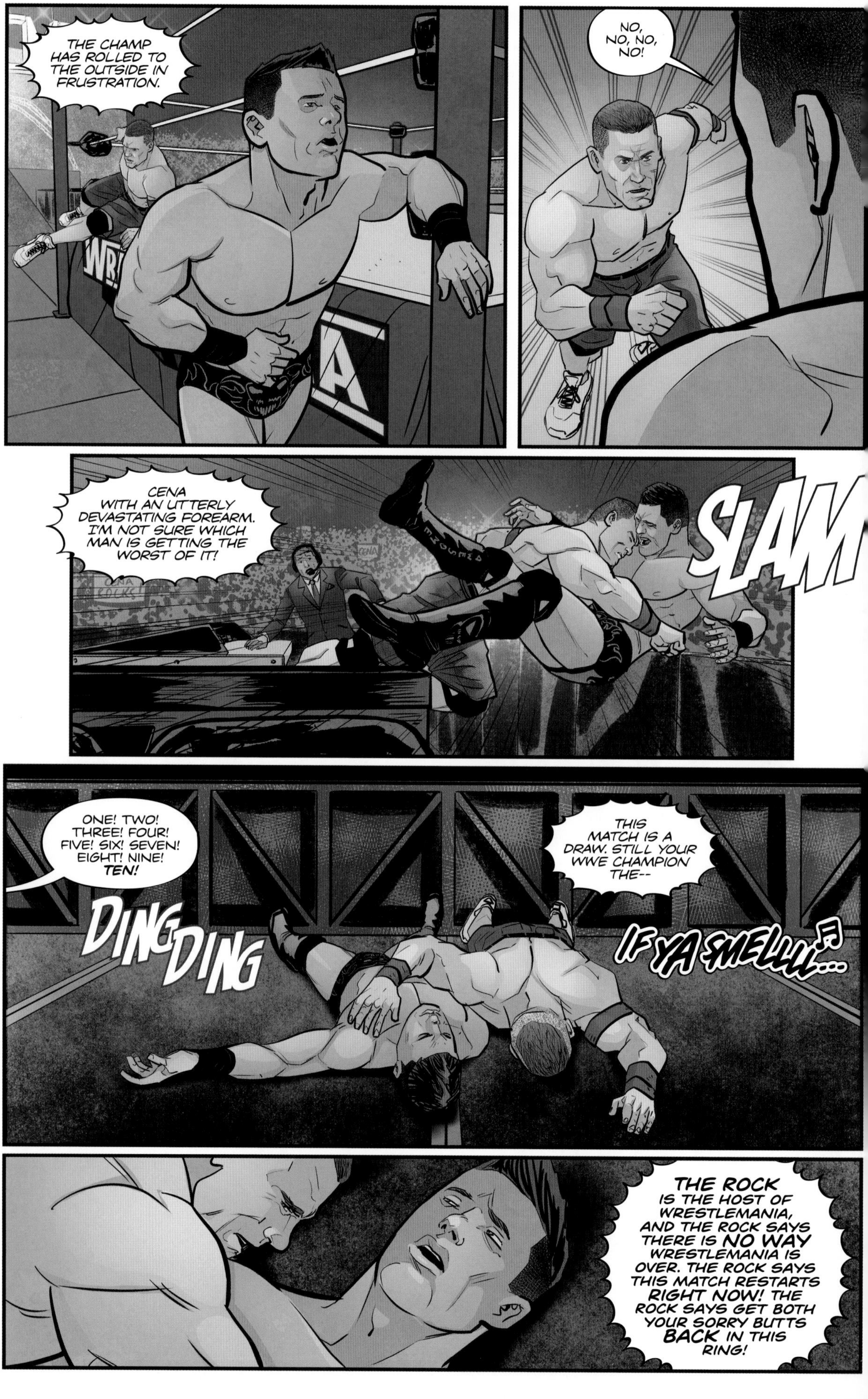

THE CHAMP HAS ROLLED TO THE OUTSIDE IN FRUSTRATION.
NO, NO, NO, NO!
CENA WITH AN UTTERLY DEVASTATING FOREARM. I'M NOT SURE WHICH MAN IS GETTING THE WORST OF IT!
SLAM
ONE! TWO! THREE! FOUR! FIVE! SIX! SEVEN! EIGHT! NINE! **TEN!**
THIS MATCH IS A DRAW. STILL YOUR WWE CHAMPION THE--
DING DING
IF YA SMELLL...
**THE ROCK** IS THE HOST OF WRESTLEMANIA, AND THE ROCK SAYS THERE IS **NO WAY** WRESTLEMANIA IS OVER. THE ROCK SAYS THIS MATCH RESTARTS **RIGHT NOW!** THE ROCK SAYS GET BOTH YOUR SORRY BUTTS **BACK** IN THIS RING!

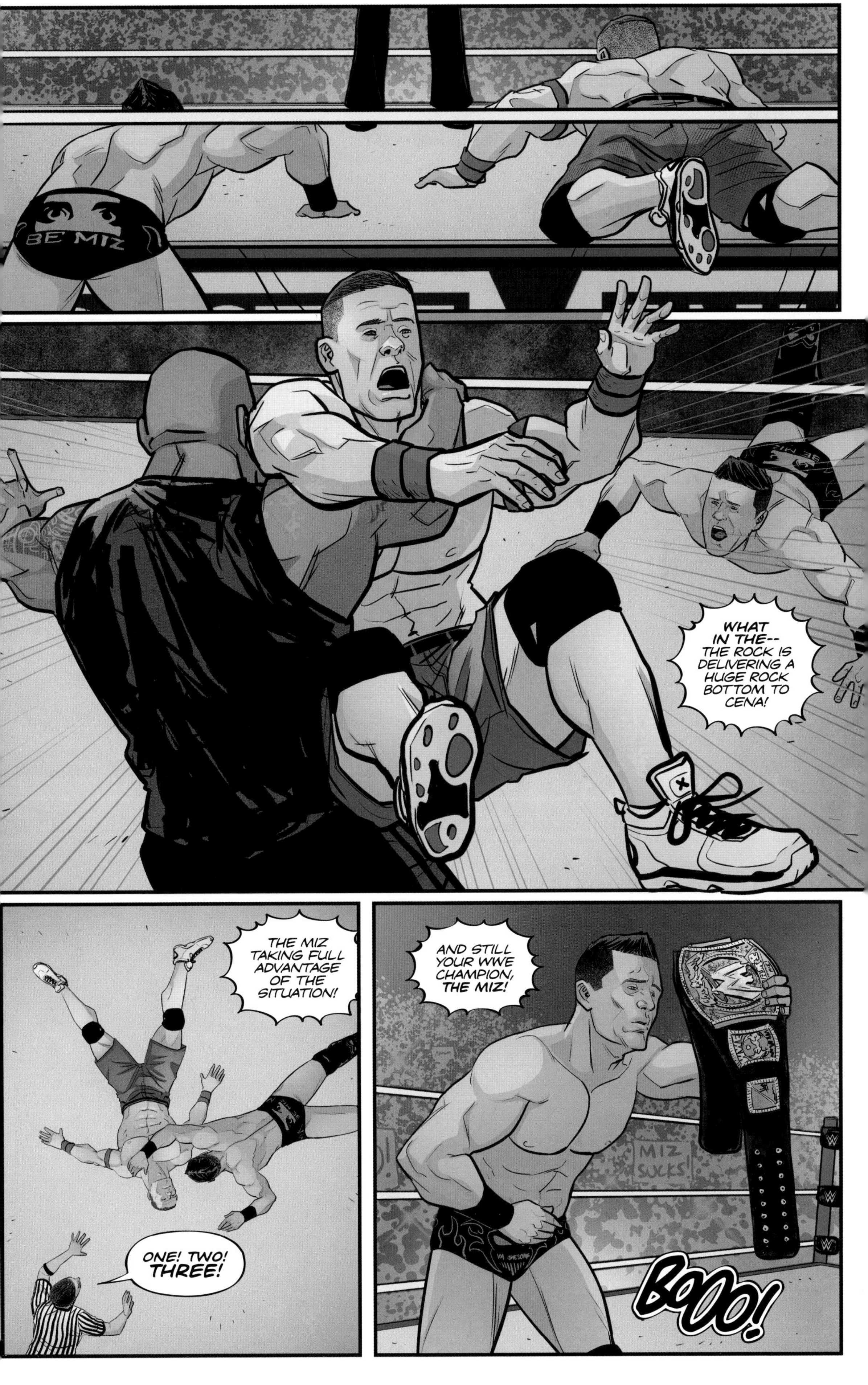
BE MIZ
WHAT IN THE-- THE ROCK IS DELIVERING A HUGE ROCK BOTTOM TO CENA!
THE MIZ TAKING FULL ADVANTAGE OF THE SITUATION!
ONE! TWO! THREE!
AND STILL YOUR WWE CHAMPION, THE MIZ!
MIZ SUCKS!
BOOO!

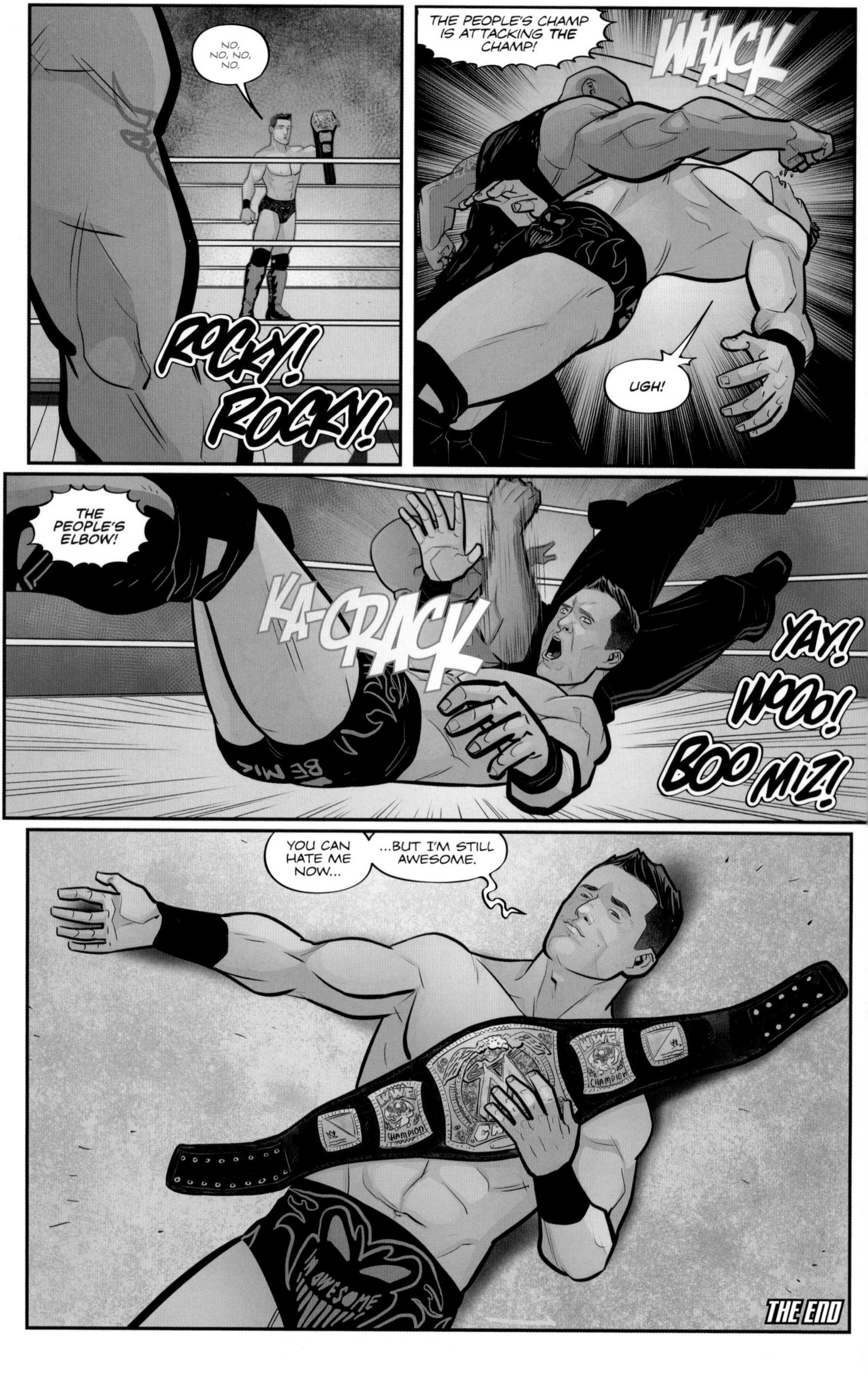
NO, NO, NO, NO.
ROCKY! ROCKY!
THE PEOPLE'S CHAMP IS ATTACKING THE CHAMP!
WHACK
UGH!
THE PEOPLE'S ELBOW!
KA-CRACK
YAY! WOOO! BOO MIZ!
YOU CAN HATE ME NOW...
...BUT I'M STILL AWESOME.
THE END

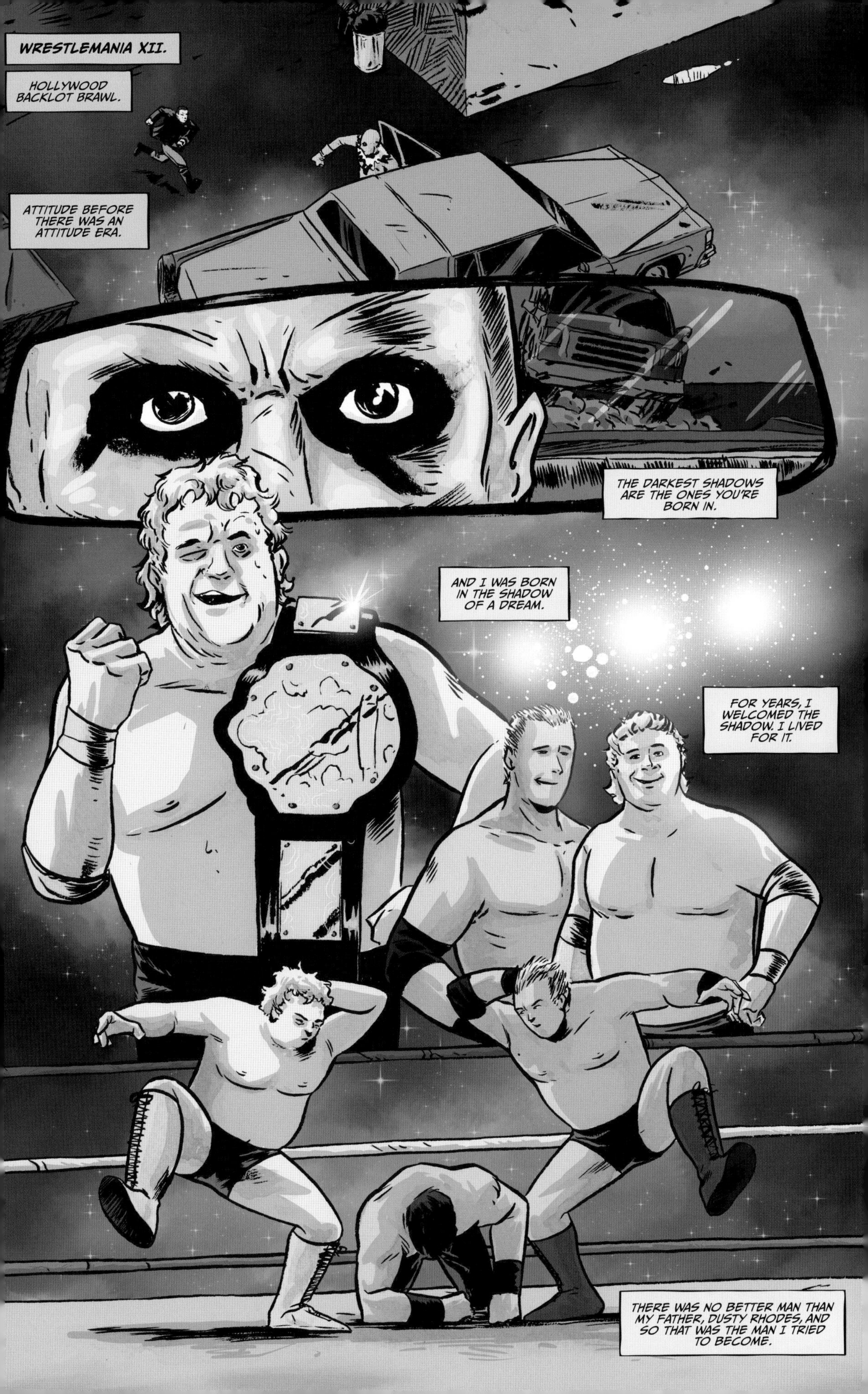
WRESTLEMANIA XII.
HOLLYWOOD BACKLOT BRAWL.
ATTITUDE BEFORE THERE WAS AN ATTITUDE ERA.
THE DARKEST SHADOWS ARE THE ONES YOU'RE BORN IN.
AND I WAS BORN IN THE SHADOW OF A DREAM.
FOR YEARS, I WELCOMED THE SHADOW. I LIVED FOR IT.
THERE WAS NO BETTER MAN THAN MY FATHER, DUSTY RHODES, AND SO THAT WAS THE MAN I TRIED TO BECOME.

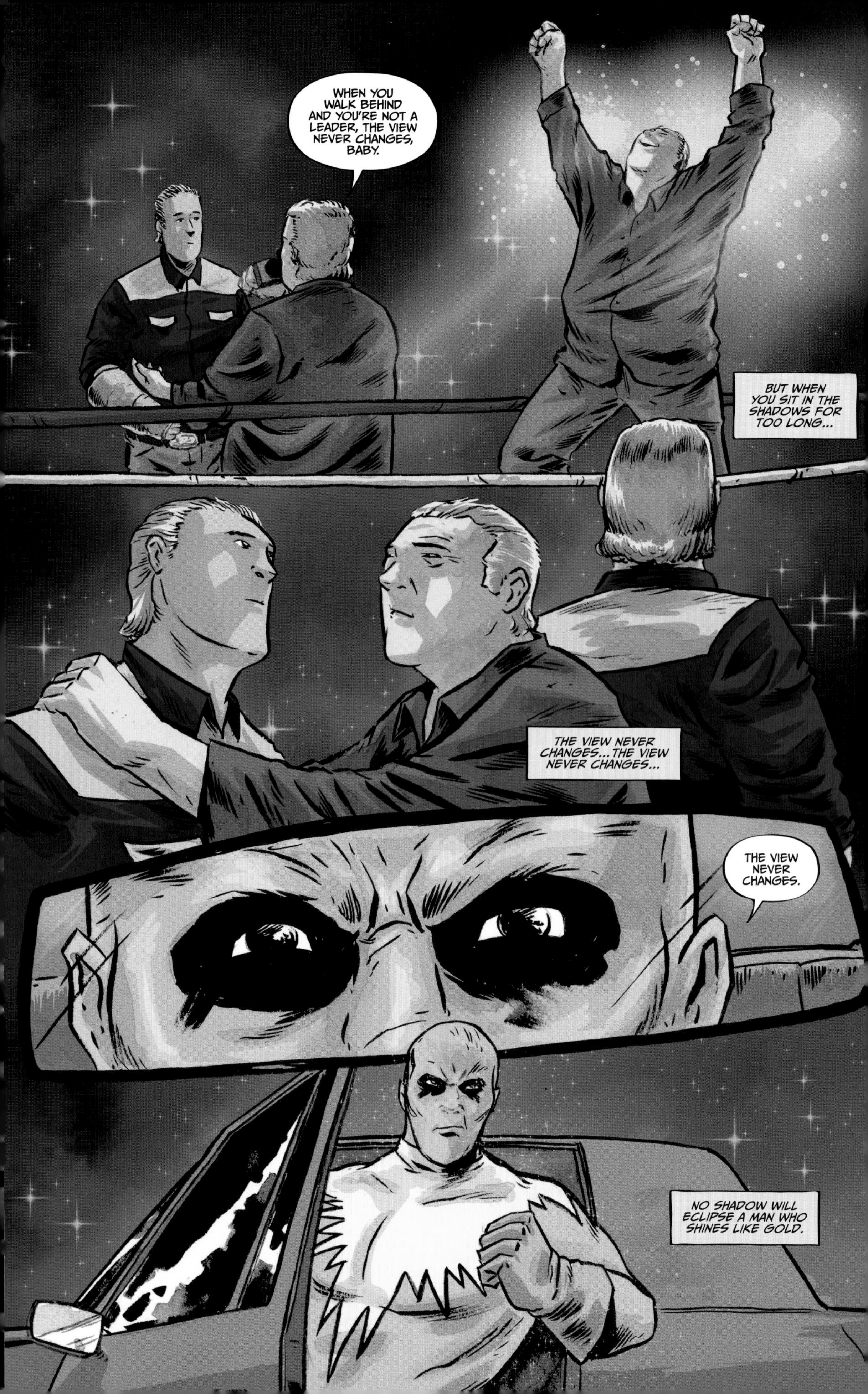
WHEN YOU WALK BEHIND AND YOU'RE NOT A LEADER, THE VIEW NEVER CHANGES, BABY.
BUT WHEN YOU SIT IN THE SHADOWS FOR TOO LONG...
THE VIEW NEVER CHANGES... THE VIEW NEVER CHANGES...
THE VIEW NEVER CHANGES.
NO SHADOW WILL ECLIPSE A MAN WHO SHINES LIKE GOLD.

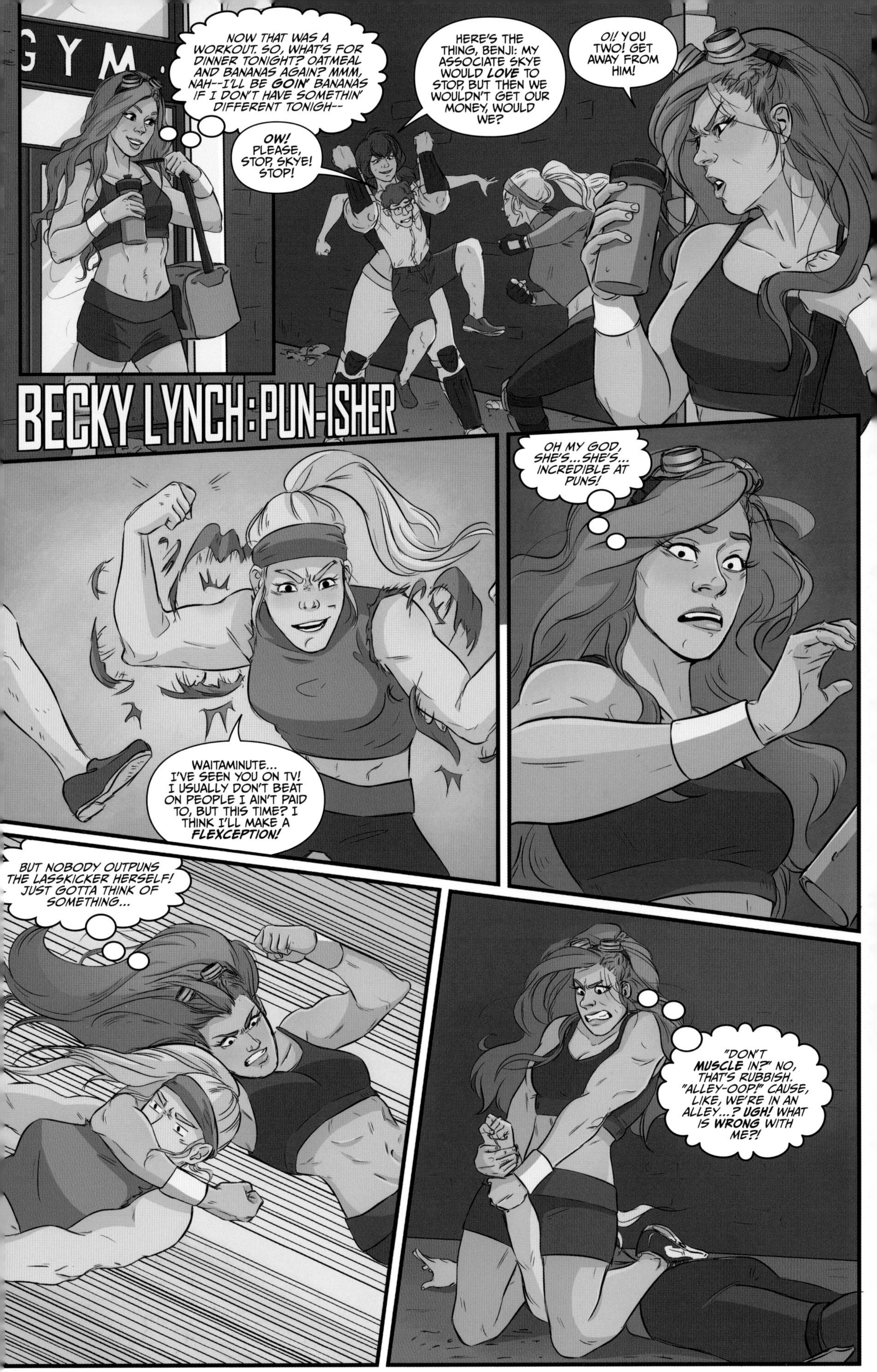
GYM
NOW THAT WAS A WORKOUT. SO, WHAT'S FOR DINNER TONIGHT? OATMEAL AND BANANAS AGAIN? MMM, NAH--I'LL BE GOIN' BANANAS IF I DON'T HAVE SOMETHIN' DIFFERENT TONIGH--
OW! PLEASE, STOP, SKYE! STOP!
HERE'S THE THING, BENJI: MY ASSOCIATE SKYE WOULD LOVE TO STOP, BUT THEN WE WOULDN'T GET OUR MONEY, WOULD WE?
OI! YOU TWO! GET AWAY FROM HIM!
BECKY LYNCH: PUN-ISHER
WAITAMINUTE... I'VE SEEN YOU ON TV! I USUALLY DON'T BEAT ON PEOPLE I AIN'T PAID TO, BUT THIS TIME? I THINK I'LL MAKE A FLEXCEPTION!
OH MY GOD, SHE'S...SHE'S... INCREDIBLE AT PUNS!
BUT NOBODY OUTPUNS THE LASSKICKER HERSELF! JUST GOTTA THINK OF SOMETHING...
"DON'T MUSCLE IN?" NO, THAT'S RUBBISH. "ALLEY-OOP!" CAUSE, LIKE, WE'RE IN AN ALLEY...? UGH! WHAT IS WRONG WITH ME?!

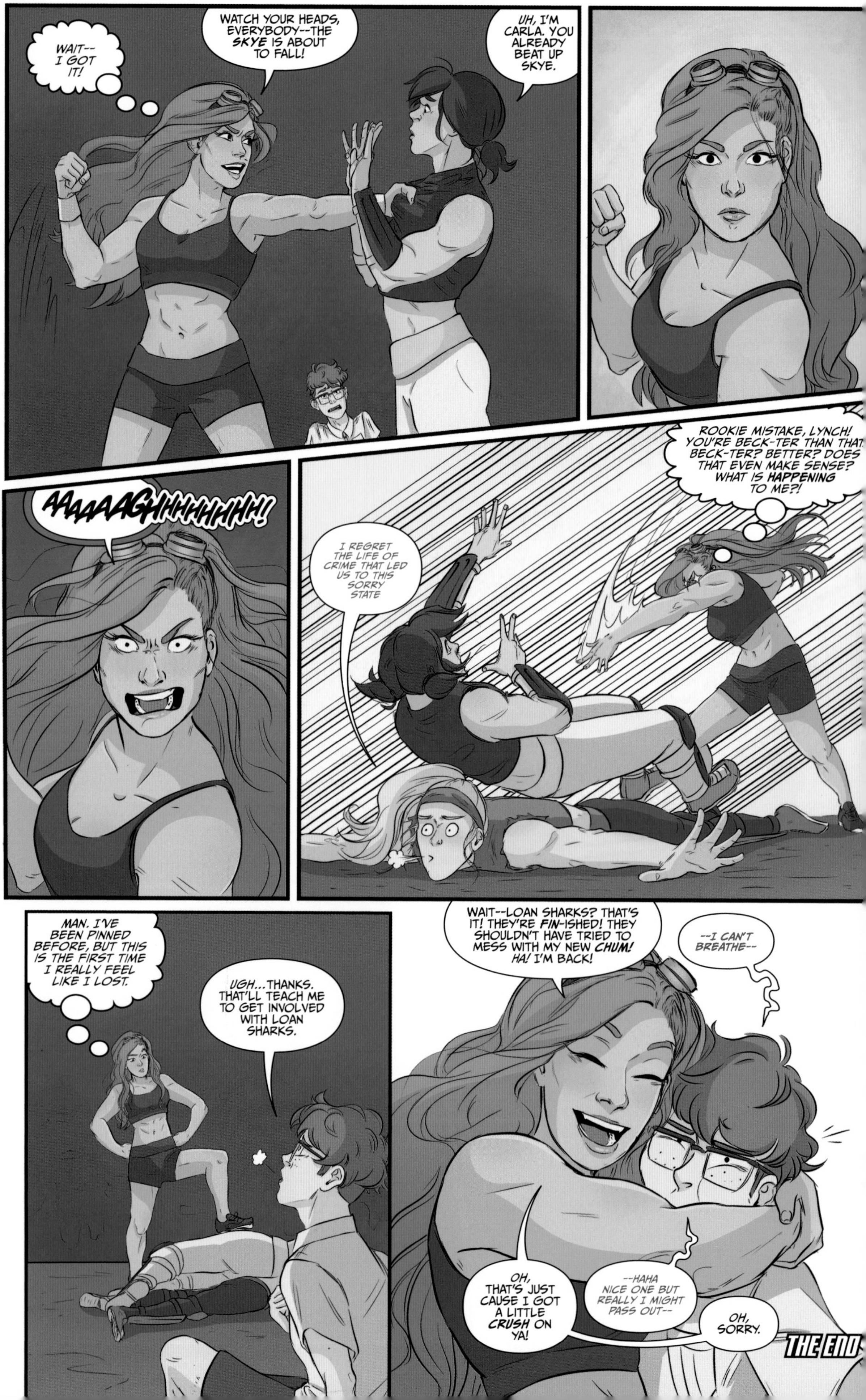
WAIT-- I GOT IT!
WATCH YOUR HEADS, EVERYBODY--THE SKYE IS ABOUT TO FALL!
UH, I'M CARLA. YOU ALREADY BEAT UP SKYE.
AAAAAAGHHHHHHHH!
ROOKIE MISTAKE, LYNCH! YOU'RE BECK-TER THAN THAT! BECK-TER? BETTER? DOES THAT EVEN MAKE SENSE? WHAT IS HAPPENING TO ME?!
I REGRET THE LIFE OF CRIME THAT LED US TO THIS SORRY STATE
MAN. I'VE BEEN PINNED BEFORE, BUT THIS IS THE FIRST TIME I REALLY FEEL LIKE I LOST.
UGH... THANKS. THAT'LL TEACH ME TO GET INVOLVED WITH LOAN SHARKS.
WAIT--LOAN SHARKS? THAT'S IT! THEY'RE FIN-ISHED! THEY SHOULDN'T HAVE TRIED TO MESS WITH MY NEW CHUM! HA! I'M BACK!
--I CAN'T BREATHE--
OH, THAT'S JUST CAUSE I GOT A LITTLE CRUSH ON YA!
--HAHA NICE ONE BUT REALLY I MIGHT PASS OUT--
OH, SORRY.
THE END

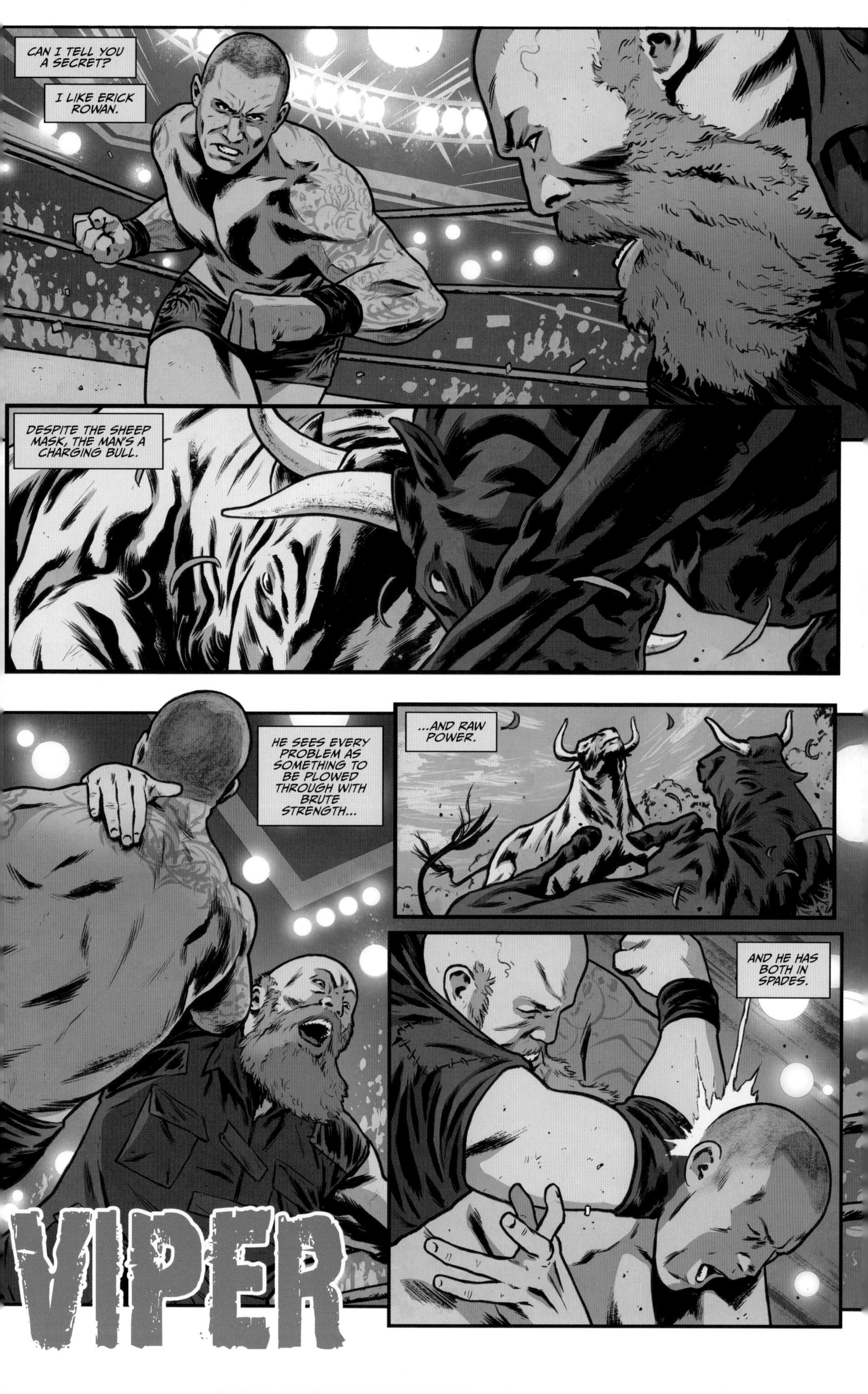
CAN I TELL YOU A SECRET?
I LIKE ERICK ROWAN.
DESPITE THE SHEEP MASK, THE MAN'S A CHARGING BULL.
HE SEES EVERY PROBLEM AS SOMETHING TO BE PLOWED THROUGH WITH BRUTE STRENGTH...
...AND RAW POWER.
AND HE HAS BOTH IN SPADES.
VIPER

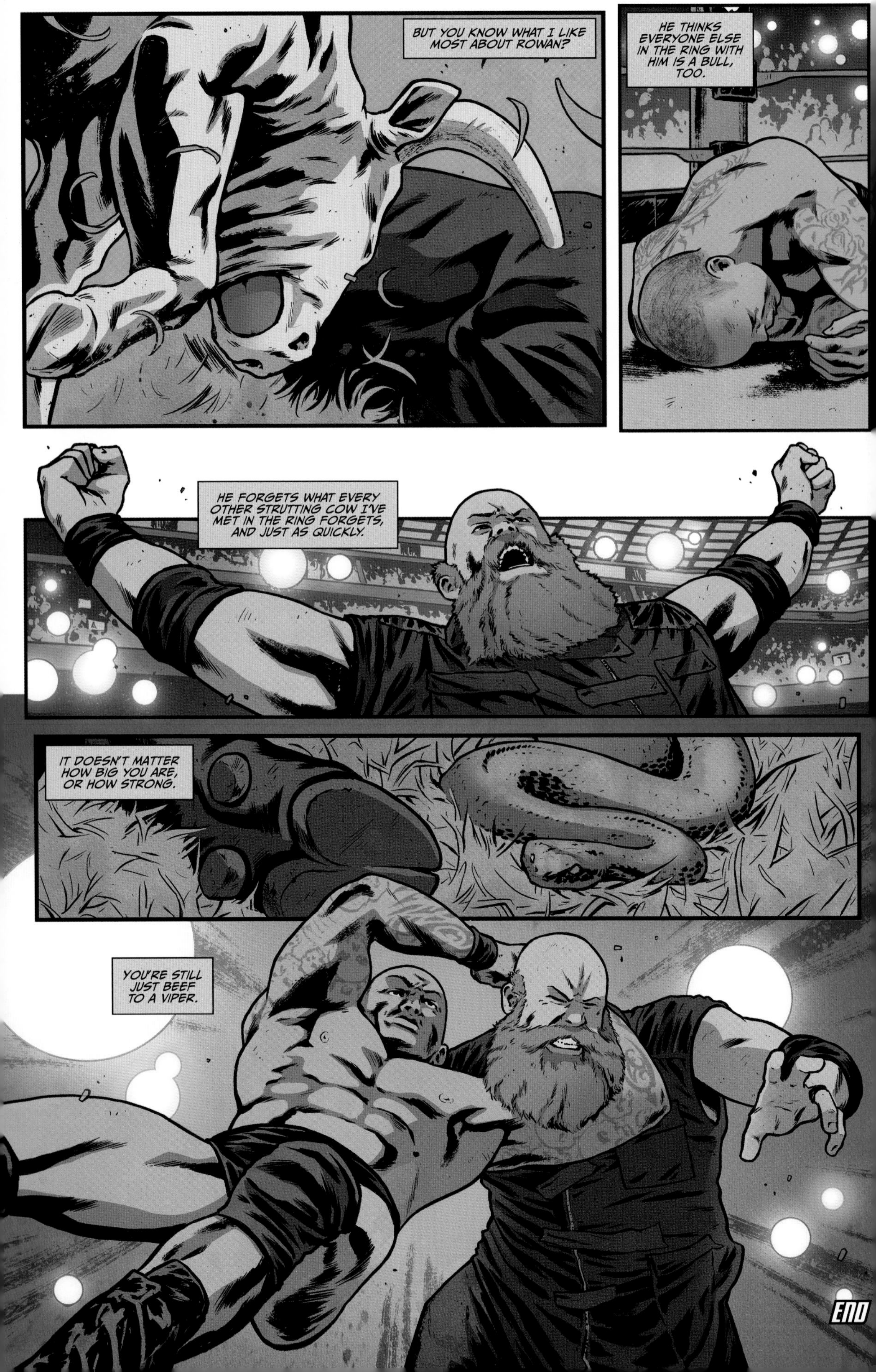
BUT YOU KNOW WHAT I LIKE MOST ABOUT ROWAN?
HE THINKS EVERYONE ELSE IN THE RING WITH HIM IS A BULL, TOO.
HE FORGETS WHAT EVERY OTHER STRUTTING COW I'VE MET IN THE RING FORGETS, AND JUST AS QUICKLY.
IT DOESN'T MATTER HOW BIG YOU ARE, OR HOW STRONG.
YOU'RE STILL JUST BEEF TO A VIPER.
END

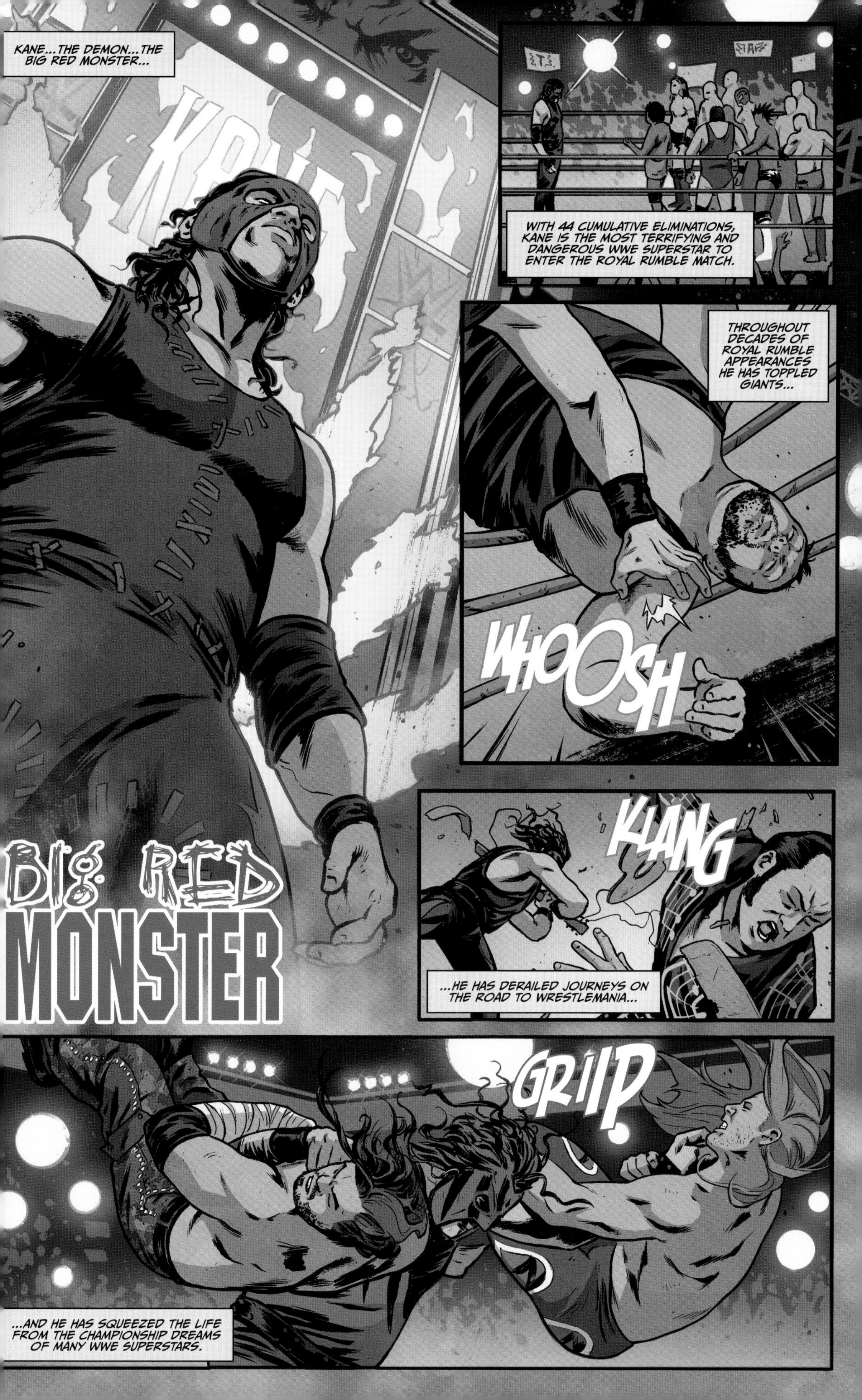
KANE...THE DEMON...THE BIG RED MONSTER...
WITH 44 CUMULATIVE ELIMINATIONS, KANE IS THE MOST TERRIFYING AND DANGEROUS WWE SUPERSTAR TO ENTER THE ROYAL RUMBLE MATCH.
THROUGHOUT DECADES OF ROYAL RUMBLE APPEARANCES HE HAS TOPPLED GIANTS...
WHOOSH
BIG RED
MONSTER
KLANG
...HE HAS DERAILED JOURNEYS ON THE ROAD TO WRESTLEMANIA...
GRIIP
...AND HE HAS SQUEEZED THE LIFE FROM THE CHAMPIONSHIP DREAMS OF MANY WWE SUPERSTARS.

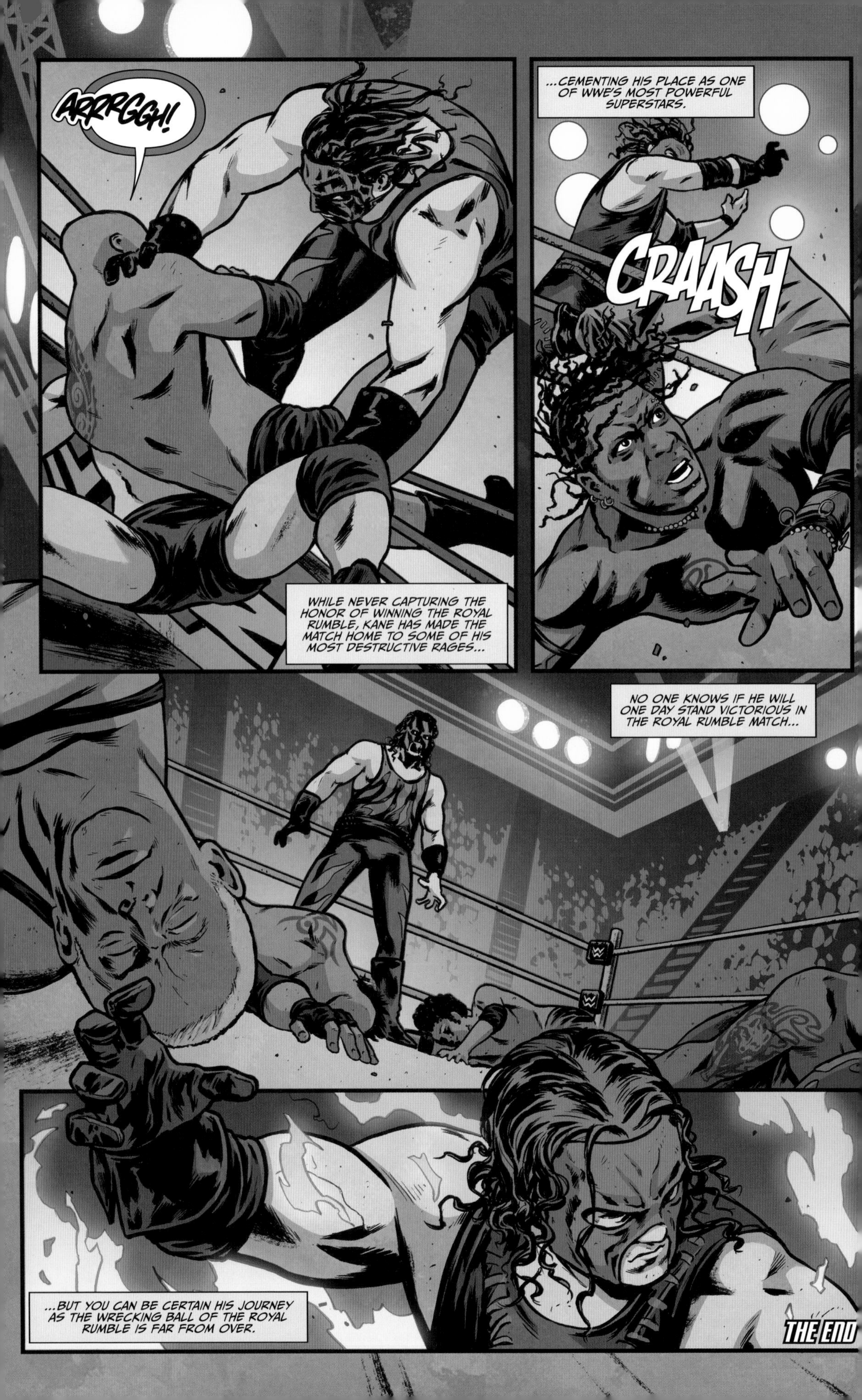
ARRRGGH!
WHILE NEVER CAPTURING THE HONOR OF WINNING THE ROYAL RUMBLE, KANE HAS MADE THE MATCH HOME TO SOME OF HIS MOST DESTRUCTIVE RAGES...
...CEMENTING HIS PLACE AS ONE OF WWE'S MOST POWERFUL SUPERSTARS.
CRAASH
NO ONE KNOWS IF HE WILL ONE DAY STAND VICTORIOUS IN THE ROYAL RUMBLE MATCH...
...BUT YOU CAN BE CERTAIN HIS JOURNEY AS THE WRECKING BALL OF THE ROYAL RUMBLE IS FAR FROM OVER.
THE END

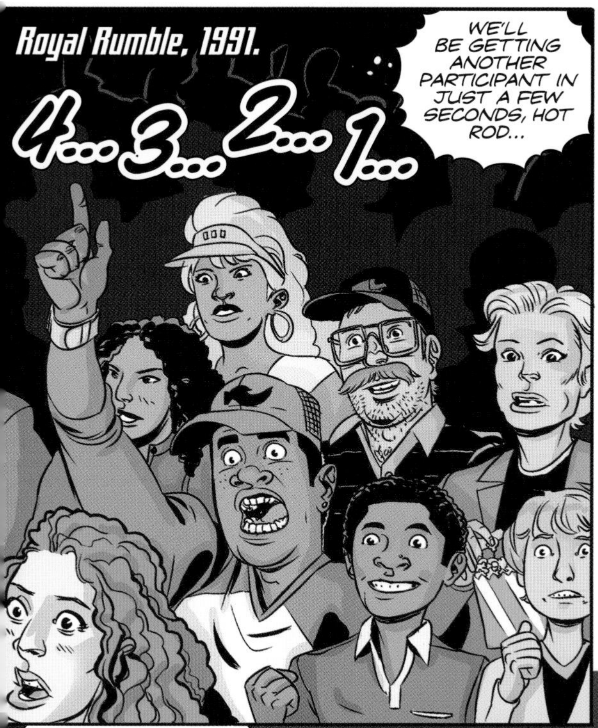
Royal Rumble, 1991.
4... 3... 2... 1...
WE'LL BE GETTING ANOTHER PARTICIPANT IN JUST A FEW SECONDS, HOT ROD...

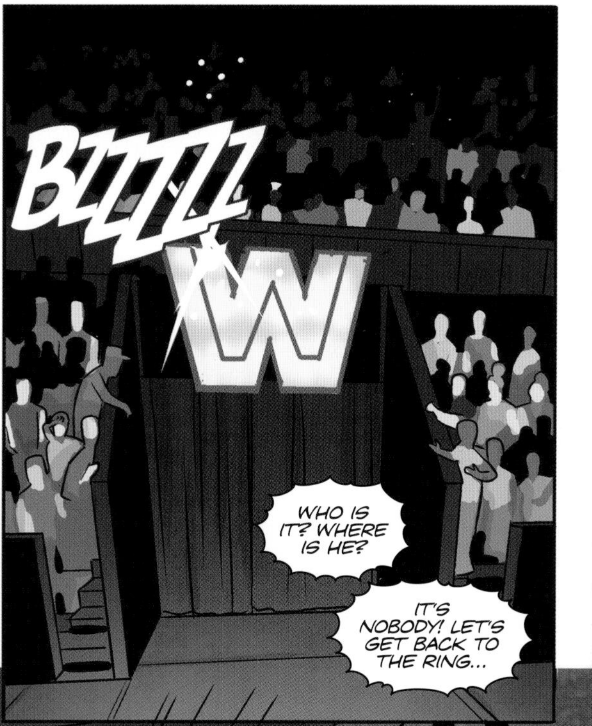
BZZZZ
W
WHO IS IT? WHERE IS HE?
IT'S NOBODY! LET'S GET BACK TO THE RING...

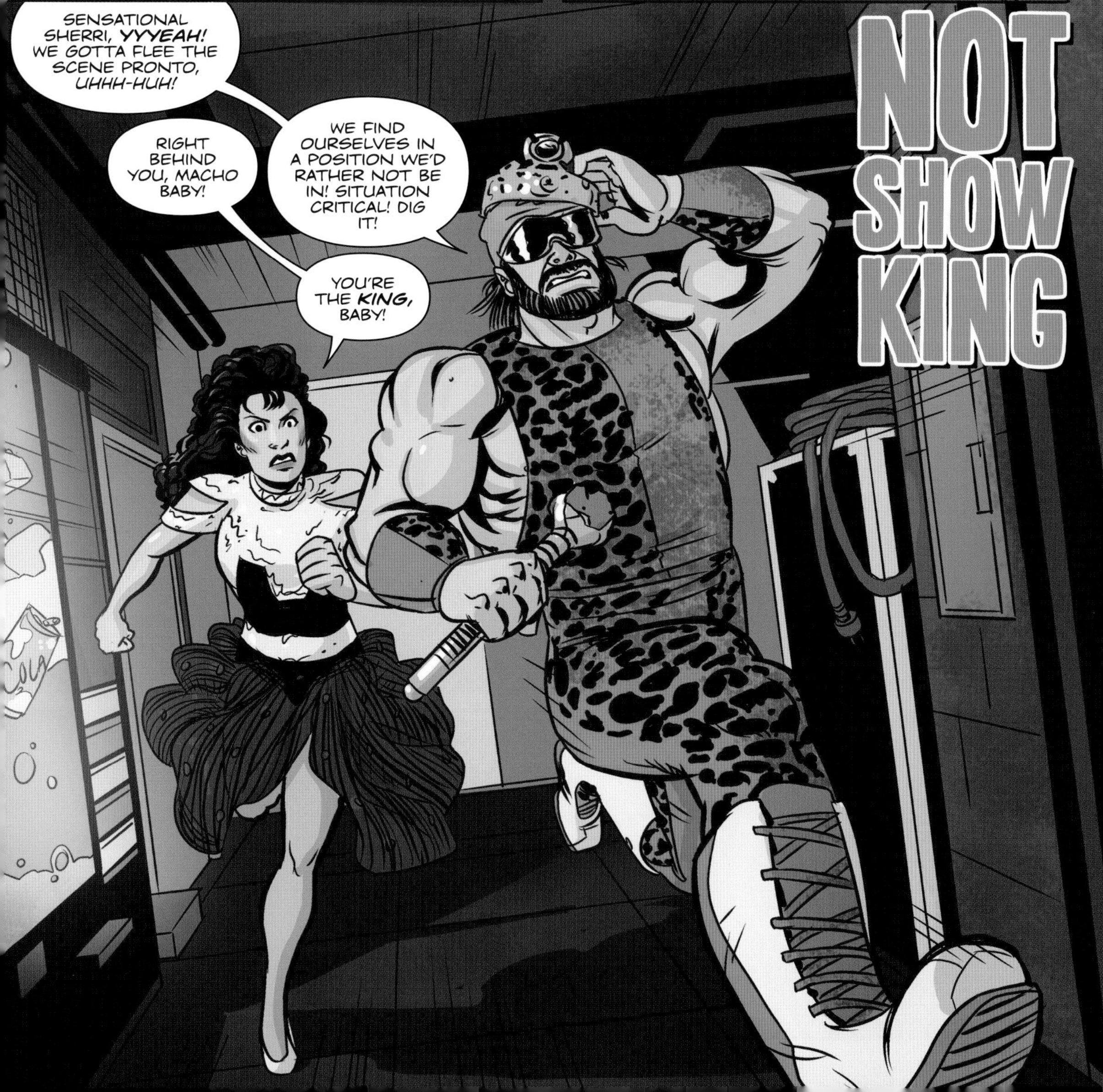
NOT SHOW KING
SENSATIONAL SHERRI, YYYEAH! WE GOTTA FLEE THE SCENE PRONTO, UHHH-HUH!
RIGHT BEHIND YOU, MACHO BABY!
WE FIND OURSELVES IN A POSITION WE'D RATHER NOT BE IN! SITUATION CRITICAL! DIG IT!
YOU'RE THE KING, BABY!
COLA

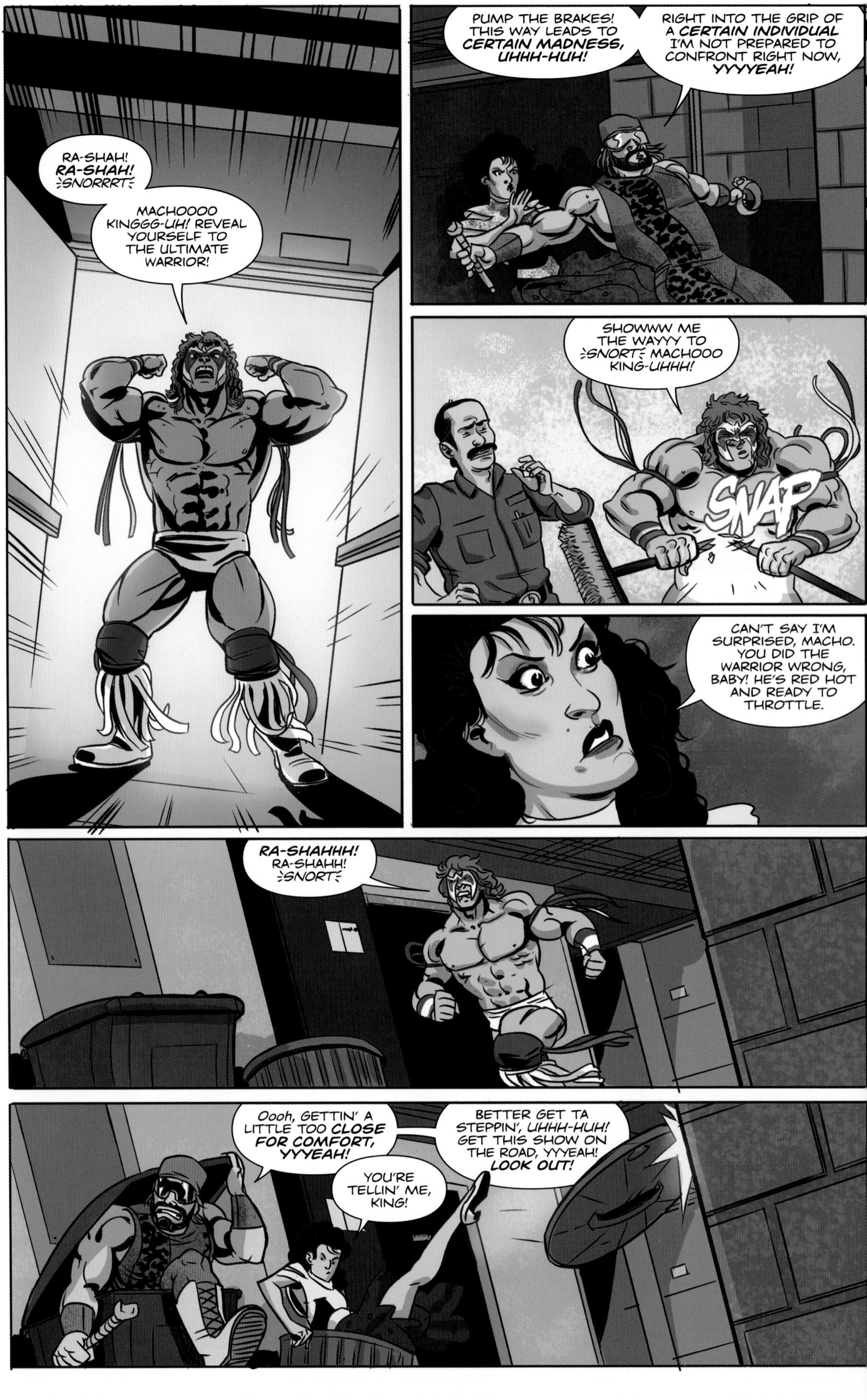
RA-SHAH! RA-SHAH! SNORRRT
MACHOOOO KINGGG-UH! REVEAL YOURSELF TO THE ULTIMATE WARRIOR!
PUMP THE BRAKES! THIS WAY LEADS TO CERTAIN MADNESS, UHHH-HUH!
RIGHT INTO THE GRIP OF A CERTAIN INDIVIDUAL I'M NOT PREPARED TO CONFRONT RIGHT NOW, YYYYEAH!
SHOWWW ME THE WAYYY TO SNORT MACHOOO KING-UHHH!
SNAP
CAN'T SAY I'M SURPRISED, MACHO. YOU DID THE WARRIOR WRONG, BABY! HE'S RED HOT AND READY TO THROTTLE.
RA-SHAHHH! RA-SHAHH! SNORT
Oooh, GETTIN' A LITTLE TOO CLOSE FOR COMFORT, YYYEAH!
BETTER GET TA STEPPIN', UHHH-HUH! GET THIS SHOW ON THE ROAD, YYYEAH! LOOK OUT!
YOU'RE TELLIN' ME, KING!

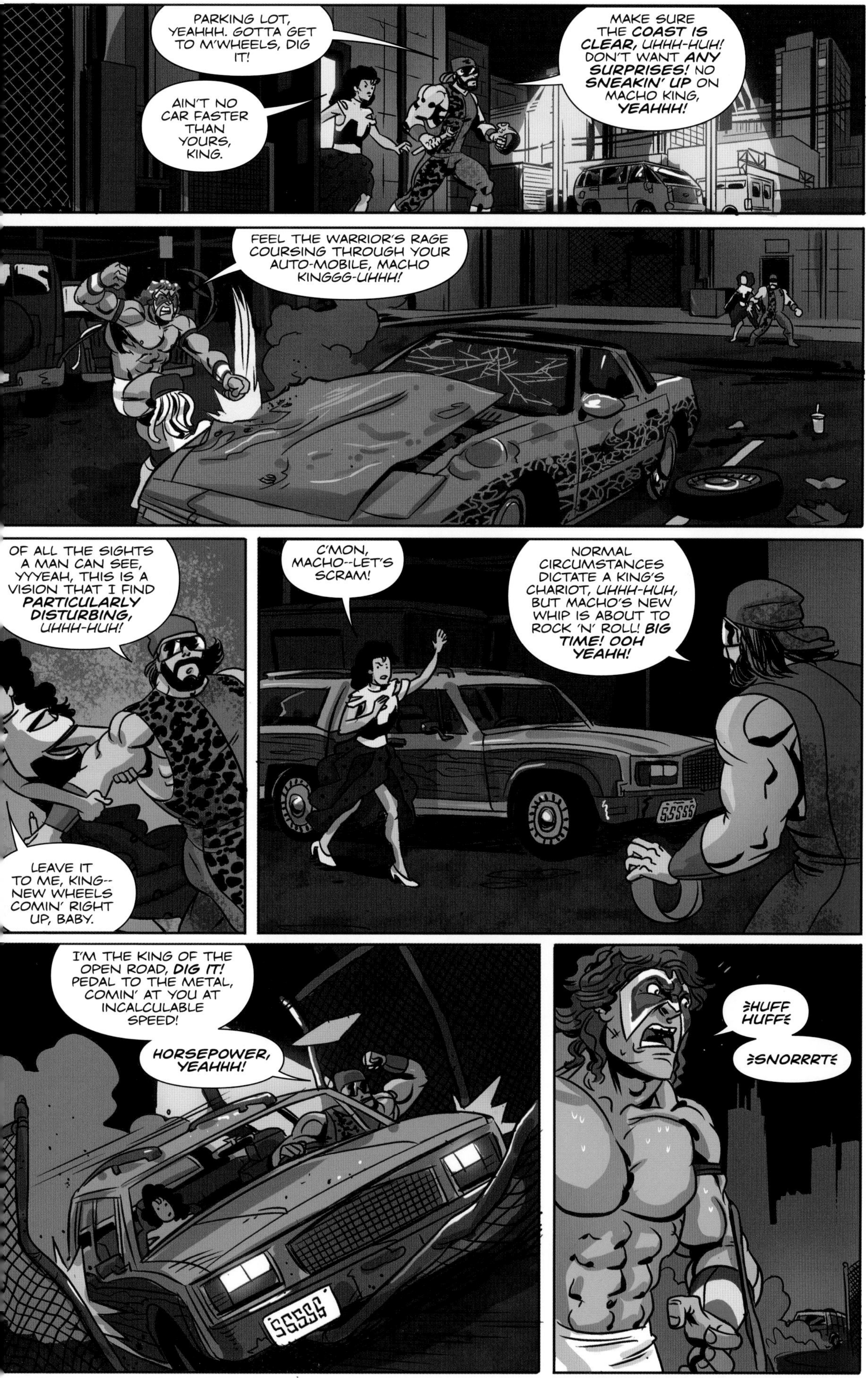
PARKING LOT, YEAHHH. GOTTA GET TO M'WHEELS, DIG IT!
AIN'T NO CAR FASTER THAN YOURS, KING.
MAKE SURE THE COAST IS CLEAR, UHHH-HUH! DON'T WANT ANY SURPRISES! NO SNEAKIN' UP ON MACHO KING, YEAHHH!
FEEL THE WARRIOR'S RAGE COURSING THROUGH YOUR AUTO-MOBILE, MACHO KINGGG-UHHH!
OF ALL THE SIGHTS A MAN CAN SEE, YYYEAH, THIS IS A VISION THAT I FIND PARTICULARLY DISTURBING, UHHH-HUH!
LEAVE IT TO ME, KING-- NEW WHEELS COMIN' RIGHT UP, BABY.
C'MON, MACHO--LET'S SCRAM!
NORMAL CIRCUMSTANCES DICTATE A KING'S CHARIOT, UHHH-HUH, BUT MACHO'S NEW WHIP IS ABOUT TO ROCK 'N' ROLL! BIG TIME! OOH YEAHH!
SSSSS
I'M THE KING OF THE OPEN ROAD, DIG IT! PEDAL TO THE METAL, COMIN' AT YOU AT INCALCULABLE SPEED!
HORSEPOWER, YEAHHH!
SSSSS
HUFF HUFF
SNORRRT

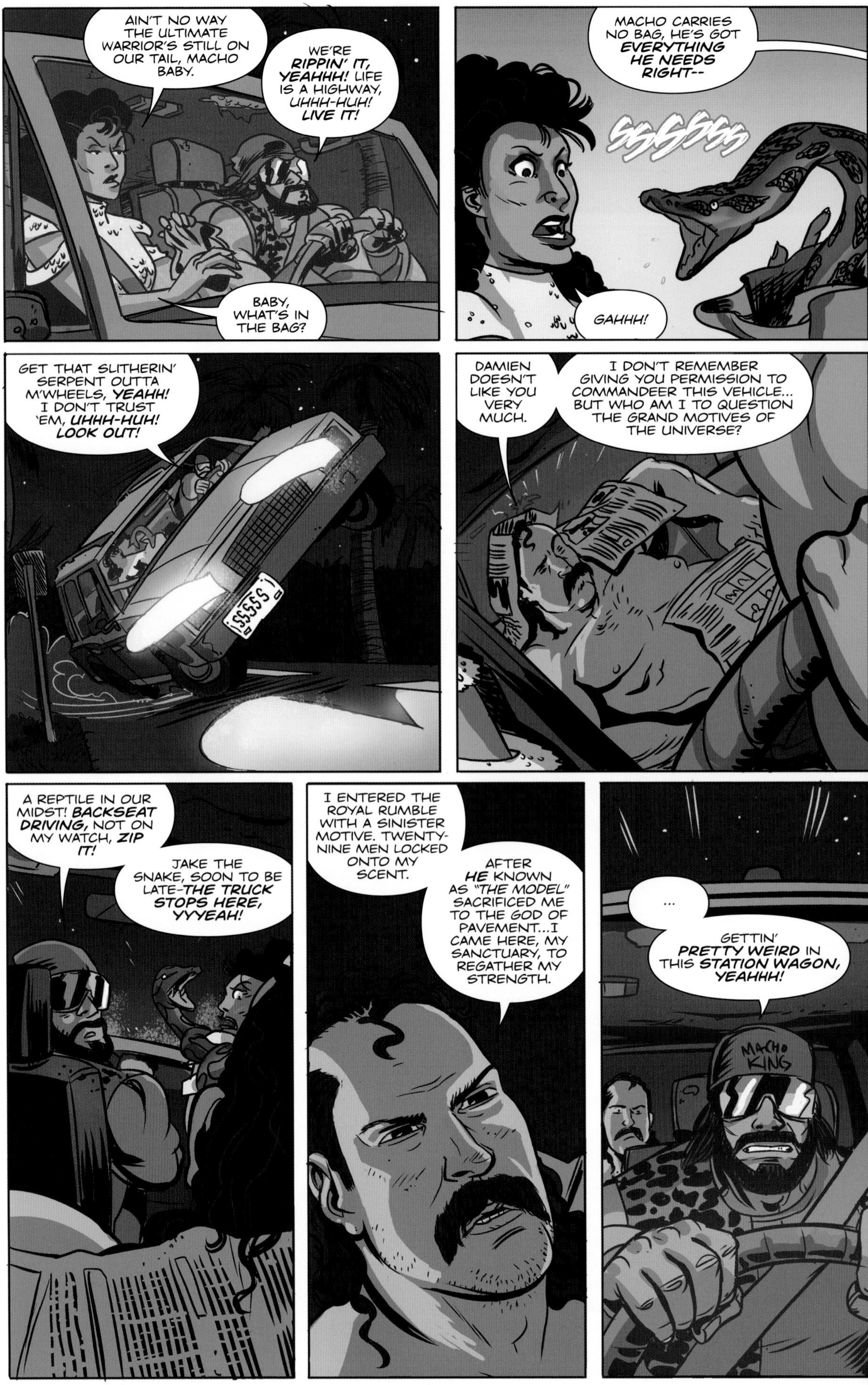
AIN'T NO WAY THE ULTIMATE WARRIOR'S STILL ON OUR TAIL, MACHO BABY.
WE'RE RIPPIN' IT, YEAHHH! LIFE IS A HIGHWAY, UHHH-HUH! LIVE IT!
BABY, WHAT'S IN THE BAG?
MACHO CARRIES NO BAG, HE'S GOT EVERYTHING HE NEEDS RIGHT--
SSSSSS
GAHHH!
GET THAT SLITHERIN' SERPENT OUTTA M'WHEELS, YEAHH! I DON'T TRUST 'EM, UHHH-HUH! LOOK OUT!
SSSSS
DAMIEN DOESN'T LIKE YOU VERY MUCH.
I DON'T REMEMBER GIVING YOU PERMISSION TO COMMANDEER THIS VEHICLE... BUT WHO AM I TO QUESTION THE GRAND MOTIVES OF THE UNIVERSE?
A REPTILE IN OUR MIDST! BACKSEAT DRIVING, NOT ON MY WATCH, ZIP IT!
JAKE THE SNAKE, SOON TO BE LATE–THE TRUCK STOPS HERE, YYYEAH!
I ENTERED THE ROYAL RUMBLE WITH A SINISTER MOTIVE. TWENTY-NINE MEN LOCKED ONTO MY SCENT.
AFTER HE KNOWN AS "THE MODEL" SACRIFICED ME TO THE GOD OF PAVEMENT...I CAME HERE, MY SANCTUARY, TO REGATHER MY STRENGTH.
...
GETTIN' PRETTY WEIRD IN THIS STATION WAGON, YEAHHH!
MACHO KING

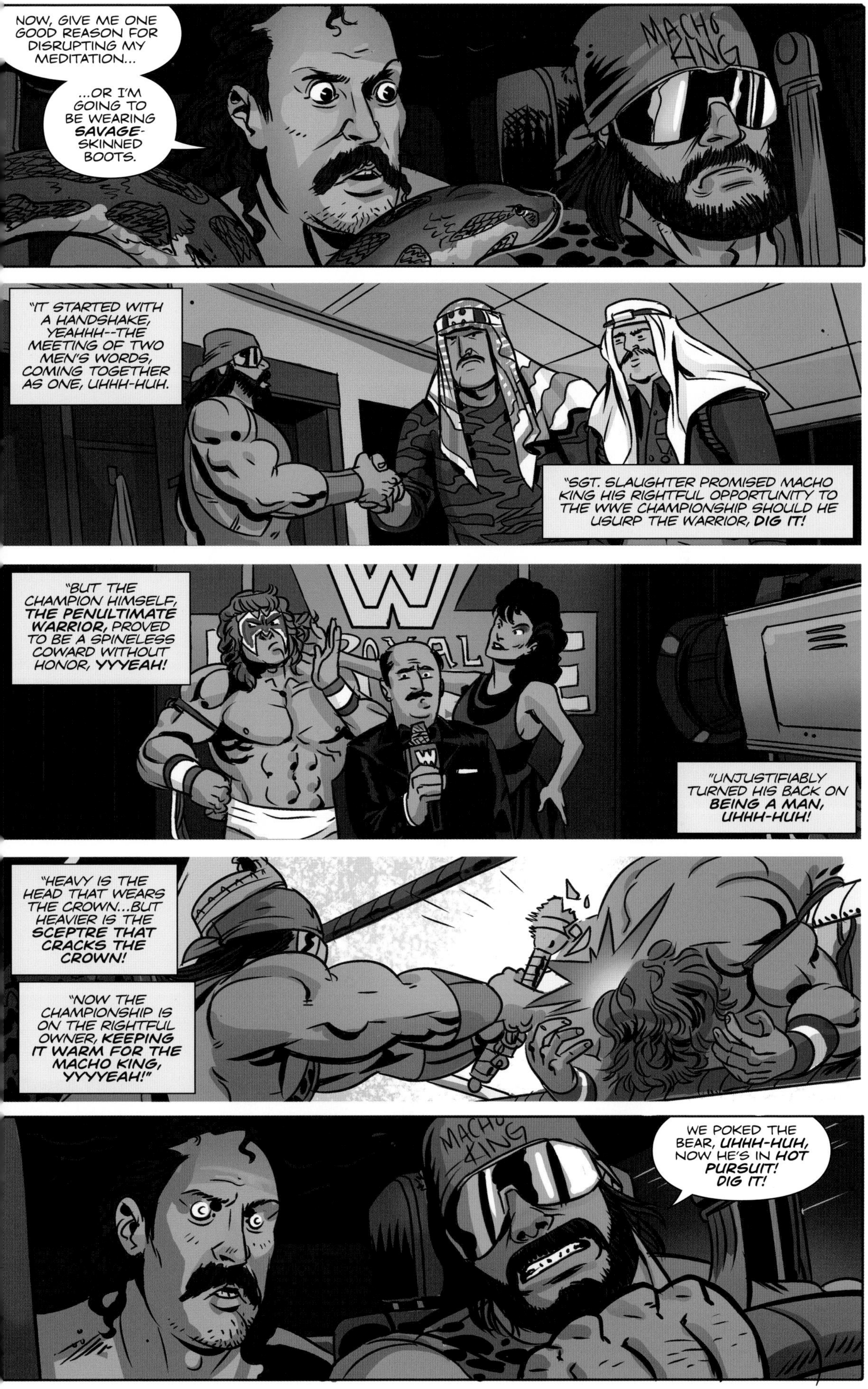
NOW, GIVE ME ONE GOOD REASON FOR DISRUPTING MY MEDITATION...
...OR I'M GOING TO BE WEARING SAVAGE-SKINNED BOOTS.
MACHO KING
"IT STARTED WITH A HANDSHAKE, YEAHHH--THE MEETING OF TWO MEN'S WORDS, COMING TOGETHER AS ONE, UHHH-HUH.
"SGT. SLAUGHTER PROMISED MACHO KING HIS RIGHTFUL OPPORTUNITY TO THE WWE CHAMPIONSHIP SHOULD HE USURP THE WARRIOR, DIG IT!
"BUT THE CHAMPION HIMSELF, THE PENULTIMATE WARRIOR, PROVED TO BE A SPINELESS COWARD WITHOUT HONOR, YYYEAH!
"UNJUSTIFIABLY TURNED HIS BACK ON BEING A MAN, UHHH-HUH!
"HEAVY IS THE HEAD THAT WEARS THE CROWN...BUT HEAVIER IS THE SCEPTRE THAT CRACKS THE CROWN!
"NOW THE CHAMPIONSHIP IS ON THE RIGHTFUL OWNER, KEEPING IT WARM FOR THE MACHO KING, YYYYEAH!"
MACHO KING
WE POKED THE BEAR, UHHH-HUH, NOW HE'S IN HOT PURSUIT! DIG IT!

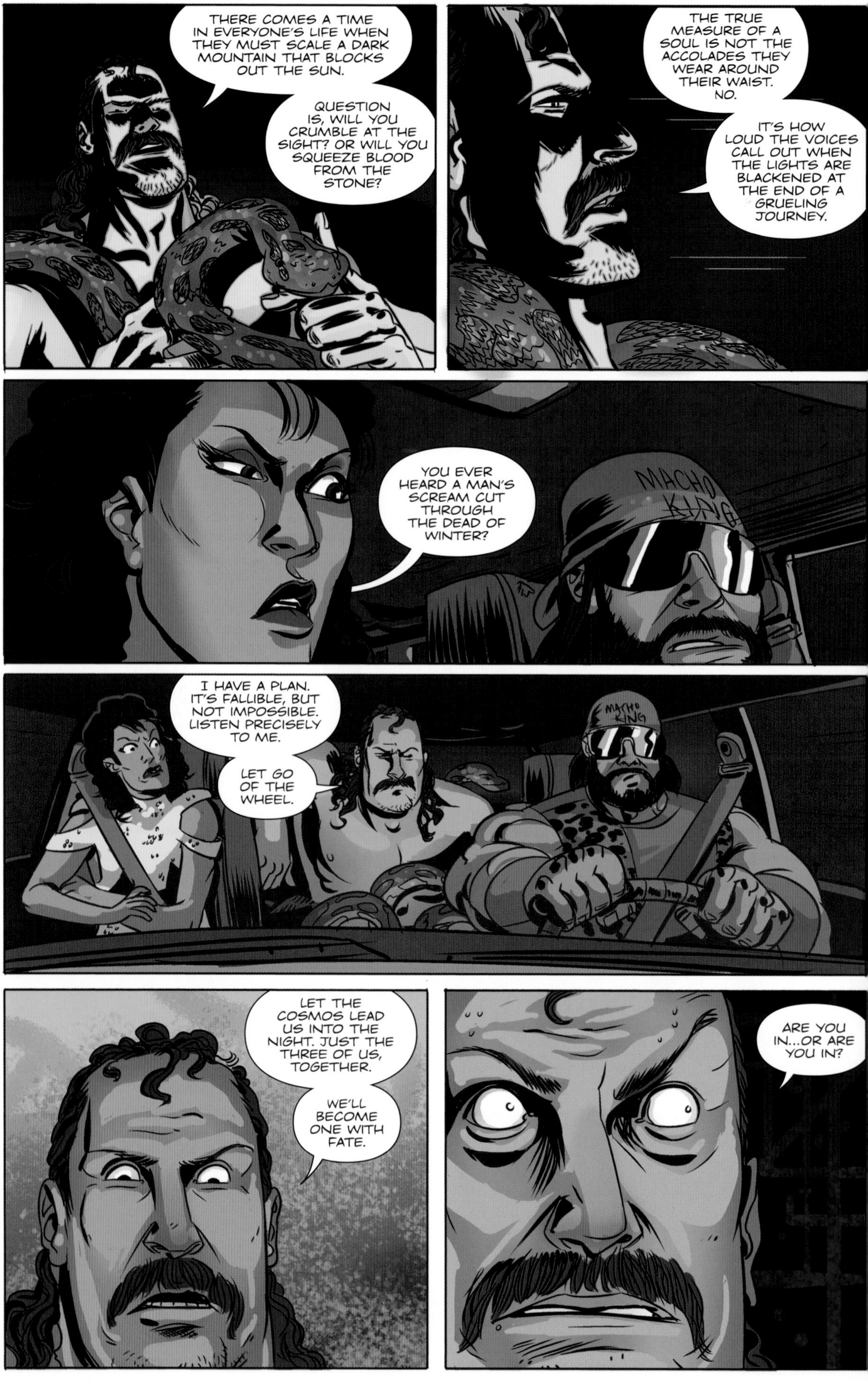
THERE COMES A TIME IN EVERYONE'S LIFE WHEN THEY MUST SCALE A DARK MOUNTAIN THAT BLOCKS OUT THE SUN.
QUESTION IS, WILL YOU CRUMBLE AT THE SIGHT? OR WILL YOU SQUEEZE BLOOD FROM THE STONE?
THE TRUE MEASURE OF A SOUL IS NOT THE ACCOLADES THEY WEAR AROUND THEIR WAIST. NO.
IT'S HOW LOUD THE VOICES CALL OUT WHEN THE LIGHTS ARE BLACKENED AT THE END OF A GRUELING JOURNEY.
MACHO KING
YOU EVER HEARD A MAN'S SCREAM CUT THROUGH THE DEAD OF WINTER?
I HAVE A PLAN. IT'S FALLIBLE, BUT NOT IMPOSSIBLE. LISTEN PRECISELY TO ME.
LET GO OF THE WHEEL.
MACHO KING
LET THE COSMOS LEAD US INTO THE NIGHT. JUST THE THREE OF US, TOGETHER.
WE'LL BECOME ONE WITH FATE.
ARE YOU IN...OR ARE YOU IN?

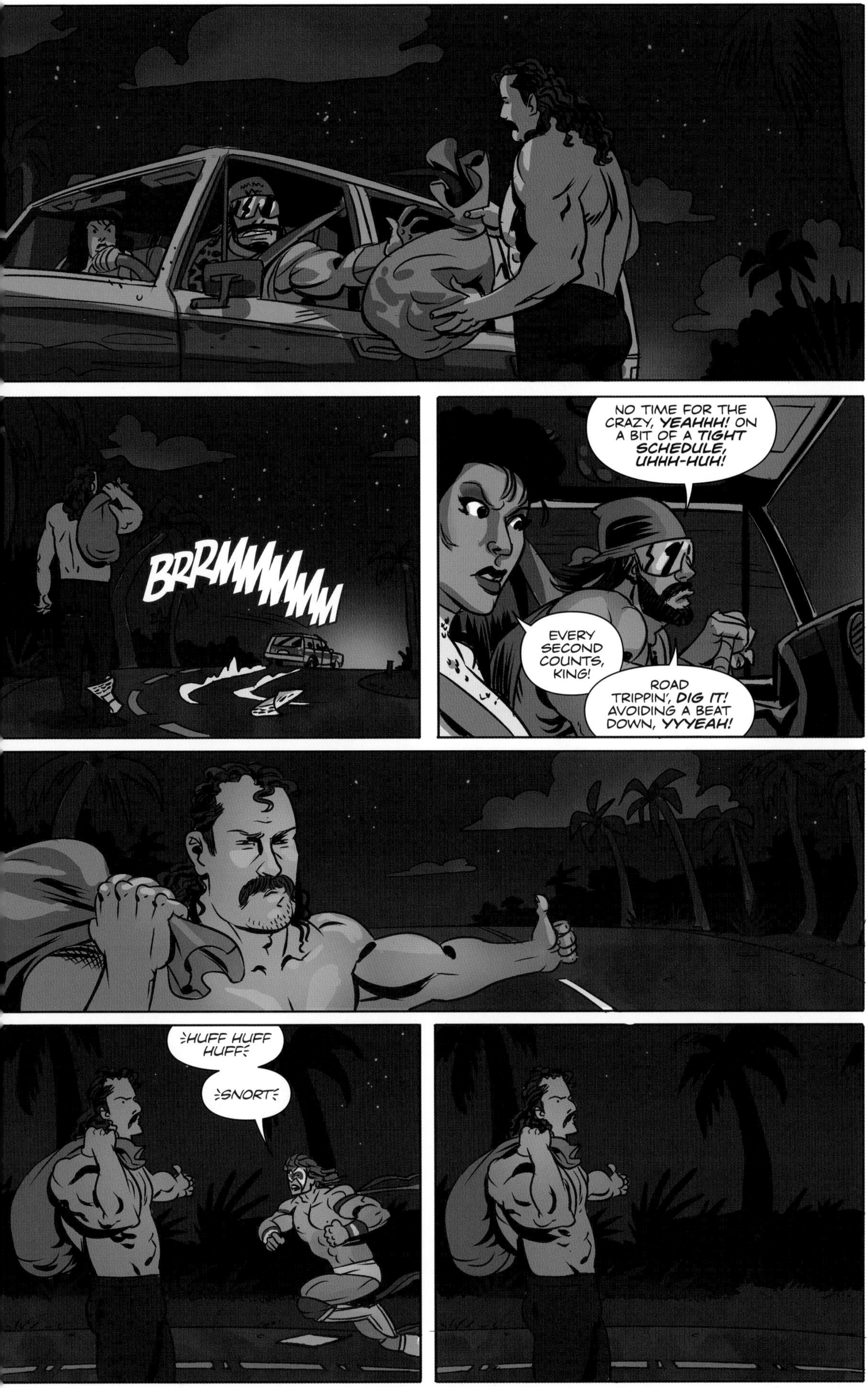
BRRMMMMMM
NO TIME FOR THE CRAZY, YEAHHH! ON A BIT OF A TIGHT SCHEDULE, UHHH-HUH!
EVERY SECOND COUNTS, KING!
ROAD TRIPPIN', DIG IT! AVOIDING A BEAT DOWN, YYYEAH!
HUFF HUFF HUFF
SNORT

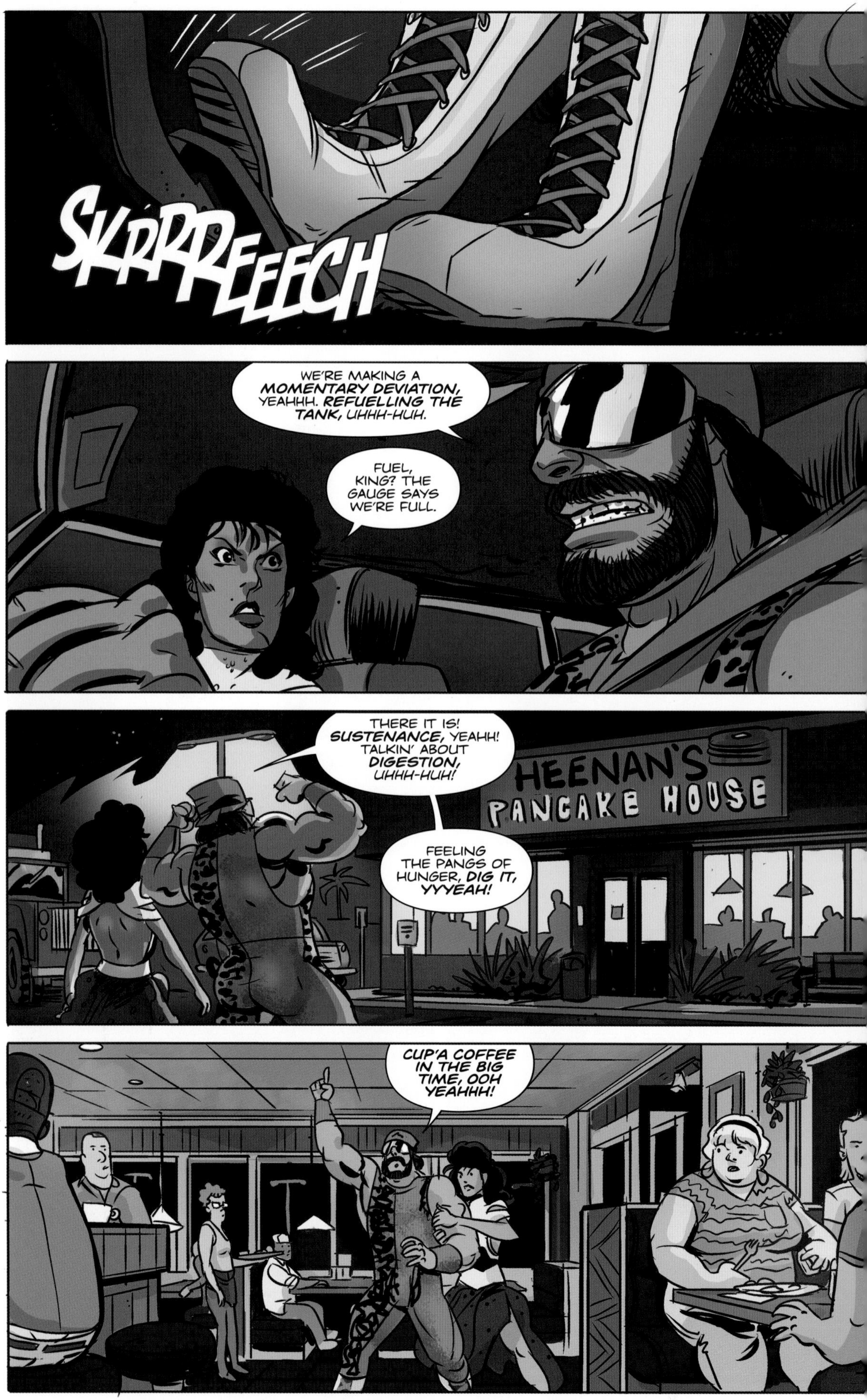
SKRRREEECH
WE'RE MAKING A MOMENTARY DEVIATION, YEAHHH. REFUELLING THE TANK, UHHH-HUH.
FUEL, KING? THE GAUGE SAYS WE'RE FULL.
THERE IT IS! SUSTENANCE, YEAHH! TALKIN' ABOUT DIGESTION, UHHH-HUH!
HEENAN'S PANCAKE HOUSE
FEELING THE PANGS OF HUNGER, DIG IT, YYYEAH!
CUP'A COFFEE IN THE BIG TIME, OOH YEAHHH!

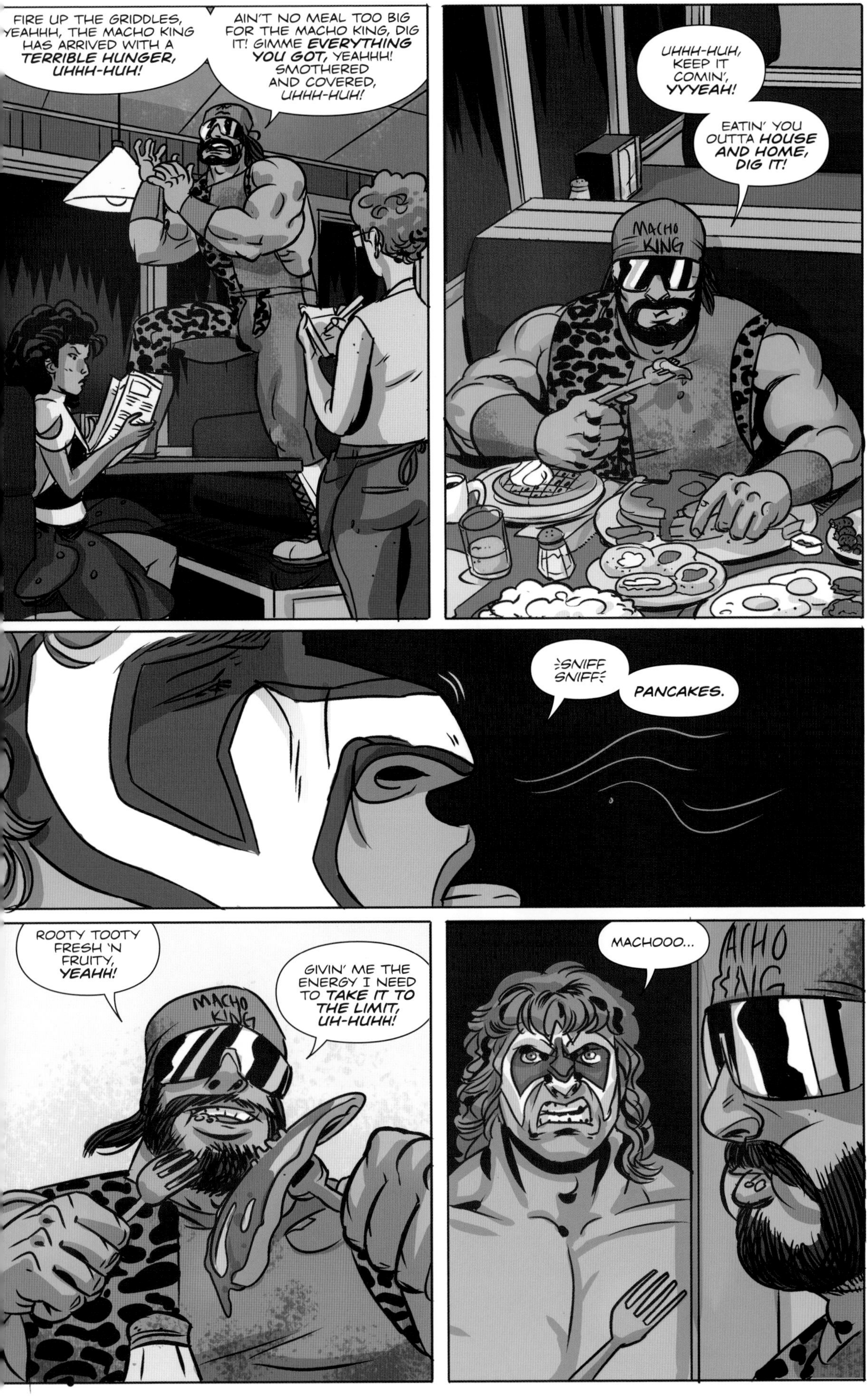
FIRE UP THE GRIDDLES, YEAHHH, THE MACHO KING HAS ARRIVED WITH A TERRIBLE HUNGER, UHHH-HUH!
AIN'T NO MEAL TOO BIG FOR THE MACHO KING, DIG IT! GIMME EVERYTHING YOU GOT, YEAHHH! SMOTHERED AND COVERED, UHHH-HUH!
UHHH-HUH, KEEP IT COMIN', YYYEAH!
EATIN' YOU OUTTA HOUSE AND HOME, DIG IT!
MACHO KING
SNIFF SNIFF
PANCAKES.
ROOTY TOOTY FRESH 'N FRUITY, YEAHH!
GIVIN' ME THE ENERGY I NEED TO TAKE IT TO THE LIMIT, UH-HUHH!
MACHO KING
MACHOOO...

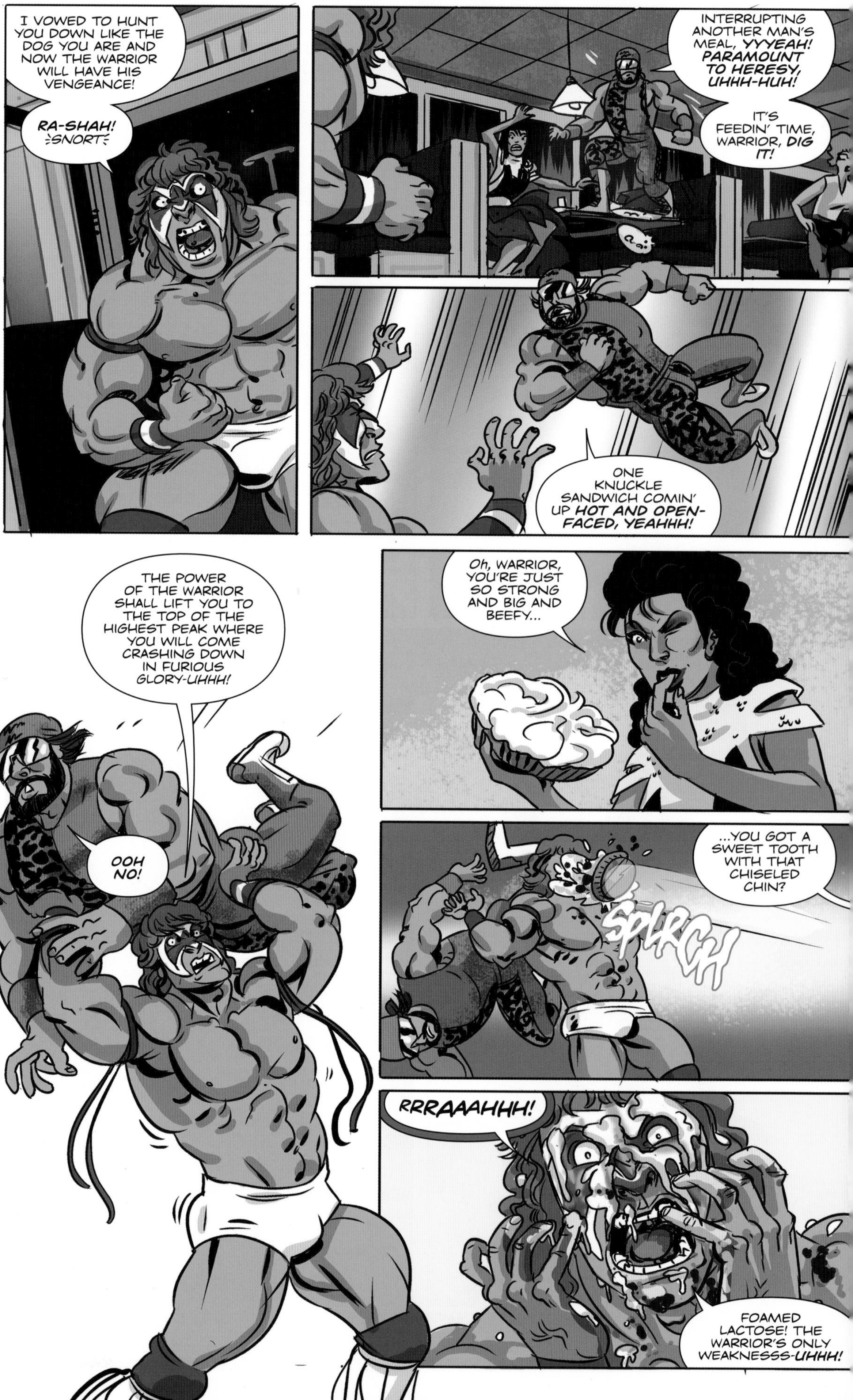
I VOWED TO HUNT YOU DOWN LIKE THE DOG YOU ARE AND NOW THE WARRIOR WILL HAVE HIS VENGEANCE!
RA-SHAH! SNORT
INTERRUPTING ANOTHER MAN'S MEAL, YYYEAH! PARAMOUNT TO HERESY, UHHH-HUH!
IT'S FEEDIN' TIME, WARRIOR, DIG IT!
ONE KNUCKLE SANDWICH COMIN' UP HOT AND OPEN-FACED, YEAHHH!
THE POWER OF THE WARRIOR SHALL LIFT YOU TO THE TOP OF THE HIGHEST PEAK WHERE YOU WILL COME CRASHING DOWN IN FURIOUS GLORY-UHHH!
OOH NO!
Oh, WARRIOR, YOU'RE JUST SO STRONG AND BIG AND BEEFY...
...YOU GOT A SWEET TOOTH WITH THAT CHISELED CHIN?
SPLRCH
RRRAAAHHH!
FOAMED LACTOSE! THE WARRIOR'S ONLY WEAKNESSS-UHHH!

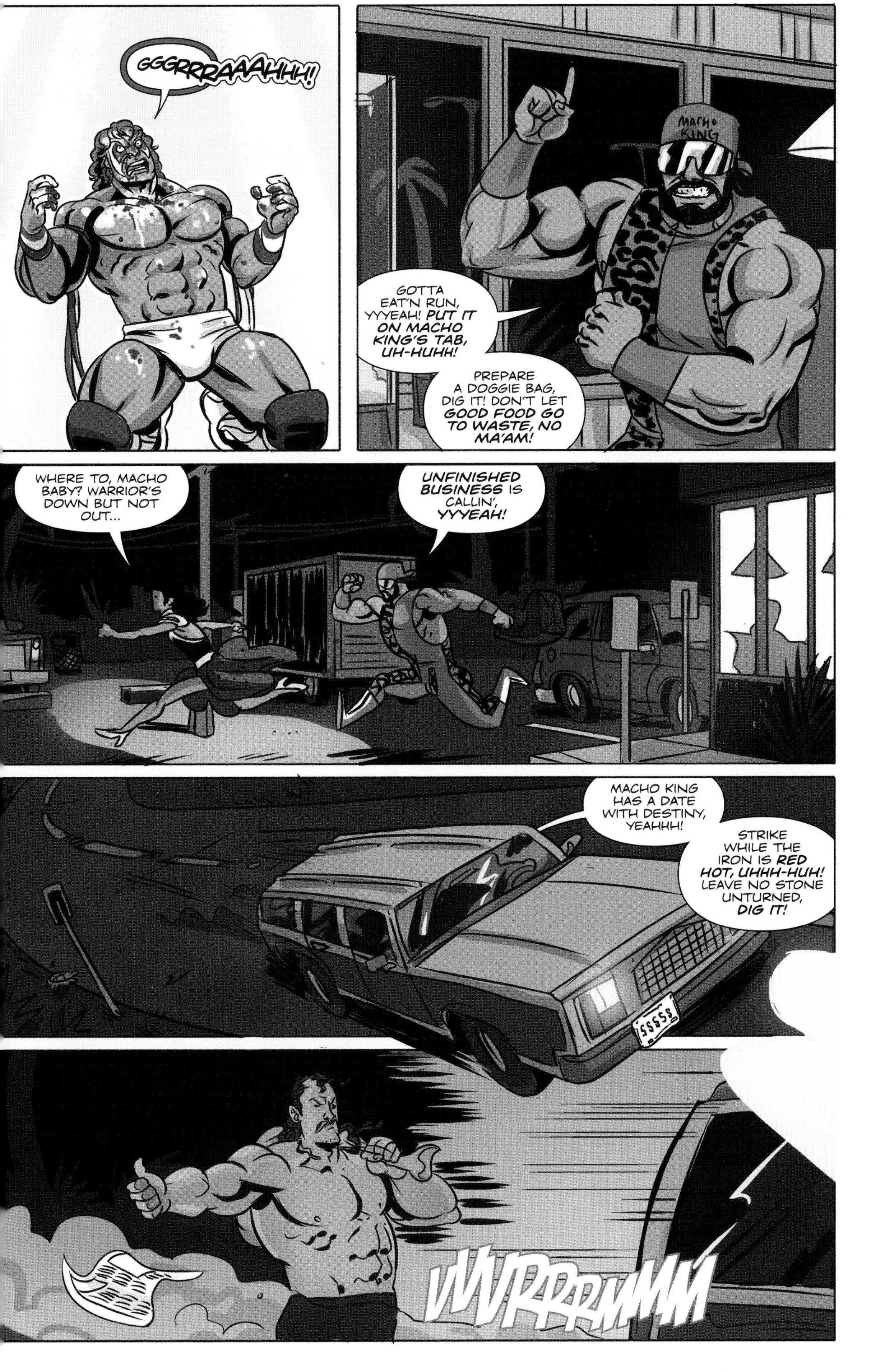
GGGRRRAAAHHH!
GOTTA EAT'N RUN, YYYEAH! PUT IT ON MACHO KING'S TAB, UH-HUHH!
PREPARE A DOGGIE BAG, DIG IT! DON'T LET GOOD FOOD GO TO WASTE, NO MA'AM!
MACHO KING
WHERE TO, MACHO BABY? WARRIOR'S DOWN BUT NOT OUT...
UNFINISHED BUSINESS IS CALLIN', YYYEAH!
MACHO KING HAS A DATE WITH DESTINY, YEAHHH!
STRIKE WHILE THE IRON IS RED HOT, UHHH-HUH! LEAVE NO STONE UNTURNED, DIG IT!
$$$$$
VVVRRRRMMMM

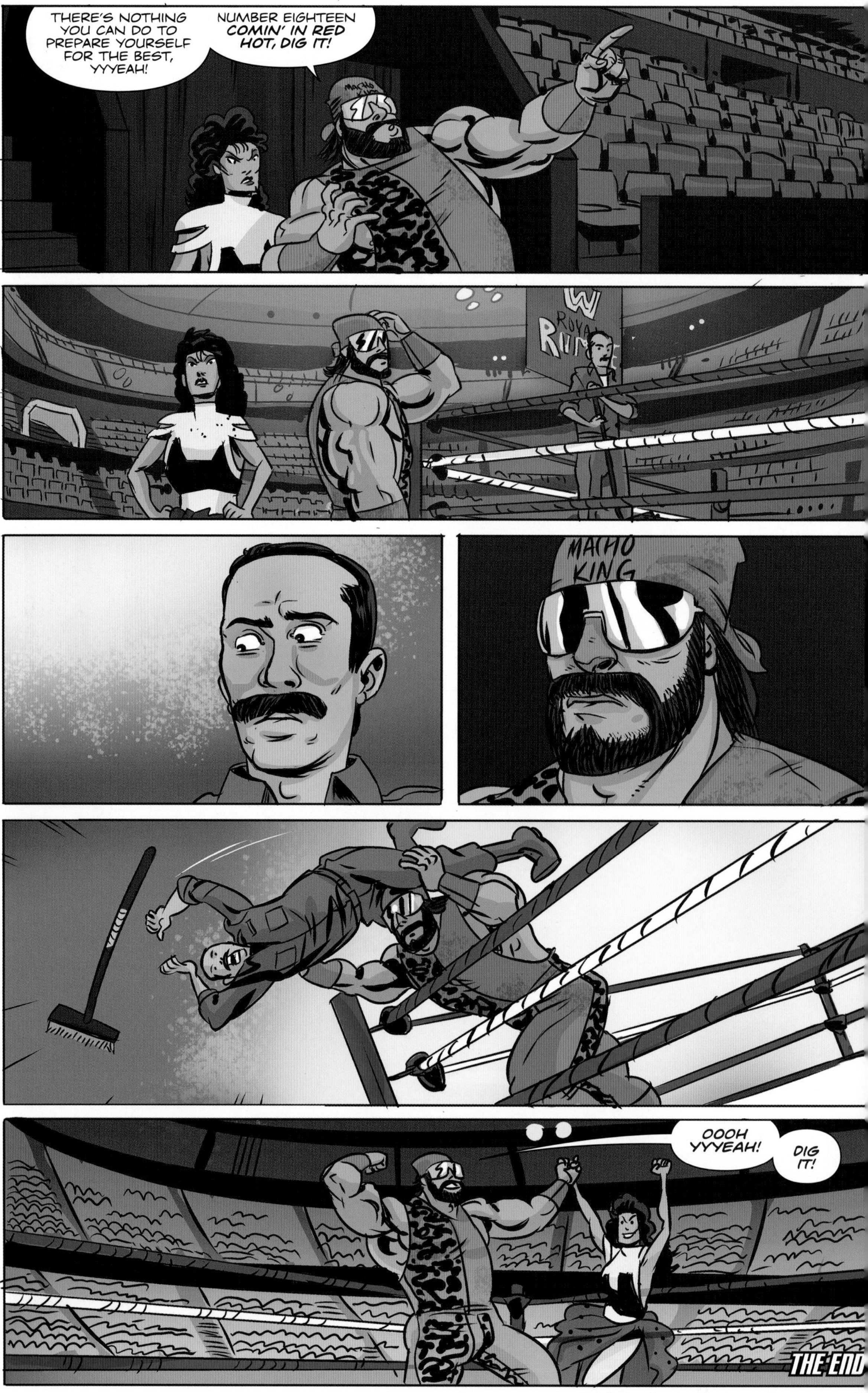
THERE'S NOTHING YOU CAN DO TO PREPARE YOURSELF FOR THE BEST, YYYEAH!
NUMBER EIGHTEEN ***COMIN' IN RED HOT, DIG IT!***
MACHO KING
OOOH YYYEAH!
DIG IT!
THE END

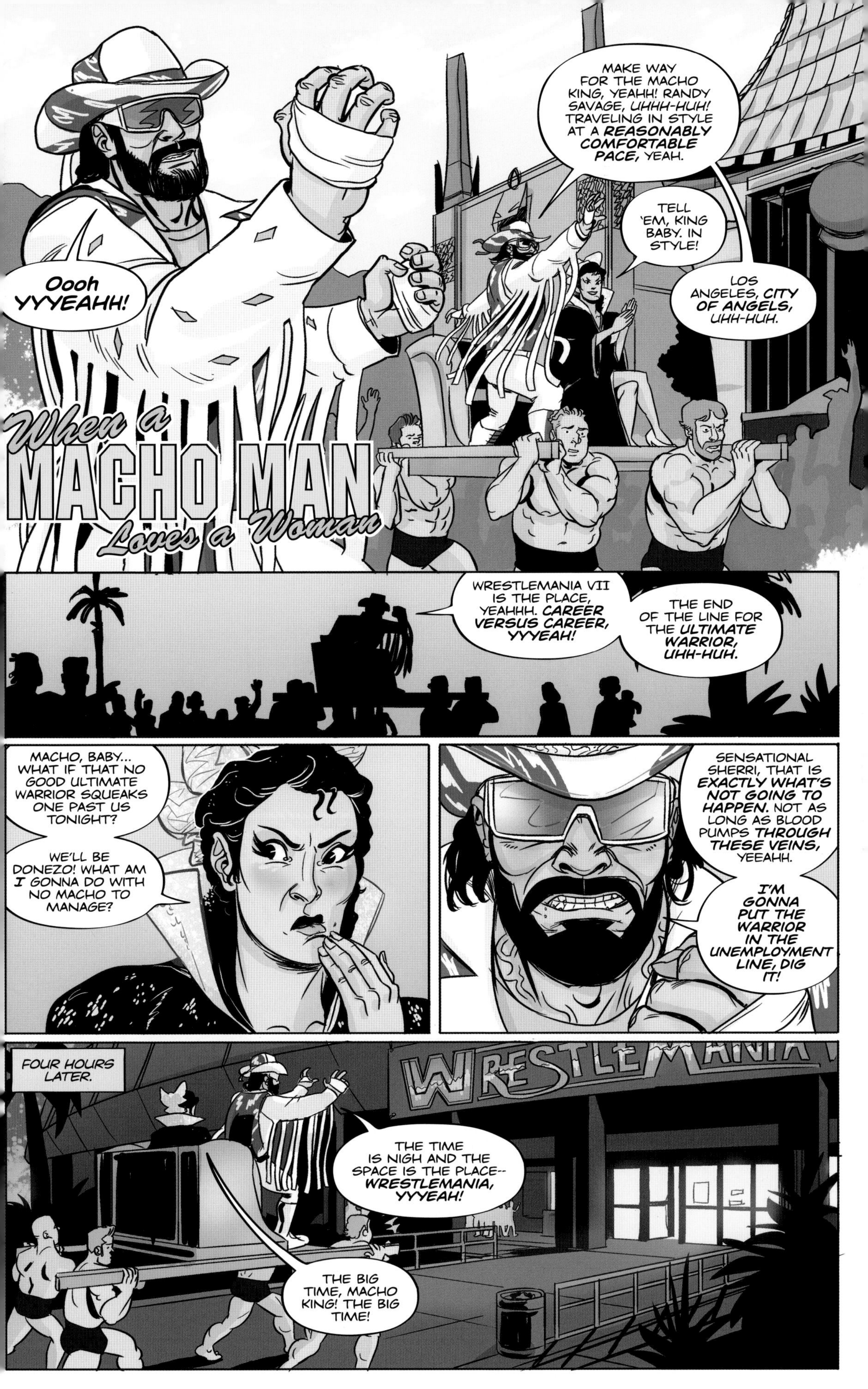
Oooh YYYEAHH!
When a MACHO MAN Loves a Woman
MAKE WAY FOR THE MACHO KING, YEAHH! RANDY SAVAGE, UHHH-HUH! TRAVELING IN STYLE AT A REASONABLY COMFORTABLE PACE, YEAH.
TELL 'EM, KING BABY. IN STYLE!
LOS ANGELES, CITY OF ANGELS, UHH-HUH.
WRESTLEMANIA VII IS THE PLACE, YEAHHH. CAREER VERSUS CAREER, YYYEAH!
THE END OF THE LINE FOR THE ULTIMATE WARRIOR, UHH-HUH.
MACHO, BABY... WHAT IF THAT NO GOOD ULTIMATE WARRIOR SQUEAKS ONE PAST US TONIGHT?
WE'LL BE DONEZO! WHAT AM I GONNA DO WITH NO MACHO TO MANAGE?
SENSATIONAL SHERRI, THAT IS EXACTLY WHAT'S NOT GOING TO HAPPEN. NOT AS LONG AS BLOOD PUMPS THROUGH THESE VEINS, YEEAHH.
I'M GONNA PUT THE WARRIOR IN THE UNEMPLOYMENT LINE, DIG IT!
FOUR HOURS LATER.
WRESTLEMANIA
THE TIME IS NIGH AND THE SPACE IS THE PLACE-- WRESTLEMANIA, YYYEAH!
THE BIG TIME, MACHO KING! THE BIG TIME!

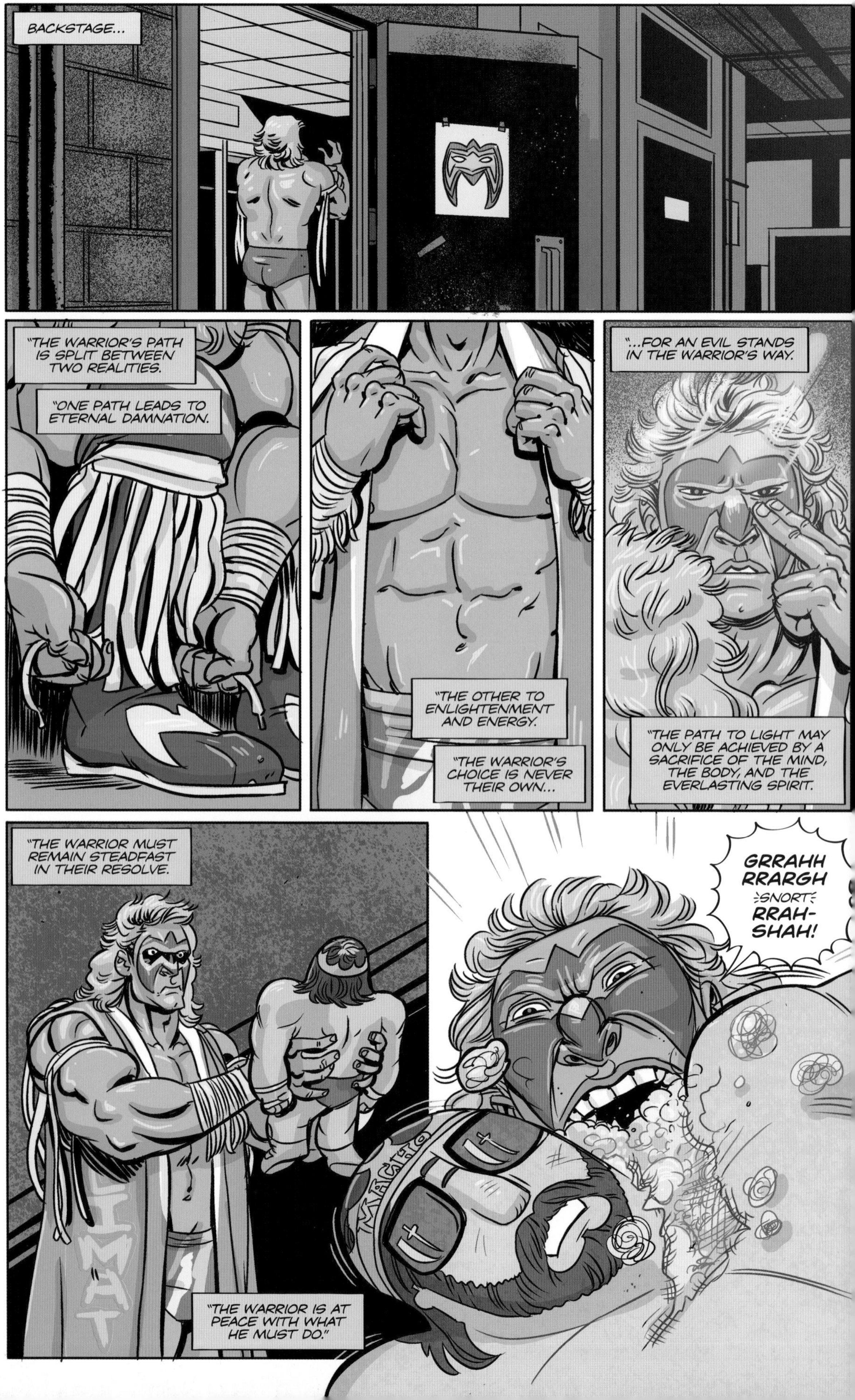
BACKSTAGE...
"THE WARRIOR'S PATH IS SPLIT BETWEEN TWO REALITIES.
"ONE PATH LEADS TO ETERNAL DAMNATION.
"THE OTHER TO ENLIGHTENMENT AND ENERGY.
"THE WARRIOR'S CHOICE IS NEVER THEIR OWN...
"...FOR AN EVIL STANDS IN THE WARRIOR'S WAY.
"THE PATH TO LIGHT MAY ONLY BE ACHIEVED BY A SACRIFICE OF THE MIND, THE BODY, AND THE EVERLASTING SPIRIT.
"THE WARRIOR MUST REMAIN STEADFAST IN THEIR RESOLVE.
"THE WARRIOR IS AT PEACE WITH WHAT HE MUST DO."
GRRAHH RRARGH SNORT RRAH-SHAH!

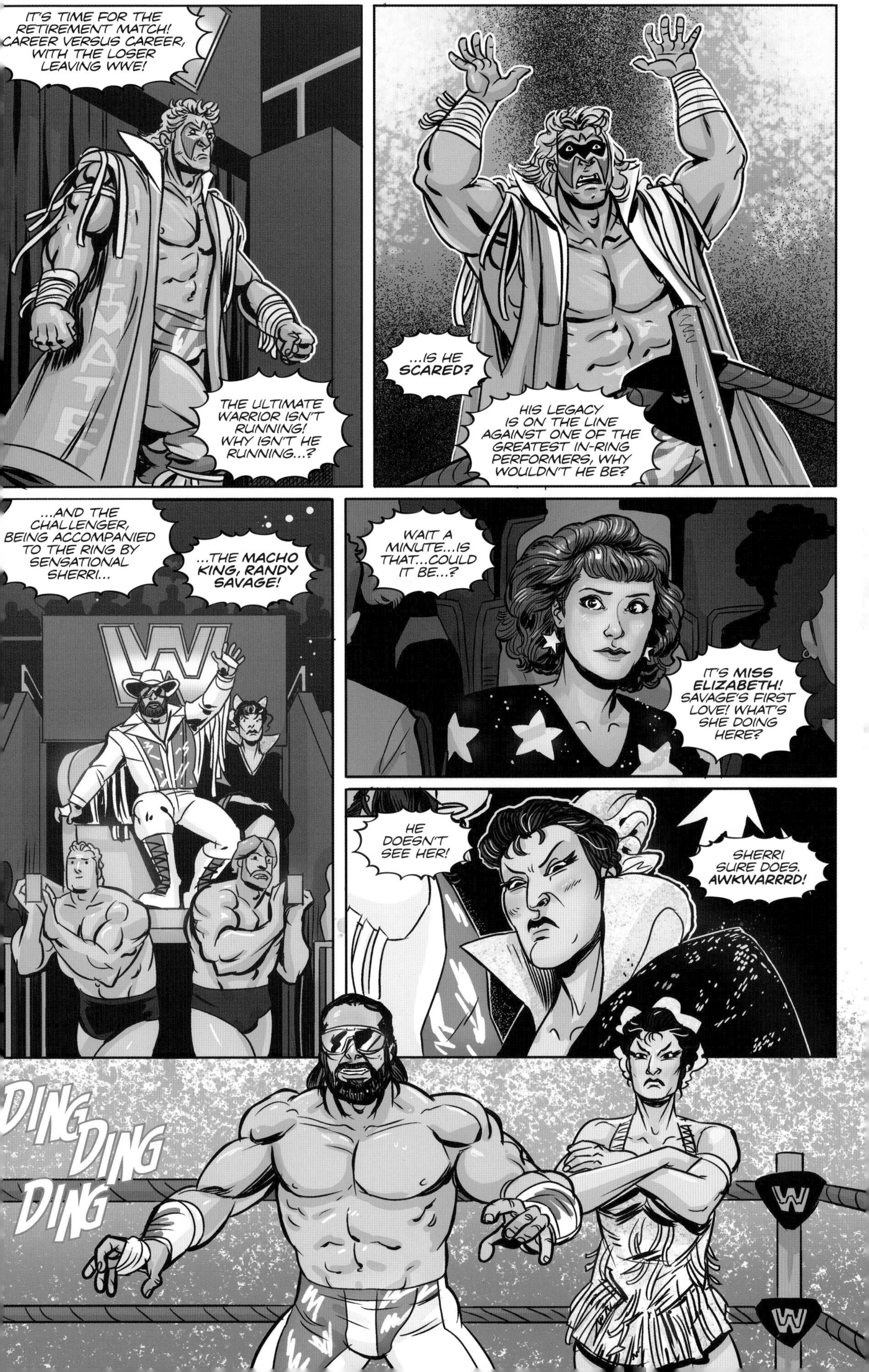
IT'S TIME FOR THE RETIREMENT MATCH! CAREER VERSUS CAREER, WITH THE LOSER LEAVING WWE!
THE ULTIMATE WARRIOR ISN'T RUNNING! WHY ISN'T HE RUNNING...?
...IS HE SCARED?
HIS LEGACY IS ON THE LINE AGAINST ONE OF THE GREATEST IN-RING PERFORMERS, WHY WOULDN'T HE BE?
...AND THE CHALLENGER, BEING ACCOMPANIED TO THE RING BY SENSATIONAL SHERRI...
...THE MACHO KING, RANDY SAVAGE!
WAIT A MINUTE...IS THAT...COULD IT BE...?
IT'S MISS ELIZABETH! SAVAGE'S FIRST LOVE! WHAT'S SHE DOING HERE?
HE DOESN'T SEE HER!
SHERRI SURE DOES. AWKWARRRD!
DING DING DING

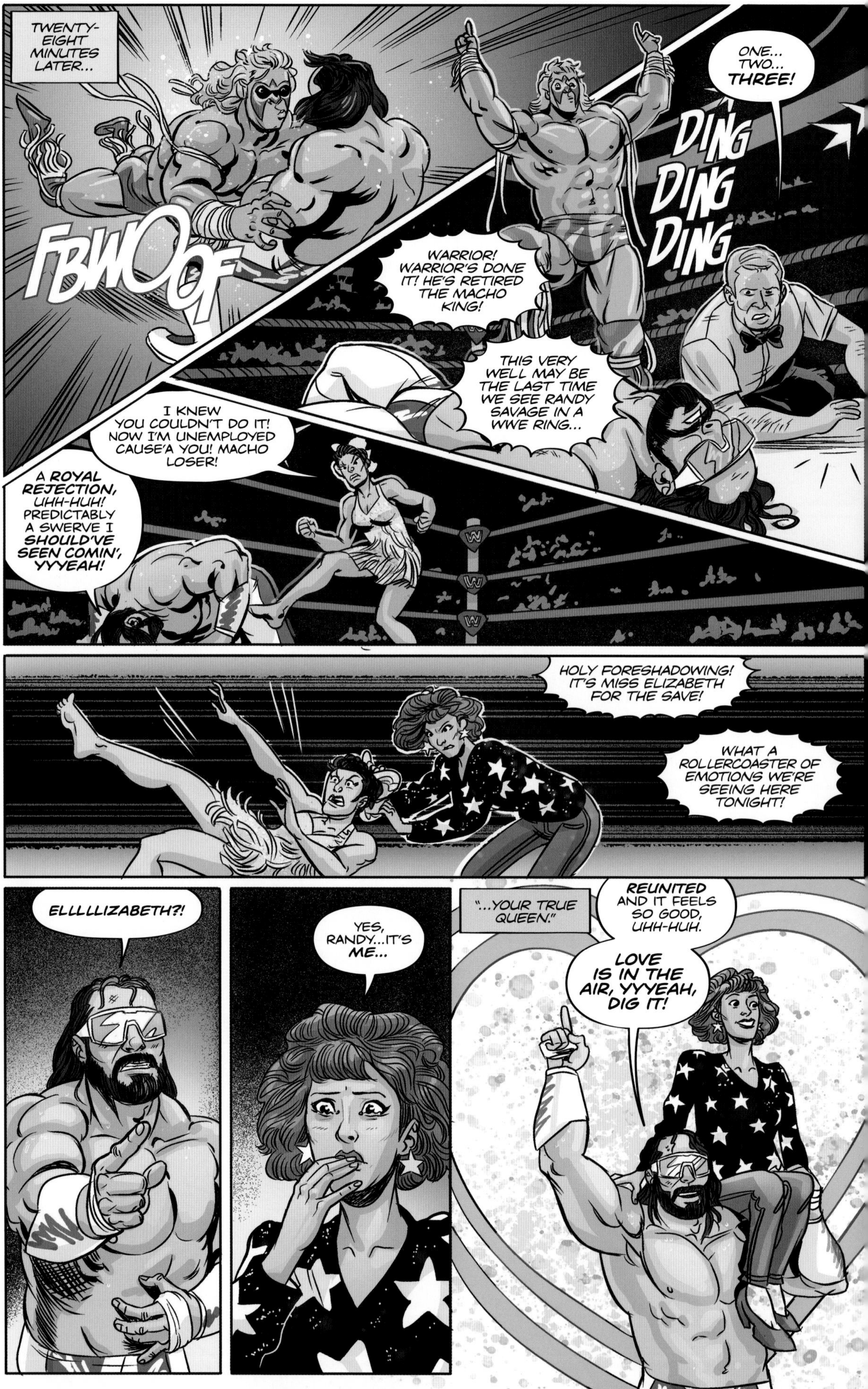

TWENTY-EIGHT MINUTES LATER...
FBWOOOF
ONE... TWO... THREE!
DING DING DING
WARRIOR! WARRIOR'S DONE IT! HE'S RETIRED THE MACHO KING!
THIS VERY WELL MAY BE THE LAST TIME WE SEE RANDY SAVAGE IN A WWE RING...
I KNEW YOU COULDN'T DO IT! NOW I'M UNEMPLOYED CAUSE'A YOU! MACHO LOSER!
A ROYAL REJECTION, UHH-HUH! PREDICTABLY A SWERVE I SHOULD'VE SEEN COMIN', YYYEAH!
HOLY FORESHADOWING! IT'S MISS ELIZABETH FOR THE SAVE!
WHAT A ROLLERCOASTER OF EMOTIONS WE'RE SEEING HERE TONIGHT!
ELLLLLIZABETH?!
YES, RANDY...IT'S ME...
"...YOUR TRUE QUEEN."
REUNITED AND IT FEELS SO GOOD, UHH-HUH.
LOVE IS IN THE AIR, YYYEAH, DIG IT!

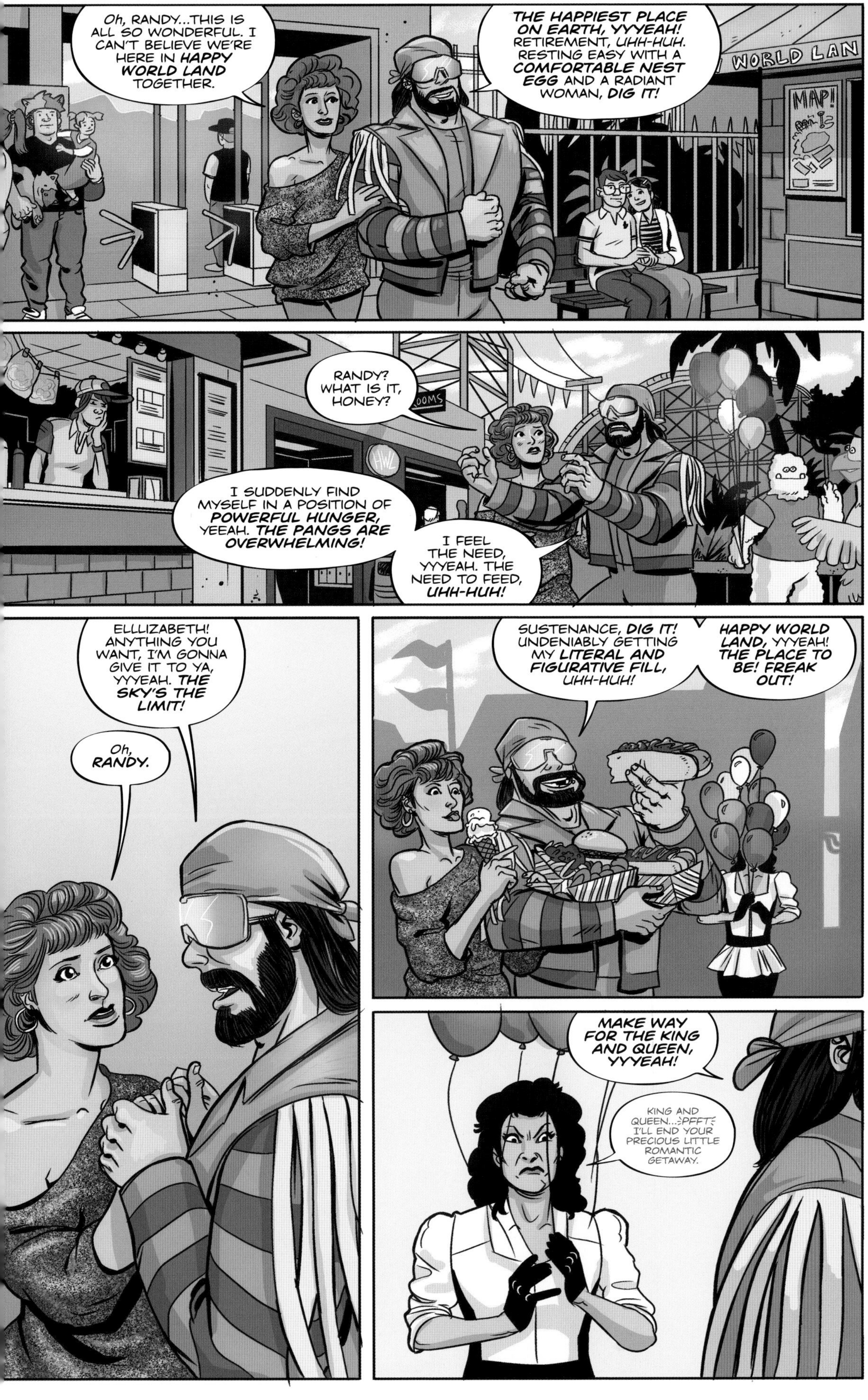

Oh, RANDY...THIS IS ALL SO WONDERFUL. I CAN'T BELIEVE WE'RE HERE IN HAPPY WORLD LAND TOGETHER.
THE HAPPIEST PLACE ON EARTH, YYYEAH! RETIREMENT, UHH-HUH. RESTING EASY WITH A COMFORTABLE NEST EGG AND A RADIANT WOMAN, DIG IT!
MAP!
RANDY? WHAT IS IT, HONEY?
HWL
I SUDDENLY FIND MYSELF IN A POSITION OF POWERFUL HUNGER, YEEAH. THE PANGS ARE OVERWHELMING!
I FEEL THE NEED, YYYEAH. THE NEED TO FEED, UHH-HUH!
ELLLIZABETH! ANYTHING YOU WANT, I'M GONNA GIVE IT TO YA, YYYEAH. THE SKY'S THE LIMIT!
Oh, RANDY.
SUSTENANCE, DIG IT! UNDENIABLY GETTING MY LITERAL AND FIGURATIVE FILL, UHH-HUH!
HAPPY WORLD LAND, YYYEAH! THE PLACE TO BE! FREAK OUT!
MAKE WAY FOR THE KING AND QUEEN, YYYEAH!
KING AND QUEEN...PFFT. I'LL END YOUR PRECIOUS LITTLE ROMANTIC GETAWAY.

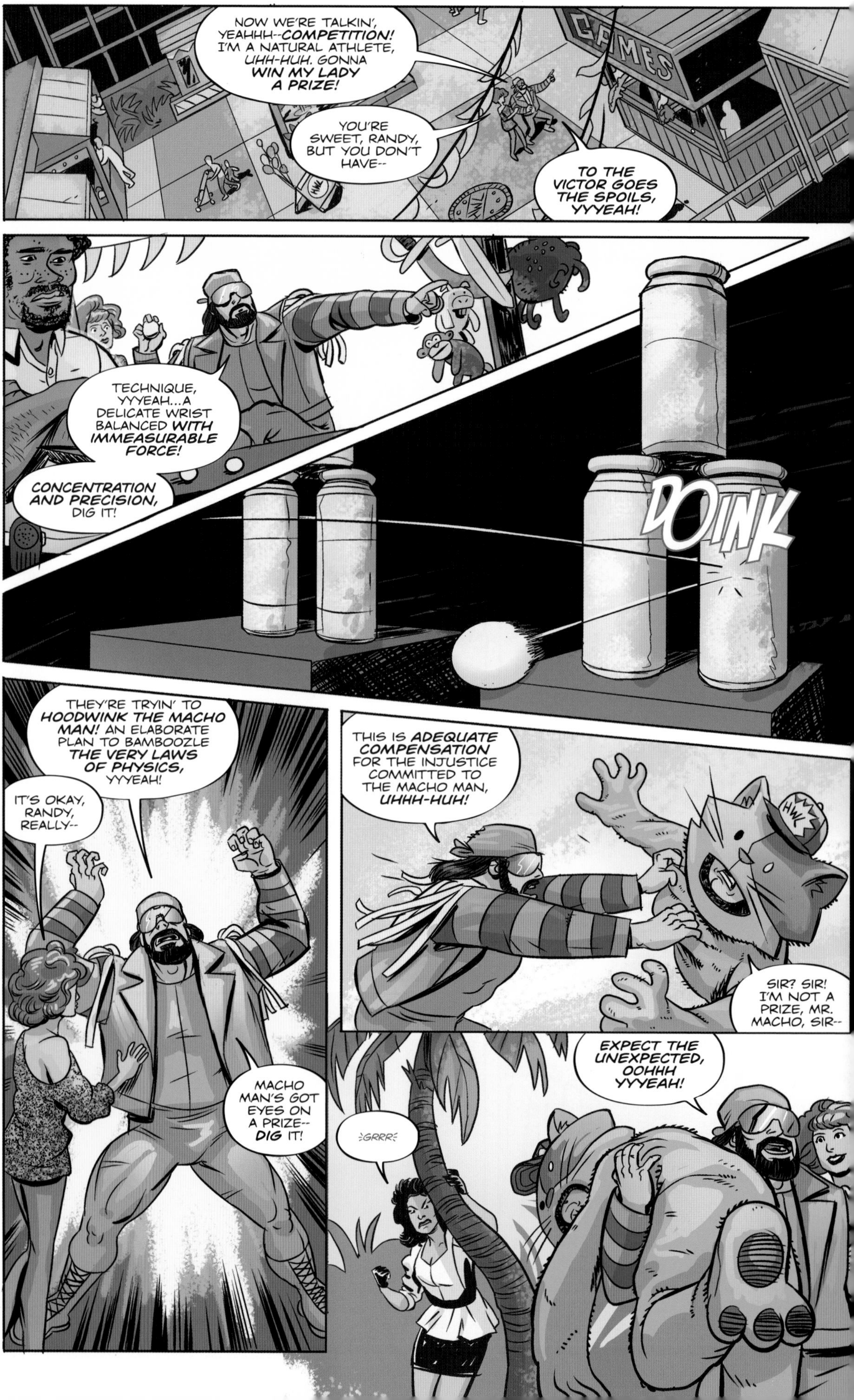
NOW WE'RE TALKIN', YEAHHH--COMPETITION! I'M A NATURAL ATHLETE, UHH-HUH. GONNA WIN MY LADY A PRIZE!
YOU'RE SWEET, RANDY, BUT YOU DON'T HAVE--
TO THE VICTOR GOES THE SPOILS, YYYEAH!
GAMES
TECHNIQUE, YYYEAH...A DELICATE WRIST BALANCED WITH IMMEASURABLE FORCE!
CONCENTRATION AND PRECISION, DIG IT!
DOINK
THEY'RE TRYIN' TO HOODWINK THE MACHO MAN! AN ELABORATE PLAN TO BAMBOOZLE THE VERY LAWS OF PHYSICS, YYYEAH!
IT'S OKAY, RANDY, REALLY--
MACHO MAN'S GOT EYES ON A PRIZE--DIG IT!
THIS IS ADEQUATE COMPENSATION FOR THE INJUSTICE COMMITTED TO THE MACHO MAN, UHHH-HUH!
SIR? SIR! I'M NOT A PRIZE, MR. MACHO, SIR--
EXPECT THE UNEXPECTED, OOHHH YYYEAH!
GRRR

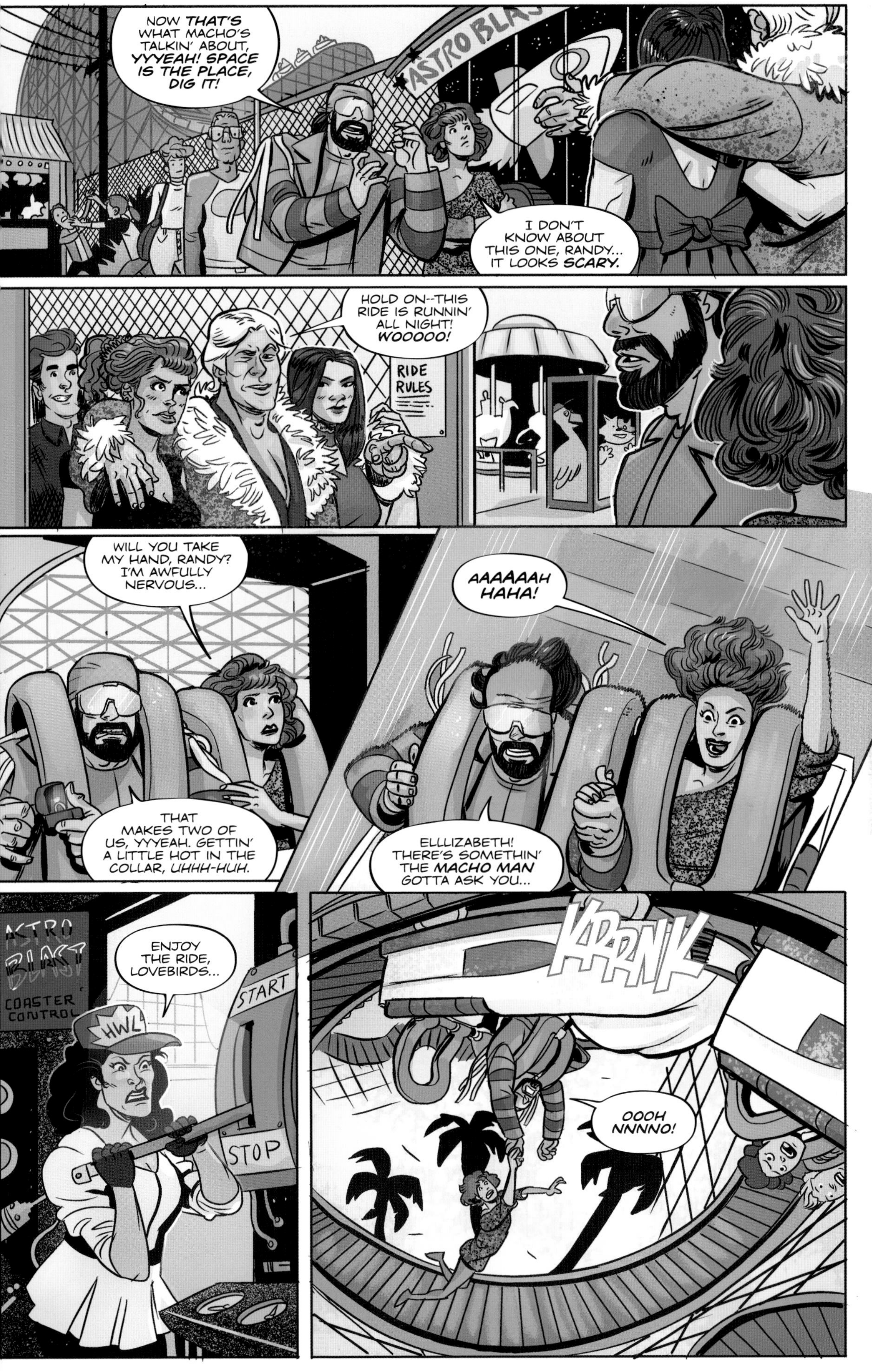
NOW **THAT'S** WHAT MACHO'S TALKIN' ABOUT, ***YYYEAH! SPACE IS THE PLACE, DIG IT!***
ASTRO BLAS
I DON'T KNOW ABOUT THIS ONE, RANDY... IT LOOKS **SCARY.**
HOLD ON--THIS RIDE IS RUNNIN' ALL NIGHT! ***WOOOOO!***
RIDE RULES
WILL YOU TAKE MY HAND, RANDY? I'M AWFULLY NERVOUS...
THAT MAKES TWO OF US, YYYEAH. GETTIN' A LITTLE HOT IN THE COLLAR, UHHH-HUH.
***AAAAAAH HAHA!***
ELLLIZABETH! THERE'S SOMETHIN' THE ***MACHO MAN*** GOTTA ASK YOU...
ASTRO BLAST
COASTER CONTROL
HWL
START
STOP
ENJOY THE RIDE, LOVEBIRDS...
KRRNK
OOOH NNNNO!

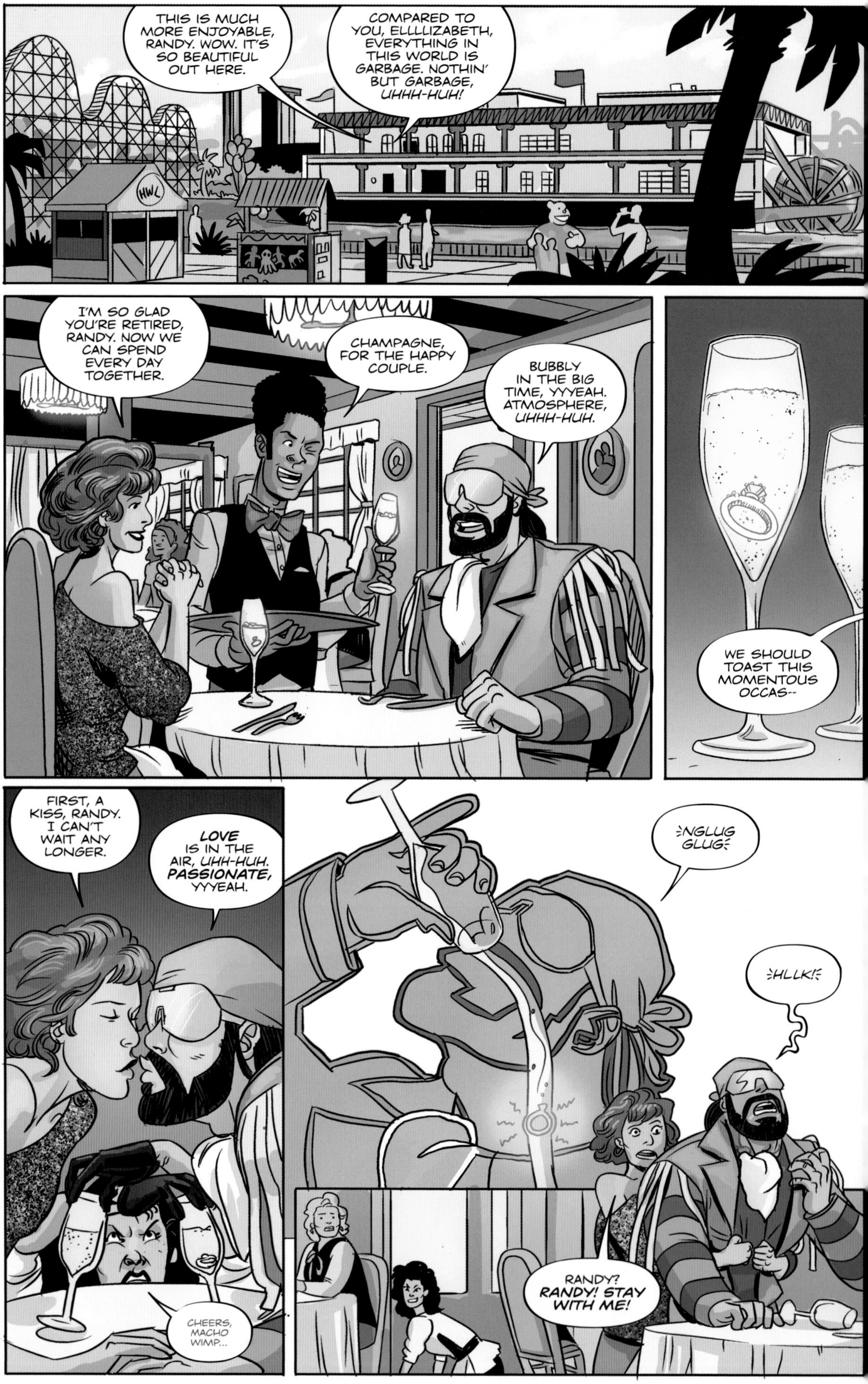
THIS IS MUCH MORE ENJOYABLE, RANDY. WOW. IT'S SO BEAUTIFUL OUT HERE.
COMPARED TO YOU, ELLLLIZABETH, EVERYTHING IN THIS WORLD IS GARBAGE. NOTHIN' BUT GARBAGE, UHHH-HUH!
HWL
I'M SO GLAD YOU'RE RETIRED, RANDY. NOW WE CAN SPEND EVERY DAY TOGETHER.
CHAMPAGNE, FOR THE HAPPY COUPLE.
BUBBLY IN THE BIG TIME, YYYEAH. ATMOSPHERE, UHHH-HUH.
WE SHOULD TOAST THIS MOMENTOUS OCCAS--
FIRST, A KISS, RANDY. I CAN'T WAIT ANY LONGER.
LOVE IS IN THE AIR, UHH-HUH. PASSIONATE, YYYEAH.
CHEERS, MACHO WIMP...
NGLUG GLUG
HLLK!
RANDY? RANDY! STAY WITH ME!

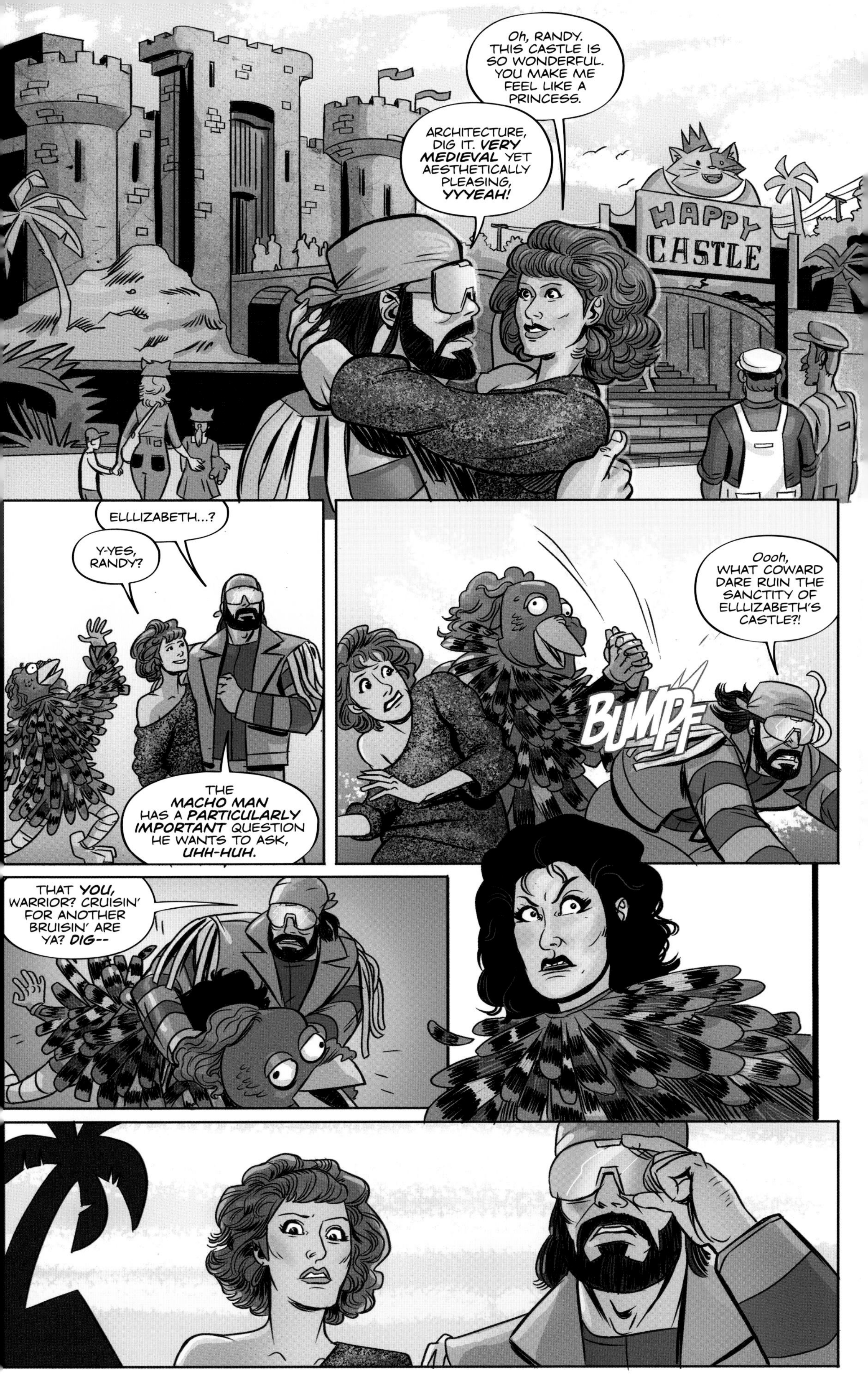

Oh, RANDY. THIS CASTLE IS SO WONDERFUL. YOU MAKE ME FEEL LIKE A PRINCESS.
ARCHITECTURE, DIG IT. VERY MEDIEVAL YET AESTHETICALLY PLEASING, YYYEAH!
HAPPY CASTLE
ELLLIZABETH...?
Y-YES, RANDY?
THE MACHO MAN HAS A PARTICULARLY IMPORTANT QUESTION HE WANTS TO ASK, UHH-HUH.
Oooh, WHAT COWARD DARE RUIN THE SANCTITY OF ELLLIZABETH'S CASTLE?!
BUMPF
THAT YOU, WARRIOR? CRUISIN' FOR ANOTHER BRUISIN' ARE YA? DIG--

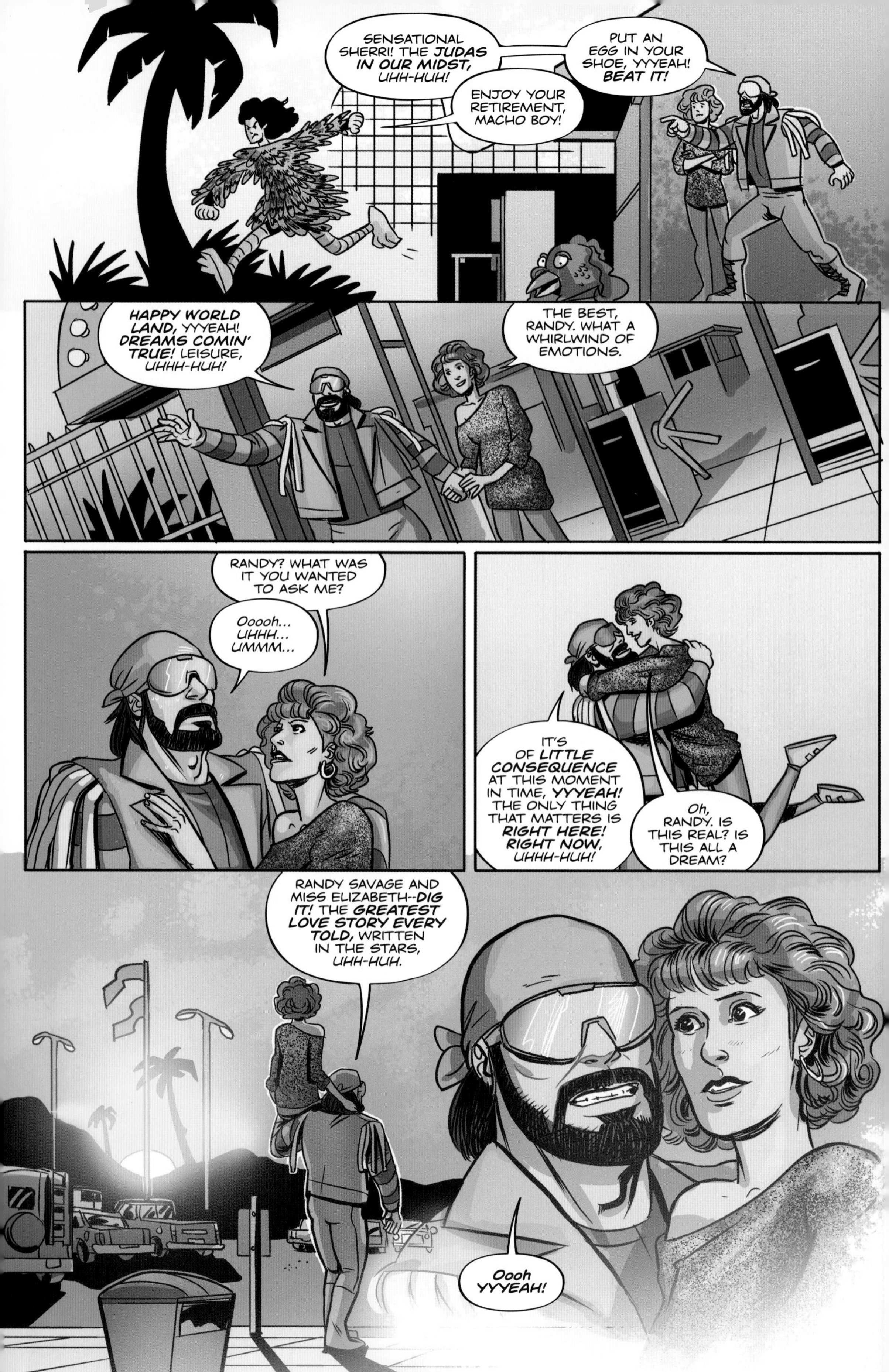
SENSATIONAL SHERRI! THE JUDAS IN OUR MIDST, UHH-HUH!
ENJOY YOUR RETIREMENT, MACHO BOY!
PUT AN EGG IN YOUR SHOE, YYYEAH! BEAT IT!
HAPPY WORLD LAND, YYYEAH! DREAMS COMIN' TRUE! LEISURE, UHHH-HUH!
THE BEST, RANDY. WHAT A WHIRLWIND OF EMOTIONS.
RANDY? WHAT WAS IT YOU WANTED TO ASK ME?
Ooooh... UHHH... UMMM...
IT'S OF LITTLE CONSEQUENCE AT THIS MOMENT IN TIME, YYYEAH! THE ONLY THING THAT MATTERS IS RIGHT HERE! RIGHT NOW, UHHH-HUH!
Oh, RANDY. IS THIS REAL? IS THIS ALL A DREAM?
RANDY SAVAGE AND MISS ELIZABETH--DIG IT! THE GREATEST LOVE STORY EVERY TOLD, WRITTEN IN THE STARS, UHH-HUH.
Oooh YYYEAH!
THE END

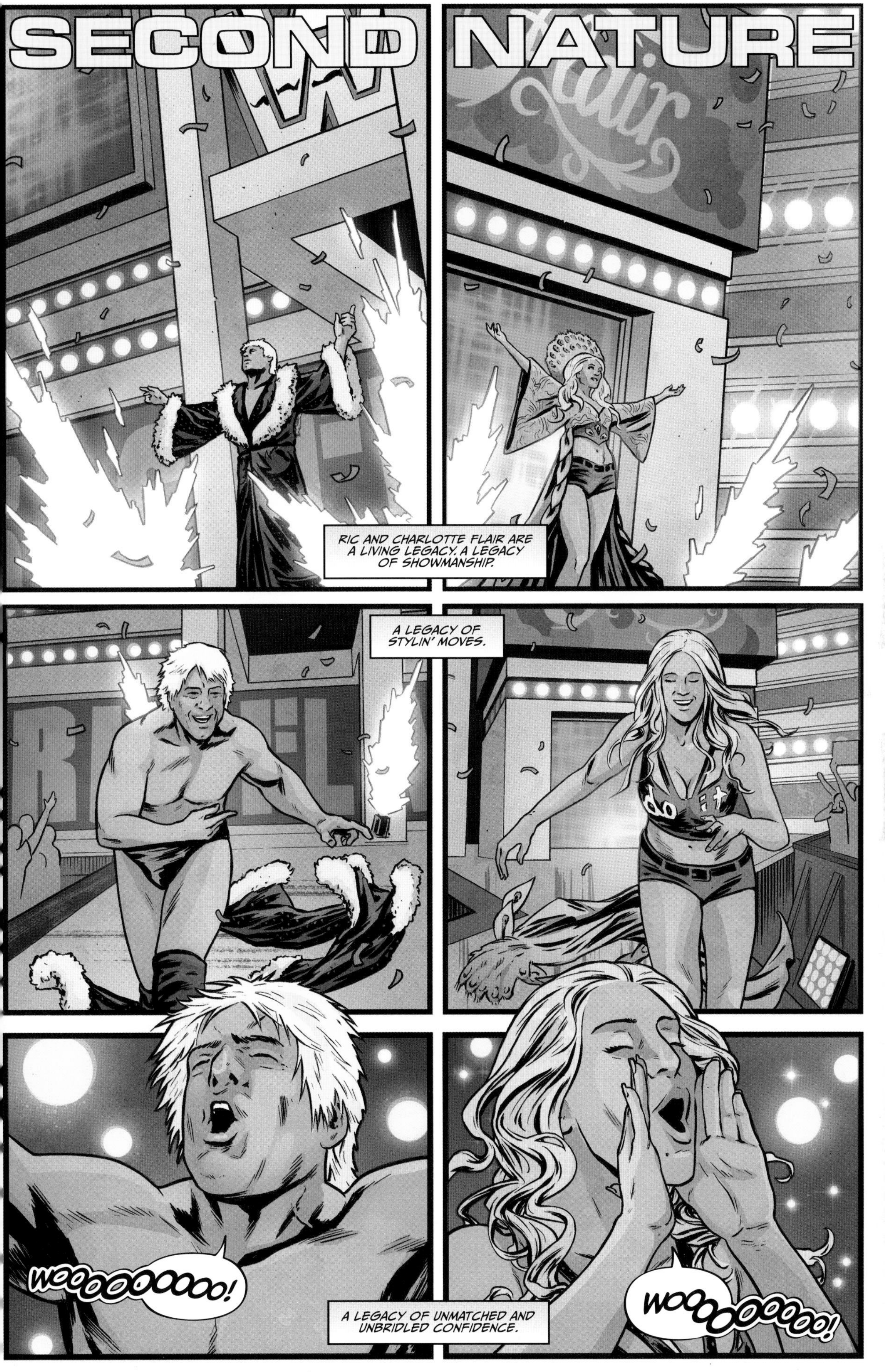
SECOND NATURE
RIC AND CHARLOTTE FLAIR ARE A LIVING LEGACY. A LEGACY OF SHOWMANSHIP.
A LEGACY OF STYLIN' MOVES.
WOOOOOOOOO!
A LEGACY OF UNMATCHED AND UNBRIDLED CONFIDENCE.
WOOOOOOOOO!

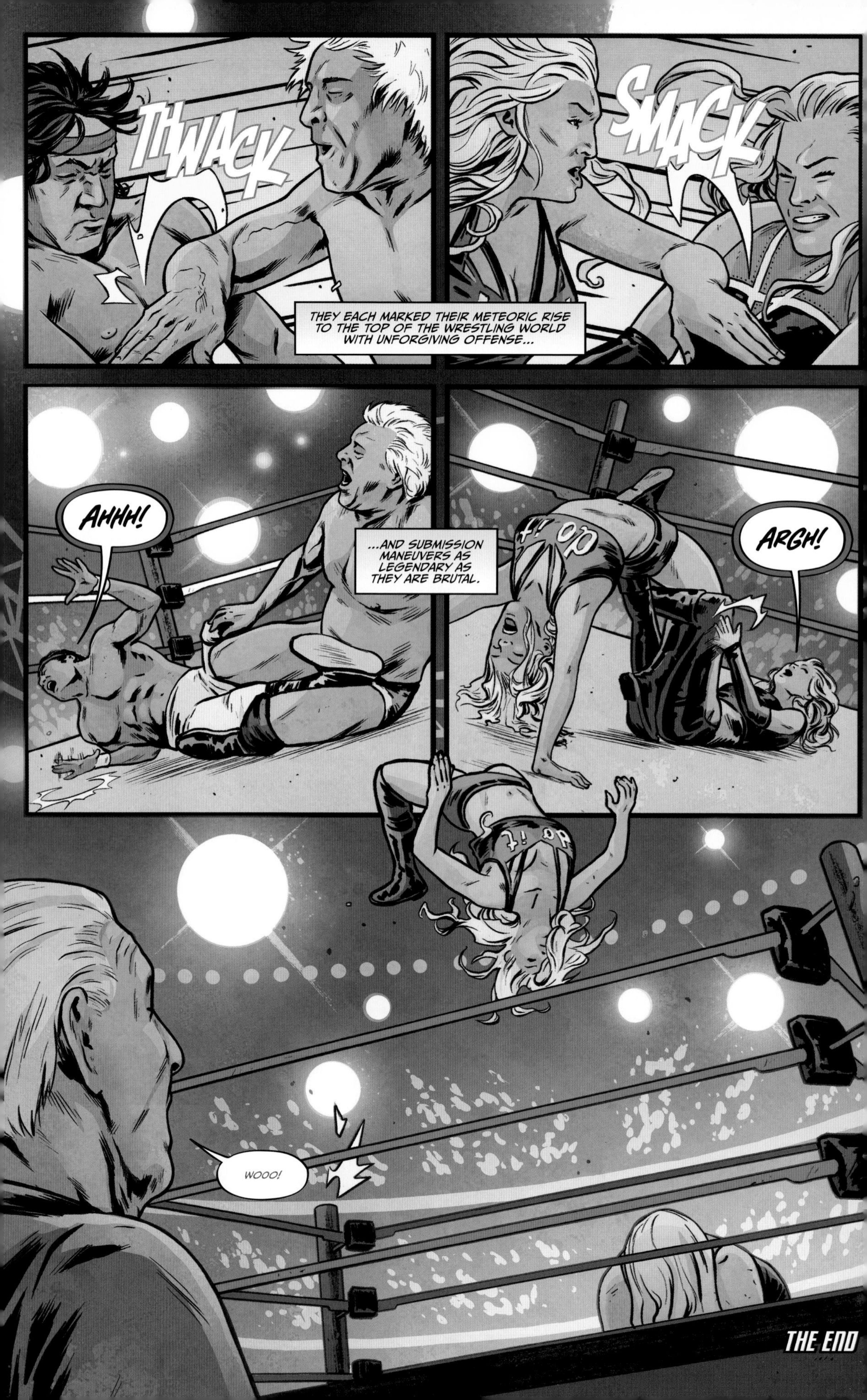
THWACK
SMACK
THEY EACH MARKED THEIR METEORIC RISE TO THE TOP OF THE WRESTLING WORLD WITH UNFORGIVING OFFENSE...
AHHH!
...AND SUBMISSION MANEUVERS AS LEGENDARY AS THEY ARE BRUTAL.
ARGH!
WOOO!
THE END

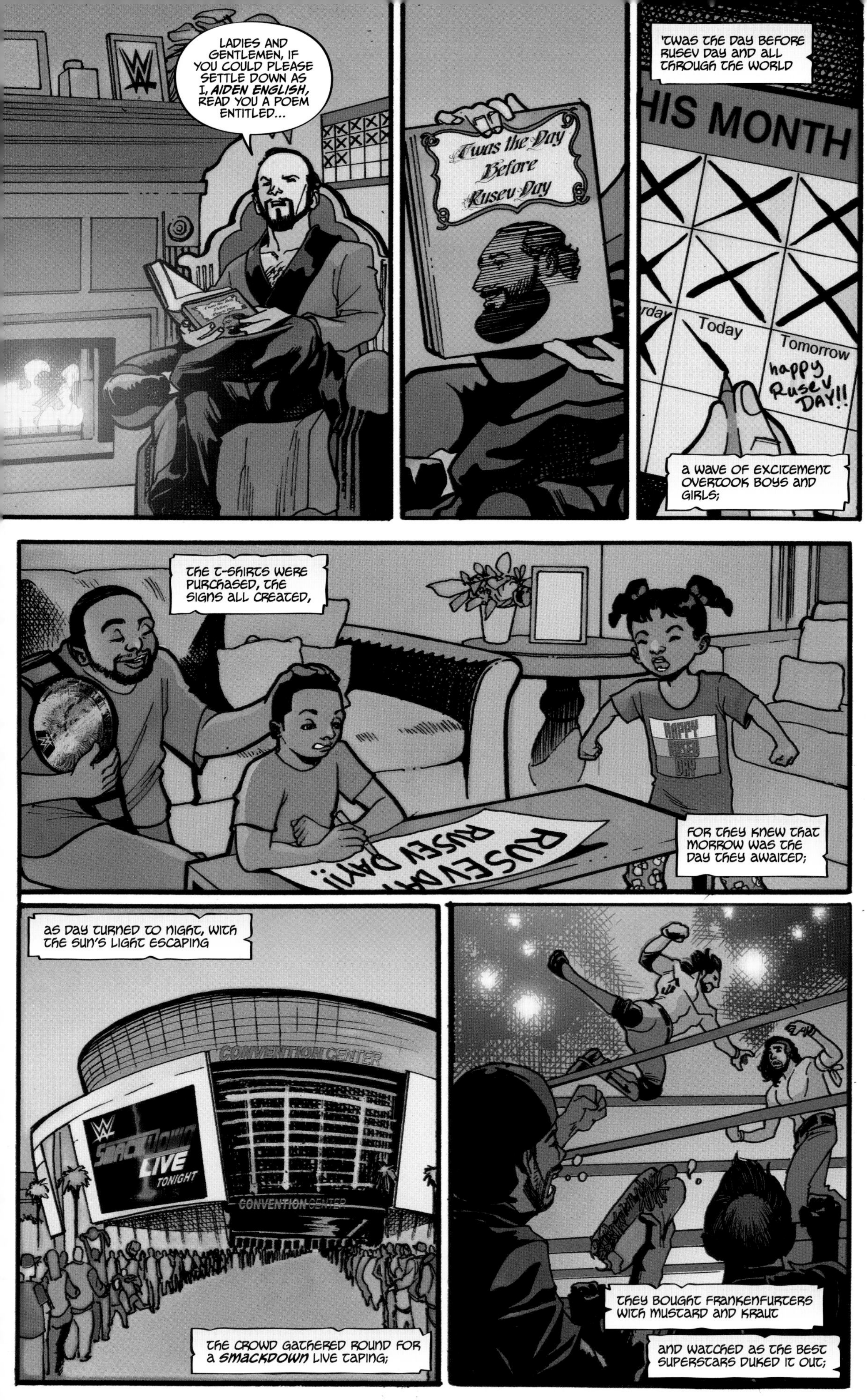
LADIES AND GENTLEMEN, IF YOU COULD PLEASE SETTLE DOWN AS I, AIDEN ENGLISH, READ YOU A POEM ENTITLED...
W
'Twas the Day Before Rusev Day
'TWAS THE DAY BEFORE RUSEV DAY AND ALL THROUGH THE WORLD
HIS MONTH
Today
Tomorrow
happy Rusev DAY!!
A WAVE OF EXCITEMENT OVERTOOK BOYS AND GIRLS;
THE T-SHIRTS WERE PURCHASED, THE SIGNS ALL CREATED,
HAPPY RUSEV DAY
RUSEV RUSEV DAY!!
FOR THEY KNEW THAT MORROW WAS THE DAY THEY AWAITED;
AS DAY TURNED TO NIGHT, WITH THE SUN'S LIGHT ESCAPING
CONVENTION CENTER
SMACKDOWN LIVE TONIGHT
CONVENTION CENTER
THE CROWD GATHERED ROUND FOR A SMACKDOWN LIVE TAPING;
THEY BOUGHT FRANKENFURTERS WITH MUSTARD AND KRAUT
AND WATCHED AS THE BEST SUPERSTARS DUKED IT OUT;

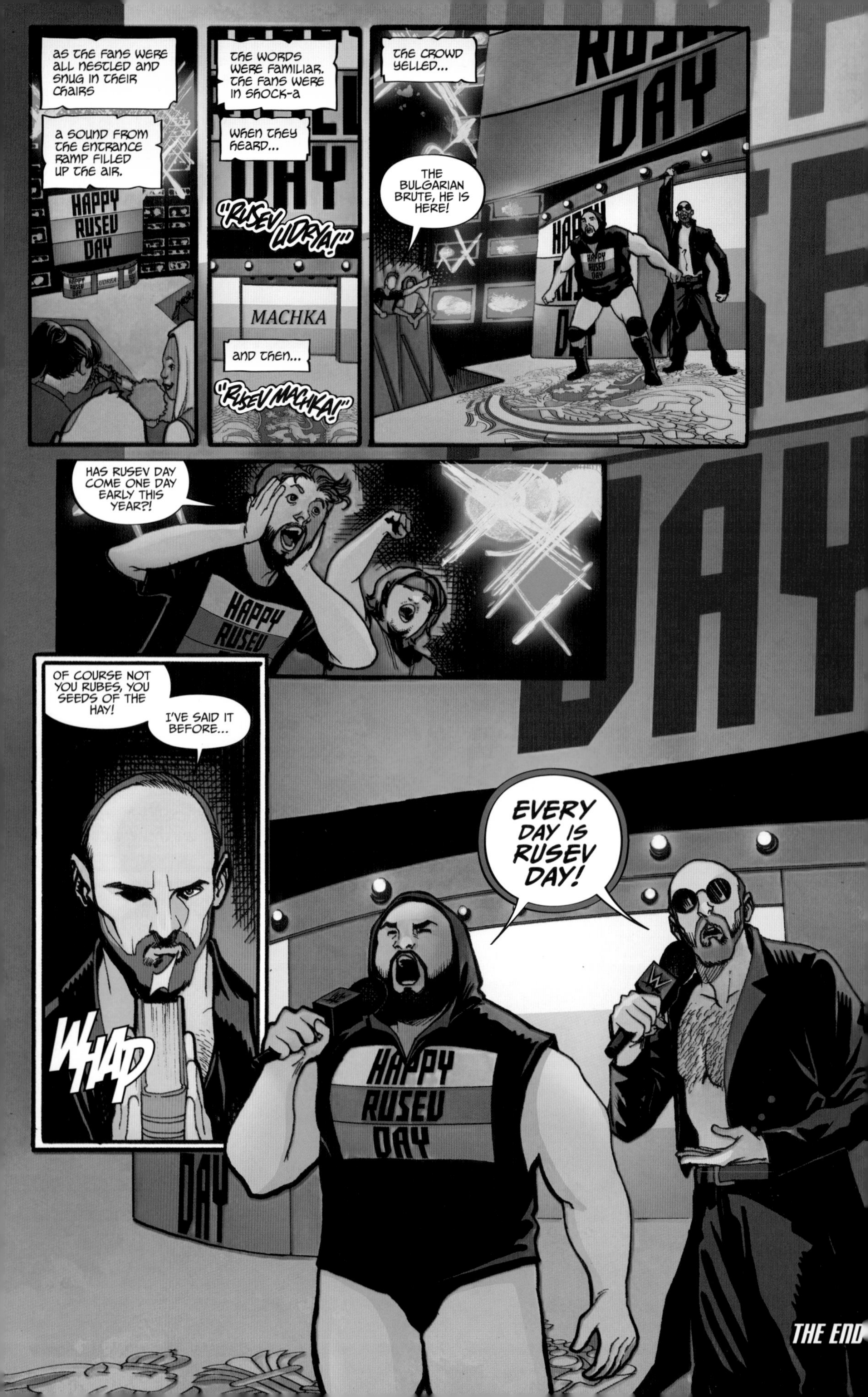
as the fans were all nestled and snug in their chairs
a sound from the entrance ramp filled up the air.
HAPPY RUSEV DAY
the words were familiar. the fans were in shock-a
when they heard...
"RUSEV UDRYA!"
MACHKA
and then...
"RUSEV MACHKA!"
the crowd yelled...
THE BULGARIAN BRUTE, HE IS HERE!
HAS RUSEV DAY COME ONE DAY EARLY THIS YEAR?!
HAPPY RUSEV
OF COURSE NOT YOU RUBES, YOU SEEDS OF THE HAY!
I'VE SAID IT BEFORE...
WHAP
EVERY DAY IS RUSEV DAY!
HAPPY RUSEV DAY
THE END

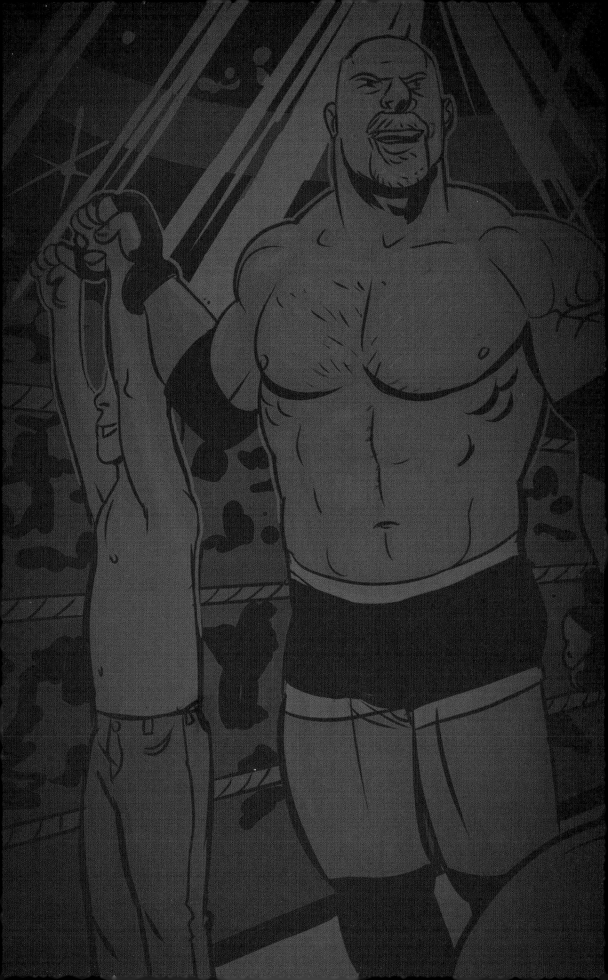

# COVER GALLERY

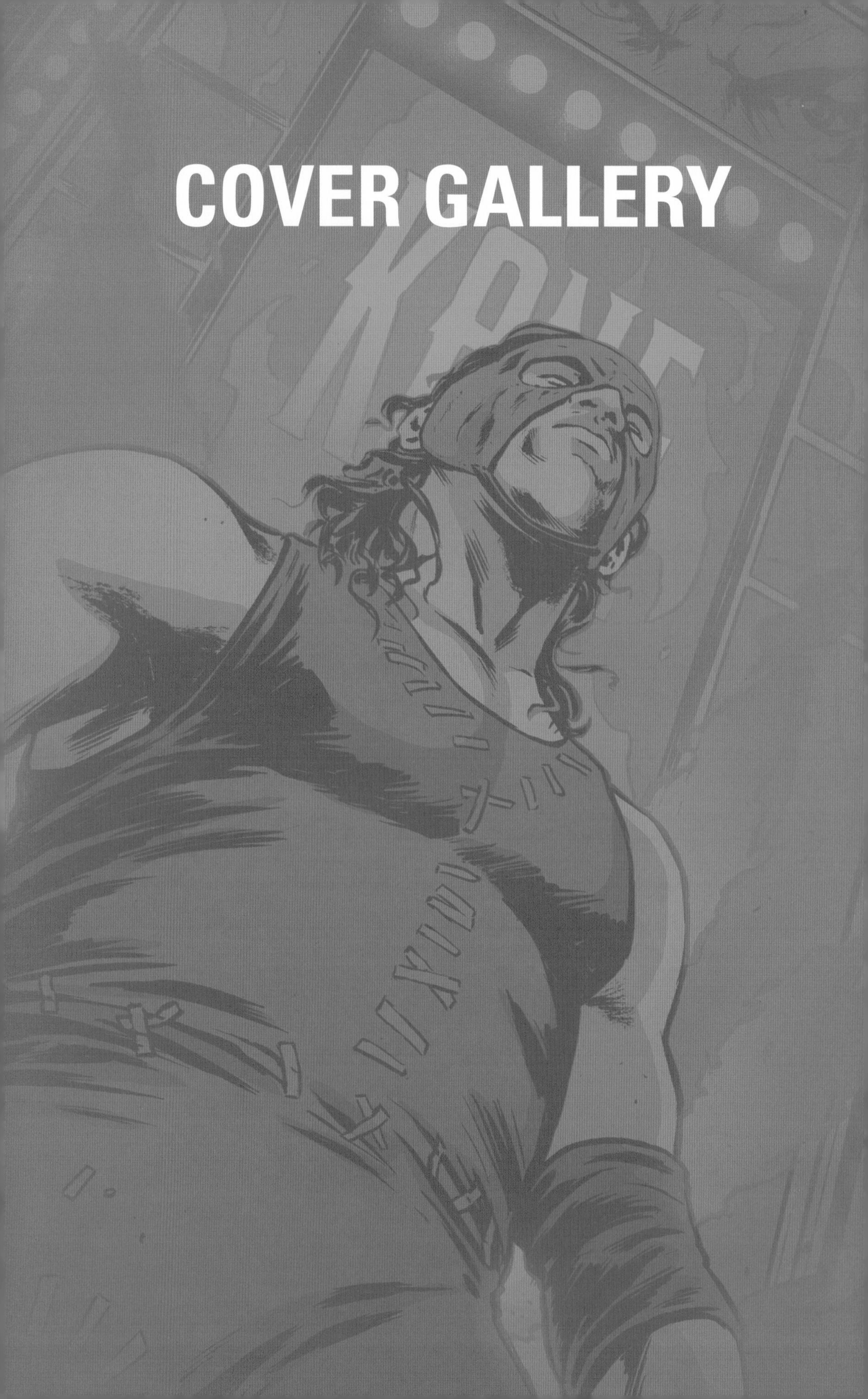

WWE SURVIVOR SERIES 2017 SPECIAL COVER BY
**RAHZZAH**

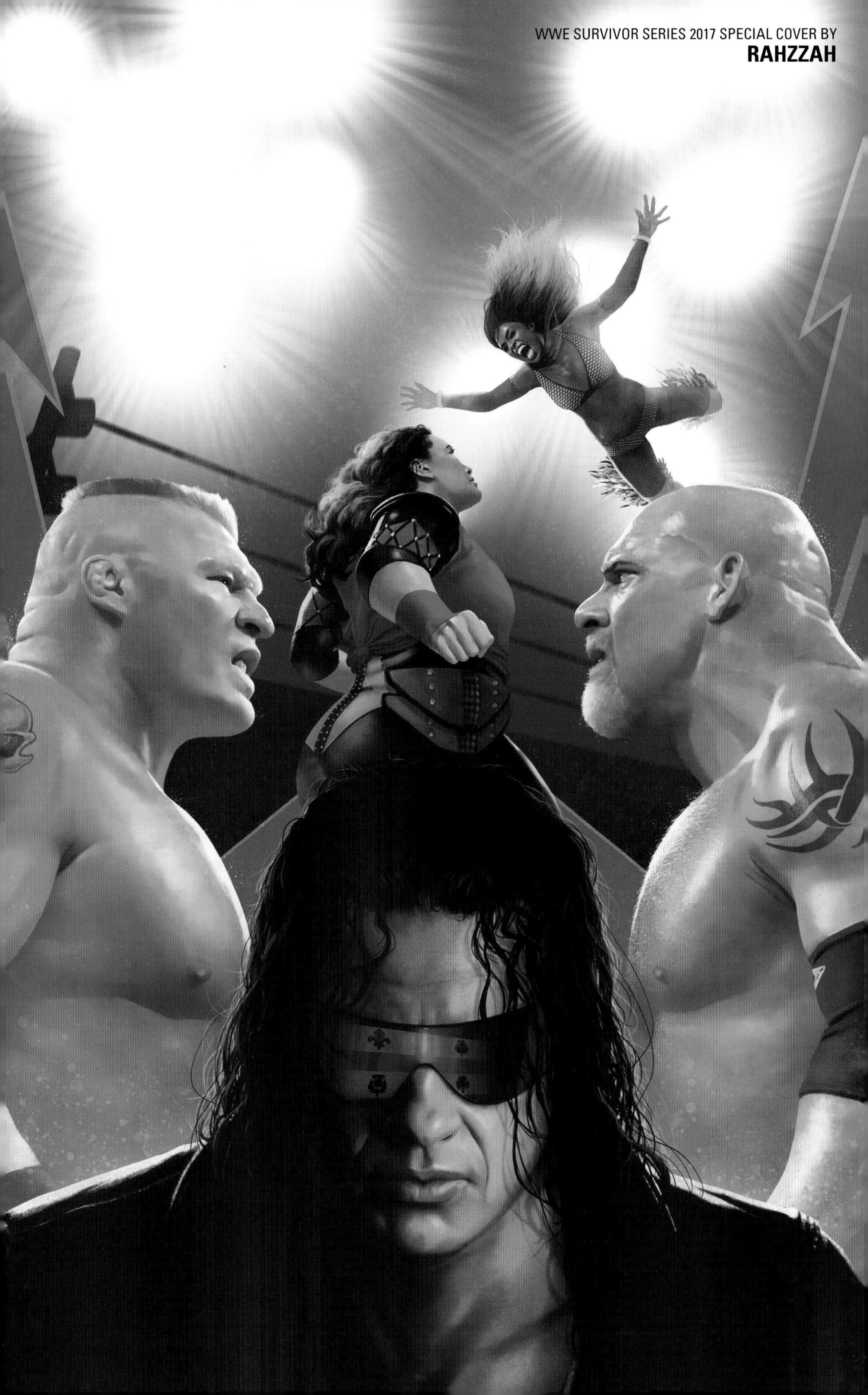

WWE SURVIVOR SERIES 2017 SPECIAL WHAT IF? VARIANT COVER BY
**JIM RUGG**

WWE SURVIVOR SERIES 2017 SPECIAL UNDERTAKER VARIANT COVER BY
**JUAN DOE**

WWE ROYAL RUMBLE 2018 SPECIAL COVER BY
**XERMÁNICO**

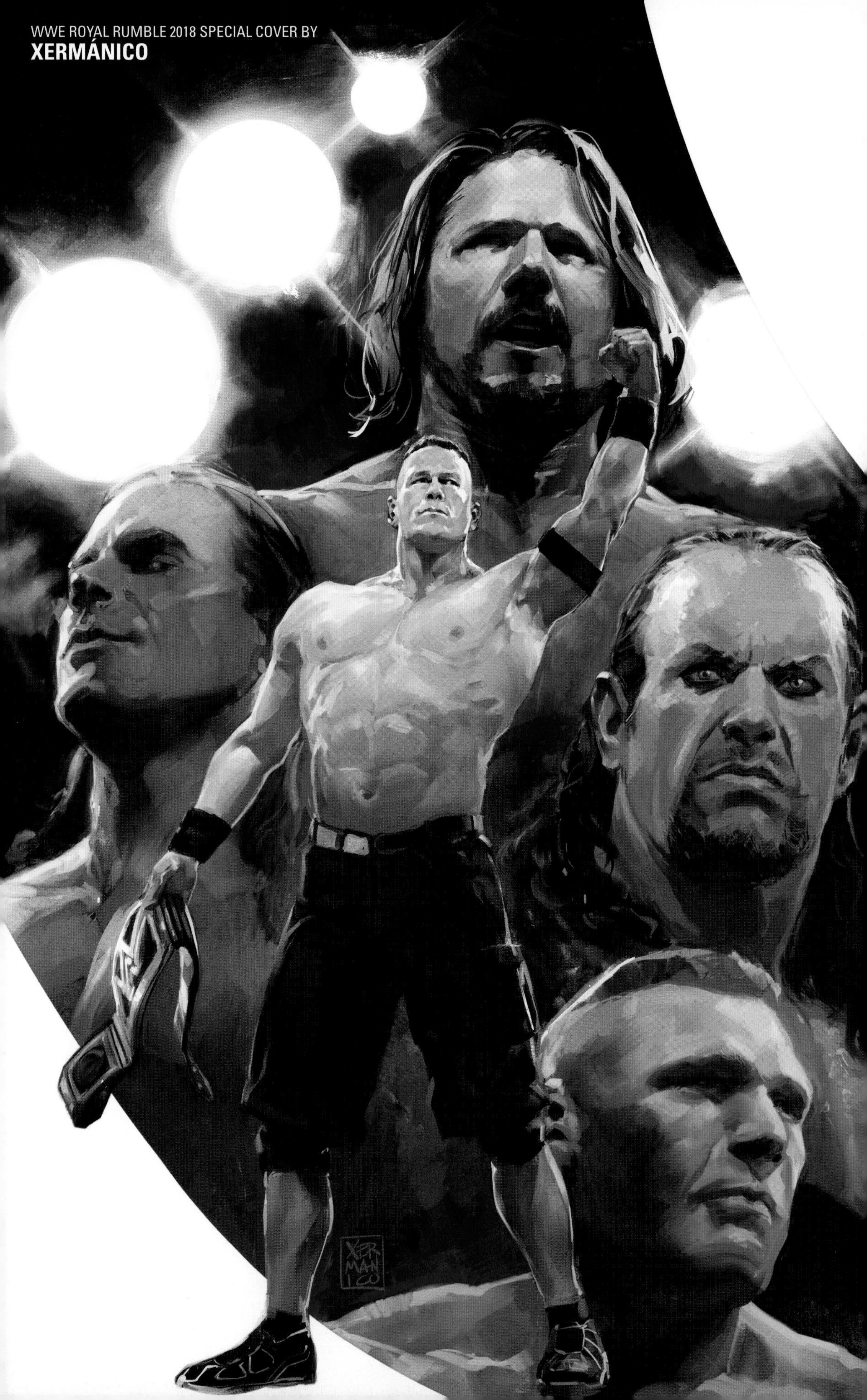

WWE ROYAL RUMBLE 2018 SPECIAL BROCK LESNAR AND PAUL HEYMAN COVER BY

**JUAN DOE**

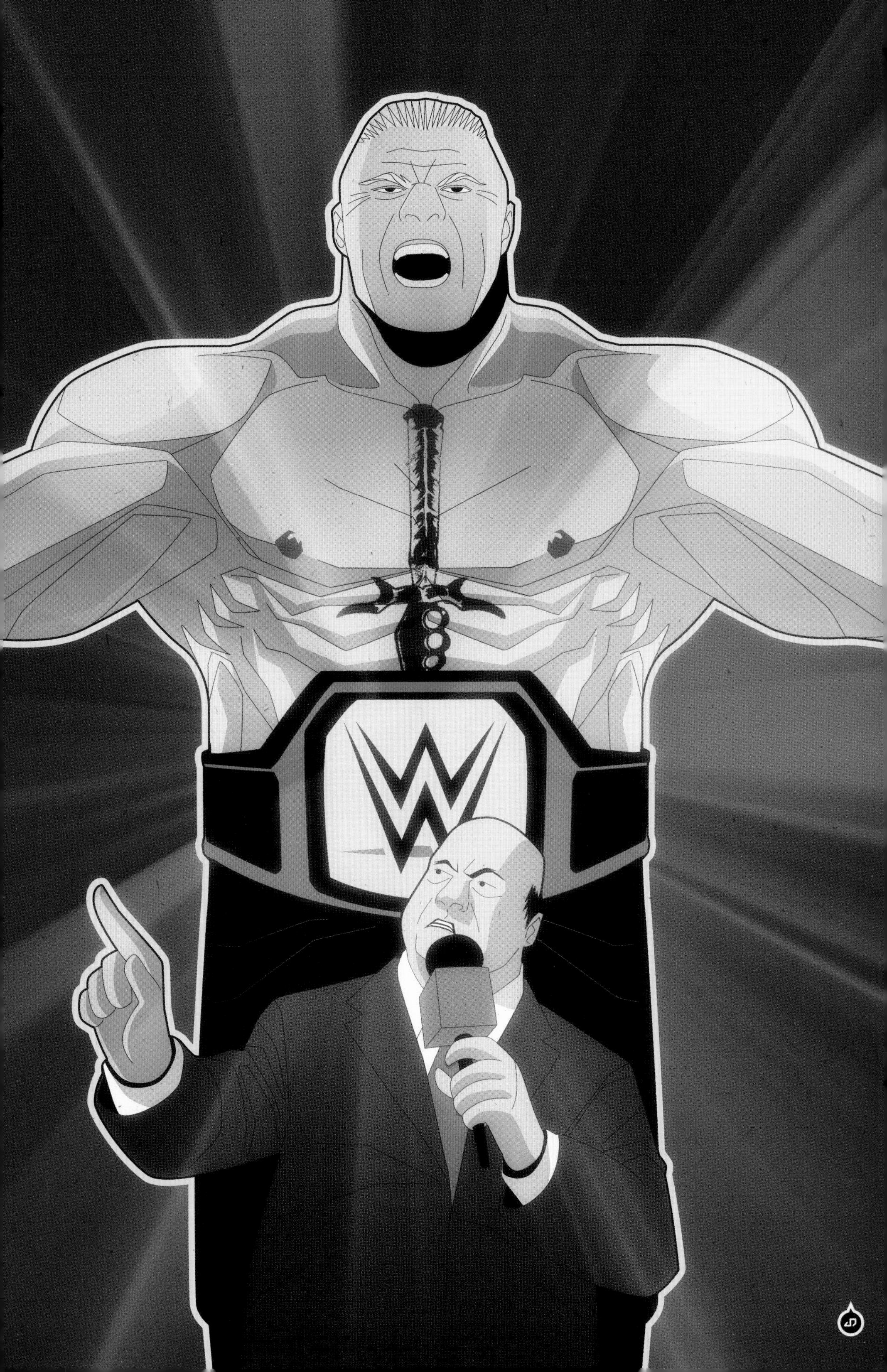

WWE ROYAL RUMBLE 2018 SPECIAL HARDY BOYZ VARIANT COVER BY
**ROB GUILLORY**

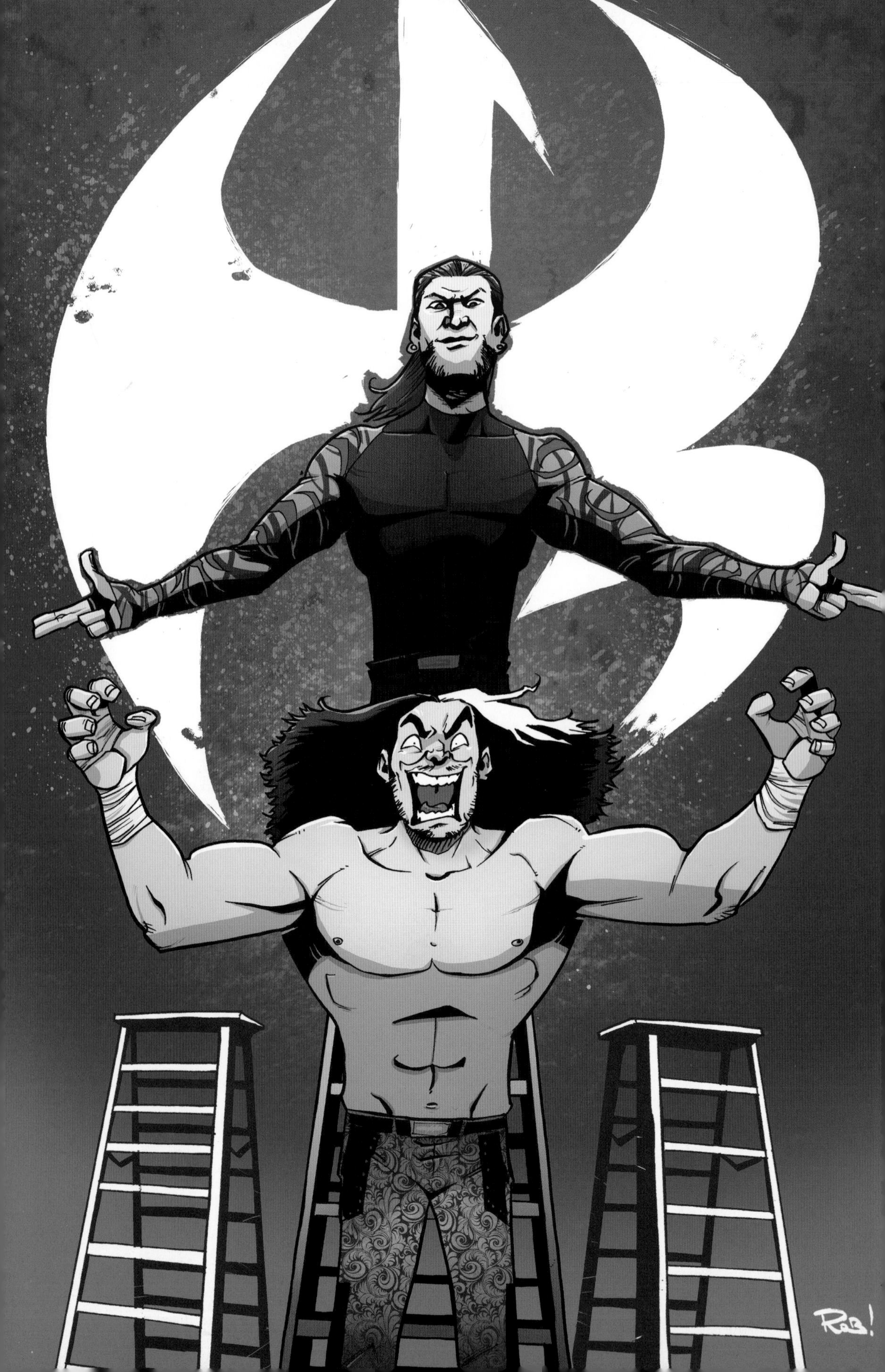

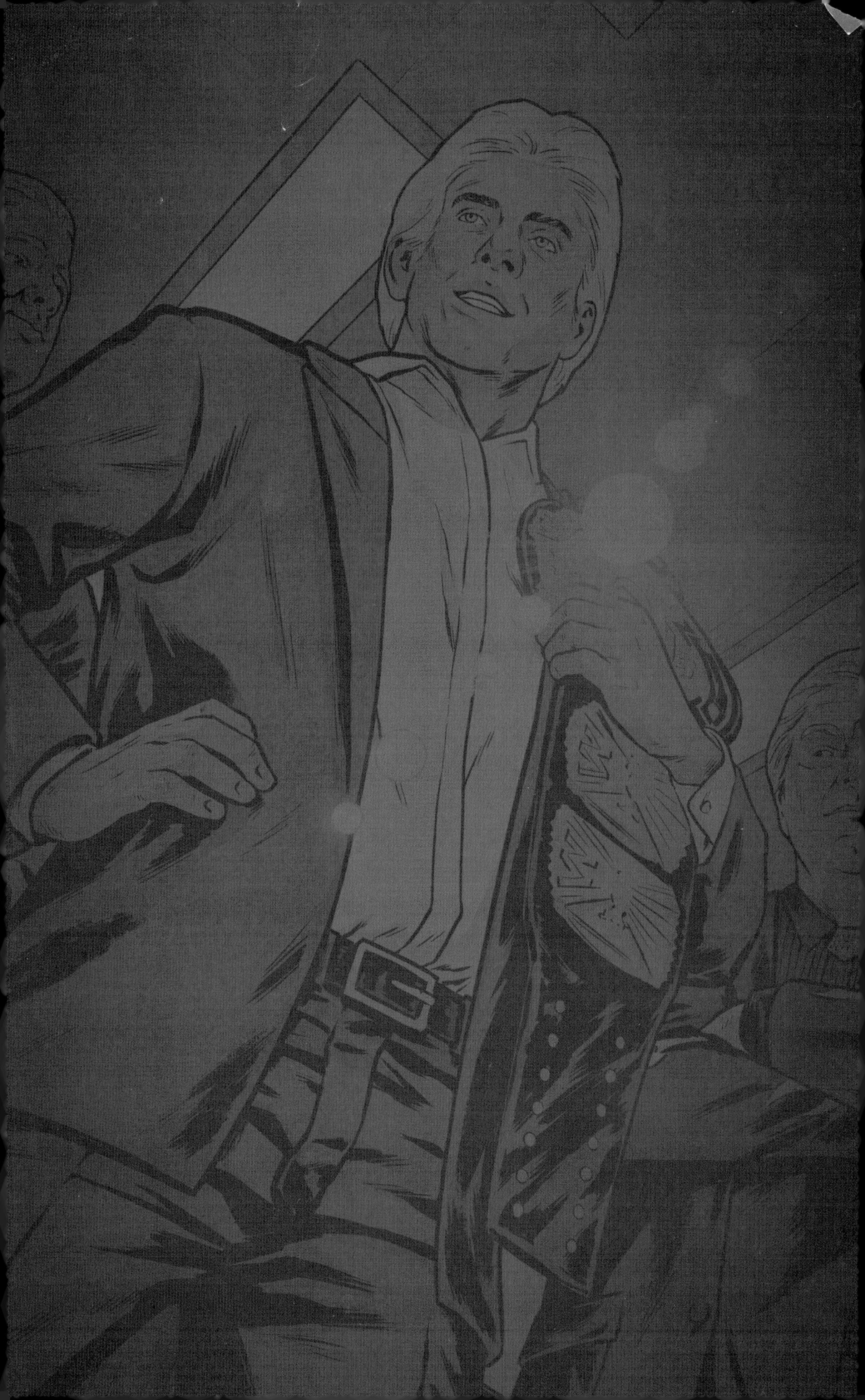

DISCOVER
# VISIONARY CREATORS

THE WOODS
JAMES TYNION IV • MICHAEL DIALYNAS
"The Woods is creepy, funny, charming, and mysterious. My favorite kind of comic, a deep mythology mixed with equally deep character work. Get in on the ground floor of something great!" —Jeff Lemire
VOL. 1
THE ARROW

"The Spire is fantastic! My kind of genre free-for-all." —BRIAN K. VAUGHAN (Saga)
THE SPIRE
SIMON SPURRIER
JEFF STOKELY
ANDRÉ MAY
Will Eisner
NOMINEE

MARK WAID • PETER KRAUSE
IRREDEEMABLE
AFTERWORD BY GRANT MORRISON

J.G. JONES
MARK WAID
STRANGE FRUIT
Foreword by
ELVIS MITCHELL

MICHAEL ALAN NELSON
DAN MORA
GABRIEL CASSATA
HEXED
THE HARLOT & THE THIEF VOLUME ONE

ABNETT & CULBARD
WILD'S END
FIRST LIGHT
"IT'S REALLY GREAT!"
JEFF LEMIRE

BOOM! STUDIOS

**AVAILABLE AT YOUR LOCAL COMICS SHOP AND BOOKSTORE**
WWW.**BOOM-STUDIOS**.COM



## James Tynion IV
**The Woods**
*Volume 1*
ISBN: 978-1-60886-454-6 | $9.99 US
*Volume 2*
ISBN: 978-1-60886-495-9 | $14.99 US
*Volume 3*
ISBN: 978-1-60886-773-8 | $14.99 US

**The Backstagers**
*Volume 1*
ISBN: 978-1-60886-993-0 | $14.99 US

## Simon Spurrier
**Six-Gun Gorilla**
ISBN: 978-1-60886-390-7 | $19.99 US

**The Spire**
ISBN: 978-1-60886-913-8 | $29.99 US

**Weavers**
ISBN: 978-1-60886-963-3 | $19.99 US

## Mark Waid
**Irredeemable**
*Volume 1*
ISBN: 978-1-93450-690-5 | $16.99 US
*Volume 2*
ISBN: 978-1-60886-000-5 | $16.99 US

**Incorruptible**
*Volume 1*
ISBN: 978-1-60886-015-9 | $16.99 US
*Volume 2*
ISBN: 978-1-60886-028-9 | $16.99 US

**Strange Fruit**
ISBN: 978-1-60886-872-8 | $24.99 US

## Michael Alan Nelson
**Hexed The Harlot & The Thief**
*Volume 1*
ISBN: 978-1-60886-718-9 | $14.99 US
*Volume 2*
ISBN: 978-1-60886-816-2 | $14.99 US

**Day Men**
*Volume 1*
ISBN: 978-1-60886-393-8 | $9.99 US
*Volume 2*
ISBN: 978-1-60886-852-0 | $9.99 US

## Dan Abnett
**Wild's End**
*Volume 1: First Light*
ISBN: 978-1-60886-735-6 | $19.99 US
*Volume 2: The Enemy Within*
ISBN: 978-1-60886-877-3 | $19.99 US

**Hypernaturals**
*Volume 1*
ISBN: 978-1-60886-298-6 | $16.99 US
*Volume 2*
ISBN: 978-1-60886-319-8 | $19.99 US

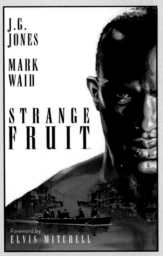